Contents

PENGUIN CLASSICS

THE PENGUIN FREUD GENERAL EDITOR:
ADAM PHILLIPS

THE PSYCHOPATHOLOGY OF EVERYDAY LIFE

SIGMUND FREUD was born in 1856 in Moravia; between the ages of four and eighty-two his home was Vienna: in 1938 Hitler's invasion of Austria forced him to seek asylum in London, where he died in the following year. His career began with several years of brilliant work on the anatomy and physiology of the nervous system. He was almost thirty when, after a period of study under Charcot in Paris, his interests first turned to psychology; and after ten years of clinical work in Vienna (at first in collaboration with Breuer, an older colleage) he invented what was to become psychoanalysis. This began simply as a method of treating neurotic patients through talking, but it quickly grew into an accumulation of knowledge about the workings of the mind in general. Freud was thus able to demonstrate the development of the sexual instinct in childhood, and largely on the basis of an examination of dreams, arrived at this fundamental discovery of the unconscious forces that influence our everyday thoughts and actions. Freud's life was uneventful, but his ideas have shaped not only many specialist disciplines, but also the whole intellectual climate of the twentieth century.

ANTHEA BELL was born in Suffolk and educated at Somerville College, Oxford. She has worked as a translator for many years, primarily from German and French. Her translations include works of nonfiction (biology, politics, social history, musicology and art history), literary and popular fiction, and books for young people including classic German works by the Grimm brothers, Clemens Brentano, Wilhelm Hauff and Christian Morgenstern. Recent translations include E. T. A. Hoffmann's *The Life and Opinions of the Tomcat Murr* (1999), Lilian Faschinger's *Vienna Passion* (2000) and W. G. Sebald's *Austerliz* (2001). Anthea Bell has also served on the committee of the Translator's Association and the jury panel of the Schlegel-Tieck German translation prize in the UK, and has received a number of translation prizes and awards, including the 1987 Schlegel-Tieck award for Hans Bemmann's *The Stone and the Flute*. She lives in Cambridge and has two adult sons.

PAUL KEEGAN was formerly editor of Penguin Classics, and is now Poetry Editor at Faber & Faber. He is the editor of *The New Penguin Book of English Verse* (2000).

ADAM PHILLIPS was formerly Principal Child Psychotherapist at Charing Cross Hospital in London. He is the author of several books on psychoanalysis including *On Kissing, Tickling and Being Bored*, *Darwin's Worms*, *Promises, Promises* and *Houdini's Box*.

SIGMUND FREUD

The Psychopathology
of Everyday Life

Translated by ANTHEA BELL
with an Introduction by PAUL KEEGAN

PENGUIN BOOKS

Published by the Penguin Group
Penguin Group (USA) Inc., 375 Hudson Street, New York, New York 10014, U.S.A.
Penguin Books Ltd, 80 Strand, London WC2R 0RL, England
Penguin Books Australia Ltd, 250 Camberwell Road, Camberwell, Victoria 3124, Australia
Penguin Books Canada Ltd, 10 Alcorn Avenue, Toronto, Ontario, Canada M4V 3B2
Penguin Books India (P) Ltd, 11 Community Centre, Panchsheel Park, New Delhi – 110 017, India
Penguin Books (N.Z.) Ltd, Cnr Rosedale and Airborne Roads, Albany, Auckland, New Zealand
Penguin Books (South Africa) (Pty) Ltd, 24 Sturdee Avenue, Rosebank, Johannesburg 2196, South Africa

Penguin Books Ltd, Registered Offices:
80 Strand, London WC2R 0RL, England

Zur Psychopathologie des Alltagsleben first published 1901 in
Monatsschrift für Psychiatrie und Neurologie 10 (1/2)
English translation published in Penguin Books (U.K.) 2002
This edition published 2003

1   3   5   7   9   10   8   6   4   2

Sigmund Freud's German text collected in *Gesammelte Werke (1940–52)*
copyright © Imago Publishing Co., Ltd, London, 1941
Translation and editorial matter copyright © Anthea Bell, 2002
Introduction copyright © Paul Keegan, 2002
All rights reserved

LIBRARY OF CONGRESS CATALOGING IN PUBLICATION DATA
Freud, Sigmund, 1856–1939.
[Zur Psychopathologie des Alltagslebens. English]
The psychopathology of everyday life / Sigmund Freud ; translated
by Anthea Bell with an introduction by Paul Keegan.
p.   cm.
Includes bibliological references.
ISNBN 0 14 24.3743 3
1. Psychoanalysis.   2. Memory.   3. Repression (Psychology)
4. Paragrammatism.   5. Freud, sigmund, 1856–1939.   I. Title.
BF173.F82513   2003
150.19'52—dc21   2003043308

Printed in the United States of America
Set in Adobe New Caledonia

Introduction

'There is a house where twice every day for six years, at regular hours, I used to wait to be let in outside a door on the second floor . . .'

While doing things, or in the interstices between doing things, we do other, less obvious things. *The Psychopathology of Everyday Life* is the inventory of what goes on when nothing much is going on, or of what we do when we think we know what we are doing. Its concern is ordinary life, using as its optic the not-so-ordinary life of the bourgeoisie at the century's turn, in Vienna and other Hapsburg capitals and resorts. The stage is largely given over to what Veblen termed 'the performance of leisure'. Doing nothing much, *circa* 1900, is all-consuming: we sit in coffee houses, wait in rooms, stand in trams; we visit each other, and effect introductions; we return from honeymoon, compose letters, consult watches and timetables; we take holidays, stay at pensione, in sanatoria, at health resorts and spas; we stroll zoos, walk mountains, wander museums. We are in thrall to travel, or to the rituals of displacement – as if places are more important than where they are. And wherever we are we repeat ourselves: we window-shop, stare at statues, scrutinize business plates, study menus. We are addicted to signs of every description, describing anything.

Above all (and Karl Kraus ridicules us for it) we read magazines and newspapers, by the avalanche. We drown in print. By the 1920s in Germany more than a thousand magazines were being founded annually. Added to which the streets are aswarm with advertise-ments, hoardings, billboards, displays. The metropolis of *Everyday Life* is as much a lexical as a visual field. And print is the omnipresent occasion for misprints, for wandering meanings. Suddenly the field of nonsense seems to have been exponentially enlarged. (Item: 'Our readers will be well aware that we have always promoted the common good in the most [un]self-interested manner.') This extends to the *non sequiturs* we ourselves generate. We seem to misread much of what comes our way: we even misread misprints. In fact, given how little we do, we get a lot of it wrong, much of the time, without paying any attention to the fact. Freud's book is all attention, and one way of reading it is as a parody, a work of pseudo-prescription, a critique of scientific method. Its starting-point is that, on the evidence all around us, we can never be as scientific, as empirical, as we might wish.

Doing nothing much is one thing; getting it wrong, suggests Freud, is something more interesting. Ordinary acts bristle with redundancy – with stumbling, slipping, falling; with dropping things, knocking things over, losing things, pouring things over ourselves; with forgetting each other's names, addressing each other by the wrong names, mislaying the names of our husbands, of our cities; with forgetting what we intend to do, omitting to carry out tasks, mixing up dates. Our days are full of farcical detour and unscripted subplots. We cannot trust ourselves to post our letters, we make mistakes in the writing, we wrongly address them to those for whose eyes their contents are specifically not intended. We put calls through to the wrong people. We take the wrong trains, we register our children with the wrong names, we forget to sign cheques. No sooner do we receive presents than we mislay them. We are inept at dodging each other in the street, and we cannot be relied on to cross an empty thoroughfare without getting run over. More generally, we produce a constant unspecified static: we fiddle with our clothes and our hair, we scribble things, we jingle coins, we hum tunes 'thoughtlessly', like Sterne's Uncle Toby; we make meaningless gestures and movements; we are obscurely 'impelled' to perform odd acts, acts which are not quite actions. We are the landing strips for all these minor furies. And through it all we say – or rather we come out with – the wrong things, with hybrid utterance, with things concealed but struggling for appearance.

The 'parapraxis' – a collective noun for all slips and errors[1] – is also a paradox: a cancelled action, so to speak. And Freud is the first observed to be philosophically struck, not by our failure rate, but by how unintrigued we are by the fact – how feckless, how innocent. In his essay 'A Plea for Excuses', discriminating the niceties of everyday usage in the matter of disclaimers, J. L. Austin wondered: 'I do not know how many of you keep a list of the kinds of fool you make of yourselves.' Freud says: I have made a list of the kinds of fool we make of ourselves. *Everyday Life* is a pattern book of examples – or of digressions, since parapraxes are detours inside the ordinary. The book is a revolving door of entrances and exits, with a largely nameless cast of hundreds. If *The Interpretation of Dreams* (Freud's previous book, published two years earlier) is structured as a journey, the Ithaca of whose discoveries comes clearly into view only near its end, *Everyday Life* is more radically peripatetic, a makeshift city comedy whose sets change so rapidly as to be superimposed rather than sequential: a café theatrical about our improvisations, the contingencies by which we live.

To maintain the focus on ordinary actions, Freud finds it necessary to admit the infra-ordinary – the micro-neurotic, the zero degree of behaviour – to focus on the unfocused, on what he calls 'occurrences which drop out of the concatenation of events' (*Introductory Lectures*, 1919). On the one hand, his concern is with the satin lining of time passing, rather than the hair shirt of obligation, and this gives the book its air of dawdle, its serpentine line of aimlessness. On the other hand, Freud is tactically committed to conveying the sense of business as usual for the psyche's functionings, given that he expected strong resistance – from empiricist and sociological accounts of the self-evidence of ordinary life – to his claims for the slipping self. He must therefore avoid the suspicion of offering an exceptionalist account. As he explained retrospectively in the *Introductory Lectures*, this meant eschewing 'the much richer material offered by my neurotic patients' so as to avoid incurring the charge that parapraxes apply to pathological states rather than to normal mental functioning. Parapraxes are not divagations from the norm, they are its measure. As if it were normal to be unable to be normal.

∗

> No wishes for today, except
> To play it out, and not become the fool.
> (Hugo Williams, 'Early Morning')

Freud offers himself up as the primary witness: in the crucible of *Everyday Life* he is his own experiment. 'I am usually obliged to take those examples of the psychic disturbance of functioning in everyday life that I am collecting in this work from my self-observations.' His own experience is the Plimsoll line, and the vessel of normality must be seen to 'steer clear of' (Freud's image) the ship of fools steaming in the other direction. In other words, Freud recruited normal life for an account of universal deviancy from the norm ('we are all slightly neurotic'), and *Everyday Life* is in this sense a satire, an *encyclopédie de la bêtise*. If W. H. Auden apostrophized normality as 'goddess of bossy underlings' (misprinted in a recent edition as goddess of bossy 'underthings'), this was to imply its reign of terror over the entire building of the self. Freud reveals the internalization of norms as something rather less successful, or threatening, or total: as a secret reign of error. Normality – the protocols of the day – is a failed regime, and Freud's cast of *personae* (in both senses: not-quite characters, but also: splintery versions of Freud) have something of the ungovernable yet self-governing oddity of Dickens's minor creations.

The rehearsal of everyday life in these pages is piled high with small (that big Freudian word) specimens. What results is a collage or palimpsest, extrapolated through recension after recension, over two decades – from its first periodical publication in 1901, and book appearance in 1904, to progressively enlarged editions in 1907, 1910, 1912, 1917, 1919, 1920 and 1924. It is Freud's *Thousand and One Days*, whose vertiginous extensios evinces a fear of closure, as if to finish would be to fail to have convinced the reader. (*Everyday Life*,

The Interpretation of Dreams and the three essays on sexuality were Freud's most revised books: he was unable to say or have the last word on sex, or slips, or dreams.) But it is a mistake to think of these examples as redundant. In a sense, they are all there is, along with their explanations, which are often as provisional and performative – or as interminable – as what they describe.

In Freud's comedy of errors, the individual scene is the isolated slip, a piece of 'incompletely suppressed psychic material which, although displaced from the conscious mind, is not, however, deprived of all ability to express itself'. The repressed returns, but this time as farce. If the Oedipus complex represents our lives as consolingly tragic, then the parapraxis presents everyday life – the placeless place where we live, flickeringly, partially – as disconsolately comic. The social comedy of *Everyday Life* is both more nuanced and more slapstick than that of *The Joke and Its Relation to the Unconscious*, which appeared four years later. Here is a symptomatic vignette (inserted in 1907) of the woman who mistook her husband for an Other:

I was once visiting a young married couple and heard the young wife, laughing, tell the tale of a recent experience of hers: the day after she came home from a journey, she had visited her unmarried sister, as she habitually did, to go shopping while her husband went out to work. She had suddenly seen a gentleman on the other side of the street, nudged her sister, and said: 'Oh, look, there's Herr L.' She had forgotten that Herr L. had actually been her husband for some weeks.

Or an example of slipped penmanship (added in 1920):

An American staying in Europe, who had parted with his wife on bad terms, thought perhaps they could now make the quarrel up and asked her to cross the Atlantic and meet him on a certain date. 'It would be a good idea if you sailed on the *Mauretania*,' he wrote. However, he did not venture to send the sheet of paper on which he had written this sentence, preferring to rewrite the whole letter in case she noticed the correction he had been obliged to make to the name of the ship. He had originally written *Lusitania*.

Freud remarks that the best slips have the 'explosiveness' of jokes. 'A lady once advanced the following opinion at a social gathering – and the words show that they were uttered with fervour and under the pressure of a host of secret impulses: "Oh yes, a woman must be pretty if she is to please men. It's much easier for a man: so long as he has his *fünf geraden Glieder* [five straight limbs] that's all he needs!"' (added in 1910). But whereas in the Joke book the self is a consumer, a net importer of jokes, in the Mistakes book the self becomes a producer. For if jokes are what we hear on their way elsewhere, ostensibly directed at others, then mistakes are jokes that the unconscious makes up, on the spot, against the self. With jokes we confine humour safely to quarters ('We can only laugh when a joke has come to our help'), whereas mistakes set it loose to roam the day.

A man walking in a strange city at around the time when, because of a course of medical treatment, he needed to open his bowels read the word *Klosetthaus* [lavatory] on a large sign over the first floor of a tall department store, although his pleasure at seeing it was mingled with some surprise at the unusual situation of this convenient place. Next moment he was less pleased to see that the signboard really read: *Korsetthaus* [corset-makers].

Parapraxes occur where our unconscious gangs up with circumstance, and gets to ridicule us merely for getting up in the morning and agreeing to appear on the stage of the day (there needs no unbuttoned fly, dear colleague, come from your bedsit to tell us this). As if our days arrive already filled with the reverse of achievement.

❋

'At dinner in the sanatorium one day I used a particularly attentive phrase to my neighbour at table during a conversation which did not much interest me, and was very conventional in tenor . . .'

Freud offers a dressing-down of *belle époque* life, and in such epitomized forms that he often seems to be riding that distinctly

Viennese observation car, the aphorism: 'Girls who are proud of their beautiful hair arrange their combs and hairpins so skilfully that their hair is bound to come down in the middle of a conversation'; 'I once treated a patient whose morbid fear of reading newspapers turned out to be a reaction against his morbid *ambition* to see himself mentioned in print'; 'aristocrats are particularly apt to distort the names of the doctors they have consulted'; women (who are forever forgetting to pay their analysts) 'pay, as it were, with their looks'. Freud breaks intellectual rank by noticing what lies below the threshold of attention, and he breaks social rank by noticing cracks in the smooth glass of ritual.[2]

At the same time he builds up a picture of *fin-de-siècle* Vienna in full dress, and *Everyday Life* is the exploded Baedeker of its rites of passage, its ordeals of civility. Think of the complexity of codes of dress or forms of address, of what it meant to be incorrectly addressed or announced, of the vertiginous decorum of family life, of the rules that govern entering ('falling') into conversation with a stranger. There is no stumbling without thresholds – the more rituals, the more trespass.

'One lady said or intended to say admiringly to another: "I expect you trimmed that pretty new hat yourself?" but instead of *aufgeputzt* [trimmed] said *aufgepatzt* [echoing the word *Patzerei*, a clumsy job].'

(inserted in 1907). Or the niece who, when asked how her uncle is, says: 'I don't know; these days I see him only *in flagranti* [for *en passant*]'; or the uncle who, when his nieces leave after paying him a long overdue visit, says with much feeling: 'Well, from now on I hope to see you *still more seldom* than before'; or this, entranced specimen, of a bungled or 'mishandled' (*vergreift*) action, supplied by Freud's colleague Stekel (also added in 1907):

I entered someone's home, and gave the lady of the house my right hand. Oddly enough, in the process I untied the bow holding her loose morning dress together. I was not aware of any dishonourable intentions, yet I had performed this unskilful movement with a conjuror's sleight of hand.

The shame-culture of *fin-d'empire* Vienna is selectively but mordantly on view throughout *Everyday Life*, as is the contemporary passion for self-betrayal, in other words, for new forms of self-display. As Stefan Zweig remarked in his memoir, *Those Were The Days* (1942): 'our entire generation was inhibited in its freedom of speech by the pressure of the times'. Contemporary Austria-Hungary was monarchical, clerical, militarist, socially and politically restrictive in respect of minorities. More significant for the culture of the parapraxis, the bourgeoisie was itself constituted as an outside caste, forever seeking assimilation with the aristocracy, and the strong assimilationist Jewish element within the Viennese bourgeoise redoubled or exemplified these emphases. The parapraxis thrives along fault-lines, and Hapsburg Vienna is the home of the slip because it is here that bourgeois rectitude encounters a highly developed critical spirit – mixing psychologism, experiment and what Zweig in his memoirs evoked as 'an atmosphere of dangerous erotic infection'.[3] In polite life a host of taboos had to be negotiated – or scrambled in the dyslexicon of the verbal slip: sex, politics, money, the Jewish question, authority, relations with colleagues, professional self-esteem. Some of these, it has been argued – such as class relations and the fear of revolution – were so censored as to be conspicuously absent even from Freud's array of examples.[4] Freud diagnoses slips of the tongue as exposing 'an inner insincerity'; but they are also forms of authenticity: sharp sayings, acts of ventriloquial outspokenness where we momentarily disown society – instead of ourselves – for teaching us manners. (Lacan: 'through slips of the tongue we discover our own voice'.)

It was often remarked, at the time, that the good citizens of Vienna flocked to the theatre so as to learn how to be Viennese. The architectural *façade-ism* of Vienna was the backdrop. Freud takes for granted the innate theatricality of everyday life, and focuses upon its gestic aspect, its surfaces. ('Where are the depths concealed?' asked Hugo von Hoffmansthal, and answered: 'On the surface.') Put differently, there can be no difference between watching an actor imitate a parapraxis on stage and seeing an acquaintance commit a parapraxis in real life. In both cases the spectacle is the same: the faultless performance of a fault. The parapraxis has something in common with the improvisings of Sartrean *mauvaise foi*. Like Sartre's waiter (the superbia of whose every gesture proclaims: 'I am a waiter in the function of being what I am not'), the parapraxis makes no mistakes. Sartre invented situations to illustrate bad faith playing out its daily script. Were we suddenly to discover that Freud's examples were all inventions – some of them undoubtedly are inventions, and some of Freud's collaborators, notably Stekel, were far from reliable as sources – it is not clear how this would compromise their validity.

There is a generalized Proustian comedy of the surface in *Everyday Life*, reminiscent of an item from Proust's own correspondence, which suggests how all slips enact the belatedness of all self-knowledge:

My dear Madam, I just noticed that I forgot my cane at your house yesterday; please be good enough to give it to the bearer of this letter. P.S. Kindly pardon me for disturbing you; I have just found my cane.

From this compound example of a forgetting accompanied by a social gesture so recondite as to be nameless, the élite could be said to have incorporated the slip into its charades, its own needy endgame ceremonies, rather than ceremony being simply exposed or compromised by the slip.[5] And Freud's text can seem like a contemporary reader's guide to *A la recherche du temps perdu*, which was appearing in instalments during the same two decades as the recensions of *Everyday Life*. In both ventures, minor arcana to do with the social presentation of the self were subject to a critique of unprecedented acuity, and rendered suddenly intelligible to themselves. The pathos of both texts consists in their intimation that, for the society they describe, this knowledge is too late, is a form of *esprit d'escalier*, more autopsy than diagnosis.

❊

'I was sitting in a café, turning over the pages of the *Leipziger Illustrierte* . . .'

Since the 1860s, urban life at large had been described along primarily sociological lines – criticized or praised for having eroded the partitions of class. In a state of uncertainty, when the categories have become equivocal, the need to find under-described but solving mechanisms in ordinary life became pressing. Freud's is not the first systematic attempt, but the first anti-sociological attempt to find a new code for interpreting social display. The city-dweller gives nothing away, except what is given away for free, and which cannot be used. Parapraxes say everything about the need to give things away, by accident, in ways that can only be paraphrased. Freud laid down rules for the investigation of these accidents. The parapraxis must be 'within the range of normality'; it must be motiveless ('if we notice the slip at all, we must not recognize any motivation for it in ourselves; instead, we must be tempted to put it down to "carelessness" or "chance"'); and it must be 'a brief and temporary disturbance' ('If someone else corrects our slip, we must immediately acknowledge the justice of the correction'). Noticeable here is that Freud makes the agent of discovery the final arbiter of intentions.

At the same time, parapraxes allow us knowledge of other minds only as passers-by. They are part of the timing of the self. Freud's individuals are mobile, in transit, caught between inside and outside. On stage so briefly, they perform actions that are incomplete, their stories are unfinished, amenable only because stalled momentarily along the *via negativa* of the mistake. The parapraxis re-imagines what William James called 'the continuous flow of the mental stream' as a stopping clock, as if these are the terms for knowing a subject who cannot be interpreted at leisure. Kafka pondered 'the picture of dissatisfaction presented by a street, where everyone is perpetually lifting his feet to escape from the place on which he stands'. Mistakes are glimpses, registered *in einem zug*, whose idiomatic sense is 'in one go', but whose literal meaning is 'on a train'. (In a recent academic misreading, we are told that Kafka's story 'The Judgement' was written on a train – rather than, as Kafka confided to his diary, 'at one sitting' – a case of an error or a slip?) Hanns Sachs, repository of Freud's many examples of the parapraxis in time of war, offered the following in 1917:

Sitting in the tram, I was thinking that many of the friends of my youth, who had always been considered delicate and frail, now seemed able to stand up to the harshest of conditions which would certainly have a shattering effect on me. In the middle of this unwelcome train of thought, as we were passing a firm's signboard, I was only half aware of registering, as we passed, a word in big black letters saying *Eisenkonstitution* [iron constitution]. A moment later it struck me that this was not really right for a business sign, and turning back quickly I caught another glimpse of the inscription, and saw that it really read *Eisenkonstruktion* [Iron Construction].

Everything in *Everyday Life* – including trains of thought – may be imagined as taking place on a train. (The railway was the most visible sign of Austria-Hungary's belated industrialization: 3,000 km of track in 1860, 20,000 km in 1910.) Or there is the moving escalator of the street – 'It was true that I had passed the display-window countless times'; 'I had gone down every other street in the area, avoiding only this single one as if it were forbidden' – which contributes to the atmospherics of the text, in thrall to the circularities and symptoms it diagnoses. There is often a dreamlike mutuality between slip and explanation, as with the patient of Freud's who

'. . . thought that recently he had seen a work on *Agoraphobia* in the display window of a bookshop, and tried to get hold of it by consulting all the publishers' catalogues. I was then able to explain why his efforts were bound to be unsuccessful: the work on agorapobia existed only in his imagination as an unconscious intention, because he was planning to write such a book himself.'

Thus do we go prospecting with our errors.

These repetitions without variation anticipate Freud's definitive account of being parapractically lost while walking the streets – in his paper on 'The Uncanny' (1919) – with its insidious intent and its overwhelming question:

Strolling one hot summer afternoon through the empty and to me unfamiliar streets of a small Italian town, I found myself in a district about whose character I could not long remain in doubt. Only heavily made-up women were to be seen at the windows of the little houses, and I hastily left the narrow street at the next turning. However, after wandering about for some time without asking the way, I suddenly found myself back in the same street, where my presence began to attract attention. Once more I hurried away, only to return there again by a different route. I was now seized by a feeling that I can only describe as uncanny . . .

The 'uncanny' (*Unheimlich*) exists in rich because apparent opposition to the *heimlich* (the 'homely', the 'familiar' – the 'concealed'). In *Everyday Life* Freud praises Strindberg for the 'uncanny faithfulness' of his depiction of the 'secret nature' of minor symptomatic acts and parapraxes, for example in his novel *The Gothic Rooms*. Home is the heart of the matter, because everything uncanny entails an act of recognition, and the power of E. T. A. Hoffmann's story 'The Sand Man' (the text at the heart of Freud's essay) is that he invades the home. As Baudelaire put the matter in a memo to himself: 'Study of The Great Malady: horror of Home'. The parapraxis is an unhoused action, and it wires the outdoors for gothic recognitions. Many of Freud's examples casually fix upon this aspect of a situation, as with the woman who gets run over in the street, in the chapter on bungled actions: 'That morning there were almost no vehicles about, since the trams, omnibuses, etc., were on strike – there was almost *absolute calm* at the time.'

❊

Here men walk alone
For most of their lives,
What with hydrants for dogs,
And windows for wives.
       (Ogden Nash, 'City')

Everyday Life is a *plein-air* forum of individual acts both joined and isolated inside collective life, as of a turning away from privacy and its reticences towards improvised forms: streets, cafés, resorts. Always a model of the unconscious, for Freud, the *agora* joins sleeping with waking and walking, since the structure of the dream has its equivalent in ordinary waking life, and the city is the topographical and psychic, mnemonic and syntactical form that the day takes. It is a marketplace, but for the exchange of what? – if not mistakes. Freud's focus upon citizens recalls Marx's dictum that the bourgeoisie can never arrive at a perfectly clear awareness of itself. As if parapraxes and their acknowledgement are the attempt of a certain historical type to pinch himself awake before it is too late. Freud focuses a general nomadism, the picaresque of selves caught off-balance, giving themselves away, prey to 'momentary and temporary disturbance'. And this is of a piece with the untethered drift of examples. The text contains a flotsam of decorously displaced persons ('An American staying in Europe . . .), who could be said to stand in for or are themselves displacements of an untidier reality: behind the scenes of *Everyday Life*. Vienna was filling up with an influx of settlers and *luftmenschen*, becoming a laboratory of social anomie, an old world full of new arrivals. And in later editions, when history eerily catches up with *Everyday Life*, the universal displacement of the First World War provokes a haemorrhage of new examples of error and slippage. Embedded in Freud's text – at fairytale depth – are the only real homes, the homes away from home (pensione, spas, sanatoria), a parallel world of witness and gossip beyond the everyday.

One of the locales of the parapraxis is commodity – error whose nexus is things seen, displayed, purchased, places visited and thereby colonized. Everyday life condenses into spectacle. 'When I am on holiday and walking down the street in a foreign town . . . I read every shop sign that suggests the word in any way at all as *Antiques*. This must be an expression of my interests as a collector'. Many of the examples concern things desired, hesitated over, mislaid, misconstrued. There is a constant *va-et-vient* between physical and psychic realms: to mislay something is a kind of forgetting, to forget something is a kind of mislaying ('just before the accident she had seen a pretty picture in a shop on the opposite side of the street'; 'I like to use good blotting paper, and on my afternoon walk into the inner city I meant to buy some'; 'When I saw the book . . . in the shop window I did not at first intend to buy it. However, a few days later I decided that I would, but by then the book was not in the window.') Props of potentially farcical materiality abound: rings, fountain pens, watches, keys, pipes, stairs, letters, telephones, books. More generally, the Freudian metropolis is a collapsing empire of signs, a scene of miscognition. Or of coincidence. In a renunciatory embrace, *Everyday Life* denies chance actions – which it sees everywhere, and from which Surrealism was to take its cues – in favour of examples and explanations which are themselves coincidences.

✻

> To see is to forget the names of the things one sees.
> (Paul Valéry)

'[T]emporarily forgetting names is one of the most frequent observed of all slips of the mind,' says Freud, and one of the forms of hide-and-seek played out in *Everyday Life* concerns naming and not-naming. A Herr Lederer, on honeymoon in Venice, runs across an acquaintance whom he reluctantly introduces to his new wife. Since he has forgotten the man's name he gets by with 'murmuring something indistinct'. When they meet again ('as was bound to happen in Venice') he draws him aside and asks him for help: ' "I can easily believe that you didn't remember my name," says the prescient other, " – it's *Lederer*, like yours!" ' Or there is the timid but ambitious young doctor who parapractically introduces himself to the celebrated pathologist Dr Virchow as – 'Dr Virchow'. Or the young father who presents himself before the registrar of births to give notice of the birth of his second daughter. 'When asked the child's name he replied: "Hanna". "But you already have a child called Hanna," the registrar told him.' This stealthy convergence of names occurs because your name – whatever it is – calls up my personal associations; in a sense, we all have the same name, because any name will do the job. Karl Kraus described Austria-Hungary as 'this pseudonymous civilization', and one of the poles of his satire is to regard all names as duplicitous – Germanized Jewish names above all. The pages of *Die Fackel*, the journal that Kraus edited from 1899 (and in which Freud's name often appeared) read like a telephone directory. Kraus names multitudes of names, but mockingly claims to be making them all up: in each instance the accused coincidentally bears the name of an actual person.

Freud unaccountably forgets the first name of a young man, the brother of one of his patients, who appears in his consulting room, whom he has seen countless times, and whose name is by no means unusual. 'I went out into the street to read the signboards over the business premises, and recognized the name as soon as I encountered it.' He ponders the reasons for this forgetting, in terms of the family story (what are brothers for?), but his symptomatic solution to the quandary of forgetting goes unremarked. That the privacy of a name ('the name is an integral part of the personality' we are told elsewhere) is to be found posted in the street is part of the book's uninvestigated suspensions. On the one hand, the argument of *Everyday Life* is legitimated by names (streets, shops, literary characters, historical figures, titles of books, authorities, colleagues, contributors of examples) – by the belief that objects, including slips, can be named and thereby located. On the other hand, it is a book in which no one is named. The individuals whose short stories are its concern remain unindividuated ('A certain Herr Y. fell in love with a lady who did not return his affection, and soon afterwards married another man, Herr X.'), like the hubbub of backs and faces which is our sight of each other amid the surrounding overspecification. In Freud's text, precisions as to place always ensure anonymity of persons. And when the same examples from *Everyday Life* are reproduced much later in the *Introductory Lectures*, the peripheral focus often sharpens. 'One day in the Dolomites I met two ladies in walking dress' becomes 'I once met two *Viennese* ladies in the *lovely* Dolomites . . .' The more precision, the more anonymity, rather in the manner of the Sherlock Holmes stories to which Freud was addicted.

This is dramatized in an allusion to the *Fragment of an Analysis of a Case History* ('*Dora*'), which he was writing up in the first months of 1901, interrupting *Everyday Life* to do so. 'When I was preparing the case history of a woman patient of mine for publication, I wondered what first name to give her.' There would naturally appear to be an unlimited choice of available names. 'Instead, only a single name came into my mind: – the name *Dora*.' Freud asks himself why – who else was there called Dora?

I felt like rejecting the next idea to occur to me as incredible, for it told me that the nanny who looked after my sister's children was called Dora, but I had enough self-discipline, or enough experience of analysis, to follow that idea and take it further. I immediately thought of a small incident the previous evening, which brought me the association determining the name I was seeking. I saw a letter addressed to 'Fräulein Rosa W.' lying on the table in my sister's dining room. In surprise, I asked who that was, and learned that the nanny Dora was really called Rosa, but had been obliged to change her name on entering the household because my sister is a Rosa too and could have taken the name to mean herself. I said, sympathetically: Poor servants, they can't even keep their own names! And now that I came to think of it, I said no more for a moment, but began meditating on various serious subjects. My thoughts trailed vaguely away, but I could now easily recall them to my conscious mind. So when next day I was looking for a name for someone *who could not be allowed to keep her own*, only *Dora* sprang to mind.

The Dora of *Everyday Life* is a shadow, one of the recessive governesses and servants who hover at the edges of the text, dropping fragile articles, mutely hostile to *objets d'art*. They constitute a doubling of ourselves, too close for comfort (for we too drop things), a stock from which contemporaries such as Walser and Kafka were to recruit heroes without qualities.

✿

'It reached me in a somewhat roundabout way, but comes from a reliable source . . .'

The other *Dora* belongs to another world: however 'fragmentary' in construction, the case history offers a heroine, a plot, and the display of a selfhood without precedent. The this-world of the parapraxis offers only fugitive scenarios of the possible, and *Everyday Life* is a host of walk-ons: here comes everybody. With rare exceptions, Freud's book is a study of errors rather than selves, of individual parapraxes rather than individual histories. His explanations largely refer to the recent past, to the experiences of adult life, rather than back to childhood. Which makes us wonder what children's slips would be like, and whether parapraxes are not a developmental, phase-specific achievement. One of the more buried suggestions of *Everyday Life* – considered as a collection of biographemes – is that not all memories are stories, and not all remembering is storytelling. The cumulative effect of Freud's anecdotes, far from interrupting his argument, is to replicate the mechanism of the slip as being, above all else, an interruption. As a unit of meaning, the parapraxis interrupts the narrative of our days, and as a unit of narrative it interrupts their meaning.

Moreover, knowledge of slips can be acquired unproblematically at second- or third-hand, by hearsay and anecdote. 'A good and easily explained example . . . is provided by the self-observation of one Herr J. G. while he was in a sanatorium' – a circular moment, and part of the oddity with which the text stages its evidence. It makes the debate over the unfalsifiability of Freud's explanations seem irrelevant: so unprivileged is the information from which they take their cue. The text has as many intermediaries – friends, colleagues, contributors – as characters. Moreover, it is a function of the 'thinness' of the slip – of its inauthenticity, even – that 'some other slip could have functioned just as well'. The specific form that error takes is not determined by the concealed idea that it has disturbed – just as a slip of the tongue is determined not by the near identity of sounds themselves, but by thoughts that lie outside the intended speech-act. A parapraxis marks the spot, locates the fact but not the direction of deviation, and *Everyday Life* is concerned less with selves than with situations. Hence its low-wattage intensities, its shavings from the table of selfhood, its status as a study in residua. These moments have fallen out of a novel, and *Everyday Life* contains the opening sentences of innumerable unwritten novels ('A young man staying in a mixed boarding house met an English woman . . .'; 'By a coincidence, there was a guest from Paris in her lodgings at present . . .'). These remain unintegrated, like specimen sentences, utterances for a manual or etiquette book. As if our parapraxes, far from belonging to us, serve to undifferentiate us as subjects.

Just as the slip is and is not an action, it is only partially interpretable. As an occurrence of doubtful status – did you say what I just heard you say? – its natural medium is the anecdote ('a married woman, who liked a good story . . .'), or the higher gossip ('A lady told me that when she last saw a common acquaintance . . .'). Freud notes our fascinated resistance when we are shown to have committed or are caught committing a parapraxis – 'it is worth noting that no one likes admitting to a slip of the tongue' – the slip is hearsay about ourselves, news from a foreign country. This might seem to distinguish slips from other forms of psychoanalytic knowing, but as Freud tells his audience in the *Introductory Lectures*: 'You cannot be present at a psychoanalytic treatment. You can only be told about it; and, in the strictest sense of the word, it is only by hearsay that you will get to know psychoanalysis' – as if theories are themselves anecdotes at one remove. Freud analysed Schreber on the basis of Schreber's published *Memoirs*, which 'took the place of' personal acquaintance. There is always mediation, and in the extroversions of *Everyday Life* it is as if Freud's brief lives become folkloric with accretion. ('I am afraid that all the examples above have been rather commonplace . . . since my intention is solely to collect everyday material.') Everyday life is a bush telegraph, and *Everyday Life* is an organon of the urban bungle. Experience is continuous – we all worry about the same things, we all make mistakes, our slips are interchangeable. Freud's inclusion of misprints as 'writing mistakes' on the compositor's part, or of telegram errors as writing mistakes on the telegraphist's part, are yet ghostlier demarcations, ever further from a constituted human subject. At another remove, and this has an oddly complicating effect upon our sense of what kind of book it is that we are reading, one of the witnesses most frequently called upon in this pages is that form of hearsay known as literature, considered as a store of *copia* or convenient examples from Shake-speare to Strindberg. 'We can only repeat what they said long ago,' remarks Freud – or on occasion anticipate what they have yet to say.

○

He happened to be putting some fresh water in the vase . . .

Although it takes the form of a treatise, *Everyday Life* has conti-nuities with literary texts in which the modern was clarified as that which can be brought into view only by a process of blurring. The prestige of 'accident' is implied here, and Freud's belief in the importance of the accidental – from *lapsus linguae* to quotidian routine – is part of a more general breach in the recalcitrance of the ordinary. How to make ordinary life visible is a central problem of aesthetics from Flaubert onwards: in other words, that area of experience which disqualifies itself as vestigial or discrepant, and which Freud qualified as the central concern of psychoanalysis: 'the dregs of the world of appearances' (*Introductory Lectures*).

This common enterprise has its synchronicities. Between the appearance of *The Psychopathology of Everyday Life* in periodical form in 1901 and in book form in 1904, for example, Joyce was collecting fragments of overheard dialogue or found speech, which he hoarded in a notebook and later transposed for fiction. When he began collecting these 'epiphanies' he regarded them, in the words of his brother, Stanislaus, as 'little errors and gestures – mere straws in the wind, by which people betrayed the very things they were most careful to conceal'.[6] Joyce's interest in psychology was intermit-tent, and he was more interested in the insignificant than the signifi-cant slip – in the freight of consciousness rather than in signs of psychic repression – but both Joyce and Freud were committed to the epic temporalities of the single day.

Freud's epiphanies are the audition of a language going on inside language, a rhyme which he began hearing all around him – or as Kraus remarked: 'I hear noises which others don't hear,' referring to his own apocalyptic audition of sinister meanings in the unexamined usages of ordinary life. Freud's moment of clear hearing is documented in a letter to Fliess (26 August 1898): 'I have at last grasped a little thing that I had long suspected.' Not the perception of nonsense – since 'what results from a slip of the tongue has a sense of its own', or as Wittgenstein said, you must pay attention to your nonsense – so much as the sound of sense without the sense, akin to Robert Frost's discovery (in his letter to John Bartlett, July 1913) that 'the best place to get the abstract sound of sense is from voices behind a door that cuts off the words'. In the same year Kafka noted in his diary: 'Yesterday's observation. The most appropriate situation for me: to listen to a conversation between two people who are discussing a matter that concerns them closely while I have only a very remote interest in it which is in addition completely selfless.' The free-floating attentiveness of psychoanalysis is close to the care with which these early listeners felt impelled to record motiveless moments, to conduct fieldwork amid the disjecta of the day. As if that which does not concern you, which has nothing to do with you, is of the greatest personal significance (which is what Freud meant by the unconscious). That Kafka repeatedly castigates himself in the *Diaries* for the poverty of his 'miserable observations' merely confirms their necessity to a nocturnal art constructed out of the refuse of the day.

One of the premises of psychoanalysis is that a clear-cut distinction between sleeping and waking has no meaning, from which Henri Bergson concluded that 'it is the awake-state, rather than the dream-state, which requires explanation'.[7] *Everyday Life* explains the awake-state as a state of analogy:

The inconsistencies, absurdities and mistakes of the content of dreams, which have largely prevented them from being recognized as the product of psychic processes, arise in the same way, although admittedly with freer use of the means available, as do the common slips in our everyday life.

The two are linked by more than this, however, since what has claimed our attention by day is recycled by night. More important, for present purposes, what does not claim our attention by day also shapes the dream. What Freud in *The Interpretation of Dreams* calls 'the remains' of the day – 'worthless fragments of daily life' (IV) – are the façade for what the dream wishes to conceal: they encode its latent content. In *Everyday Life* this unsuspected franchise of the banal is further extended, as if in flashback (most of *Everyday Life* concerns the tenses of adulthood) to the material of childhood memories, since these too preserve what is indifferent, as screens for other repressed memories. Like parapraxes, they owe their preservation not to their own content but to an associative relation between their content and another memory. *The Interpretation of Dreams* sets the scene for the investigation of *Everyday Life*, as if the latter were framed inside the former – as if our days are dignified by the discovery that they are in the service of our nights.

❀

What I tell you three times is true.
(Lewis Carroll, *The Hunting of the Snark*)

The notion of the dream's dependence on the disregarded lumber of the day is shocking, because this material had seemed so incapable – or so unworthy – of being editorialized. Even diaries defer to a remembered present. Freud's time-exposures (the parapraxis is a frozen moment) revealed psychic mechanisms rather as photography had amazed the day, asleep in the conviction of its own unregisterability. 'Whereas it is a commonplace that we have some idea of what is involved in the act of walking, we have no idea what happens during the fraction of a second when a person *steps out*.[8] The parapraxis shows the self as it steps out, or steps out of line. Photography revealed what Walter Benjamin called the optical unconscious. In early photographs, the human subject is caught and caught out, discomposed, error-stricken. Which is why, the more innocent the image, the more it struck the viewer as documenting a transgression. Cinema likewise made all habitual and familiar action seem as if somehow in the wrong. Whence its comedy: in keeping with Freud's account of the Joke, the first audiences did not know what they were laughing at. Cinema projected the inadvertence of our presence as witnesses (observing the unseeable) as an inadvertence in the realm of the seen – again, a mechanism outlined in *The Joke and Its Relation to the Unconscious*.

In silent cinema, the discontinuity of the action and the continuo of the music offer a convenient image of the parapraxis and what it conceals. The early cinemas were places where the public gathered to witness mistakes in motion, in real time, showing what the flow of the day ordinarily conceals from view. Writing in 1936, Walter Benjamin made the connections explicit:

Film has enriched our field of perception with methods which can be illustrated by those of Freudian theory. Fifty years ago, a slip of the tongue passed more or less unnoticed. Only exceptionally may such a slip have revealed dimensions or depth in a conversation which had seemed to be taking its course on the surface. Since *The Psychopathology of Everyday Life* things have changed. This book isolated and made analysable things which had heretofore floated along unnoticed on the broad stream of perception. For the entire spectrum of optical, and now also acoustic perception, film has brought about a similar deepening of appercepion . . . By close-ups of the things around us film extends our comprehension of the necessities that rule our lives, and manages to assure us of an immense and unsuspected field of action. Evidently a different nature opens itself to the camera than opens to the naked eye – if only because an unconsciously penetrated space is substituted for a space consciously explored.[9]

One of cinema's discoveries was that everyday life is repetition – as if our actions are constantly trying to remember something – and it turned this to account in the figure of the accident-prone hero. Mayakovsky noted that Chaplin characteristically repeats a gag three times, and he called these passages 'analytical sequences'. The parapraxis is a gag, the combined parapraxis is a serial gag whose spacing is the bearer of meaning, and in this it resembles the syntax of the dream.[10] In the *Introductory Lectures* Freud refers to combined slips (a symptomatic act combined with a case of mislaying, for example) as 'the finest flower of their kind'. A pedantically precise man forgets

his watch at home; he has to go on from work to an evening engagement, so he borrows the watch of a ladyfriend; the following day he
goes to return the borrowed watch, and finds he has left it at home,
although this time he has his own watch with him; he goes home to
recover the lady's watch, returns it to her, and finds he has now left
his watch at home ('as if his conscious mind were saying "I can't get
this business out of my head"'). The heroic waifs and strays of the
silent screen are innocents who see themselves – in Adorno's version
of the city-dweller in general – 'solely as objects of opaque processes,
who, torn between sudden shock and sudden forgetfulness, are no
longer capable of a sense of temporal continuity'.[11]

✿

This cannot possibly be an individual peculiarity of my own . . .

Freud rejected the operating idea that below a certain level whatever
we do is inadvertent, and he confronts our investment in contingency
– our superstitious tenderness towards the throwaway, the gamble,
the happy minute, the feat – with a concealed symptomatic order.
Everyday Life enlarged the number of things we do which must be
thought of as actions, by finding new ways of explaining them as
actions. This of course breaks with all our ordinary convictions of
behaving freely – automatically – in regard to unimportant things.
Instead,

'Any change of one's usual appearance, any small act of negligence – for
instance a button left undone – every exposure means something which the
person wearing that clothing does not want to say directly, indeed generally
does not intend to say at all.'

Never such innocence again. We accept this enlargement of meaning
largely under the aegis of comedy, since if we could not make
parapraxes interesting and amusing we would be oppressed and
horrified by them, by the new inescapability.

Indeed, it is just when we are being required to envisage a world in which we must take such injunctions seriously, that the unsettling and ambivalent figure of the paranoiac enters Freud's story of ordinary life. At the outset, Freud explains our forgettings as the power of the repressed in making hidden connections:

There is thus a constant stream of 'self-referentiality' going through my mind. I am not usually aware of it, but it betrays itself when I forget names in this way. It is as if I were obliged to relate everything I hear about other people to myself: as if my personal complexes were aroused by my perception of others. This cannot possibly be a quality peculiar to myself alone; instead, it must contain some indication of the way in which we perceive 'otherness'.

So far so normal. However, paranoiacs likewise 'draw conclusions from the trivial signs they observe in other people'. Everything the paranoiac observes in others is rich with disclosure. He notes how passers-by 'laugh to themselves, flourish their sticks, even spit on the ground as they go by'[12] – in other words, how they commit endless symptomatic acts. His hubris is to refer it all to himself: 'When his train was moving out of the station, everyone makes a particular gesture with one hand . . . Or he notes the way people walk in the street, how they flourish their sticks and so on.' The paranoiac takes signs for wonders, such as to render his knowledge 'useless'.[13] He orchestrates the world into what Freud, in his *Psycho-analytic Remarks on an Autobiographically Described Case of Paranoia*, calls 'the plot against Schreber'.

In a sense, the paranoiac cannot commit parapraxes, because he is destined to observe them – is perhaps their ideal observer. He sees life as it strikes a contemporary, and it all means too much. By the same token, perhaps, our parapraxes – our acts of unknowing, our refusals to notice – prevent us from becoming paranoiac. We habitually posit a zone of involuntary mental life in ourselves and those around us. Not to notice things is to fall over them, but parapraxes have a certain redemptive grace: they allow for what Beckett chastised Proustian voluntary memory as refusing to allow for: 'the mysterious element of inattention that colours our most commonplace experiences'.[14] Psychoanalysis in one mode suggests that we cannot know ourselves but that we can have knowledge of others. In another mode, that 'The way to carry out the famous injunction to *know thyself* is through studying our apparently accidental actions and omissions'. The paranoiac attempts to conflate these claims. Which is why he comes to grief (but never quite to mourning). He is none the less Freud's *semblable*, the only other proper character in *Everyday Life* – and the only sort of clairvoyant whom Freud could ever take seriously.

✿

We had fallen into conversation . . .

There runs through *Everyday Life* a 'strong current' of autobiographical reference, ranging from affectively charged moments from Freud's early adulthood ('When I was a young man living alone in a foreign city, I often enough heard my name suddenly called by a beloved and unmistakable voice'), to laconic glimpses into the later home life of the Freuds: 'Recently there was a time, when unusual quantities of glass and china were broken in my household.' One of the latter scenes involves the throwing of a slipper:

For instance, one morning as I was walking through a room in my dressing gown, wearing straw slippers, I obeyed a sudden impulse and kicked one slipper off my foot and against the wall, where it brought down a pretty little marble Venus from her bracket.

The impulse, and his calm acceptance of its consequences, are explained in terms of the sudden realization that his eldest daughter was showing signs of recovery from a grave illness: the breakage is an unconscious act of 'sacrificial' gratitude. The example and its explanation are closely fitting and fitted, self-sufficient. There is, however, a more occluded autobiographical strain in *Everyday Life* – having to do with the reluctant notion of the parapraxis as, of necessity, a conversation: as if the *faux pas* is always a *pas de deux*.

At the very outset of *Everyday Life*, Freud offers one of his major examples. It is cast in the form of a Socratic dialogue – because it means to persuade us of the general validity of his methods, and pave the way for easier examples to come.[15] He describes being on holiday the previous summer, and passing time with a young Austrian Jew who complains of the position in which Jews are currently held in Austria-Hungary – unable to develop their talents and doomed to atrophy. The young man ends his speech by quoting the passionate injunction that Virgil puts into the mouth of Dido, abandoned by Aeneas and on the point of suicide: *'Exoriar(e) aliquis nostris ex ossibus ultor!* [May someone rise, an avenger, from my bones!]'. But his memory of the line is at fault, and all he manages to recall is *Exoriar(e) ex nostris ossibus ultor!* He omits *aliquis* [someone] and he inverts the word-order.

But why forget the innocent *aliquis*? Challenged by the young man – who is familiar with Freud's publications – and in the hope of adding a new specimen to his collection, Freud accepts. He asks his companion to call up any associations that the forgotten word might hold. With Freud's assistance as *souffleur*, the process leads with dazzling rapidity, via *a-liquis* and 'fluid' connotations, to the young man's fears that a certain lady of his acquaintance, whose periods have stopped, may now be pregnant. Having expressed a desire for descendants (a new avenging generation), he has had a contrary thought – descendants, yes, but not on these terms – and the collision of contrary impulses ignites the parapraxis, a case of strategic forgetting.

However, there are not one but two encounters with Virgil's text here: there is the young man's failure to recall correctly, but there is also Freud's perfect and immediate recall: '"There's something the matter with that line. How does the whole thing really go?" "I'll be happy to tell you," – I replied, and quoted the line as it really runs.' What is elided by this suave moment, and what goes unremarked in commentaries on the *aliquis* example (as if remembering, unlike forgetting, is self-evident), is that Freud might have his own reasons for recalling the line. For Dido's cry is a prophetic augury of the coming of Hannibal – the future avenger whom Virgil, writing in retrospect, had in mind, and whom contemporary commentators called to mind – and whom Freud must also call to mind, having since childhood identified with Hannibal as the Carthaginian ('Semitic') general who defeated the Romans yet failed to take Rome.

In *The Interpretation of Dreams*, published the previous year, Freud dwells on a series of dreams which have their basis in his as yet unfulfilled longing to see Rome. He recalls that, as an adolescent, '*Hannibal* and *Rome* symbolized to me the opposition between the tenacity of Jewry and the organization of the Catholic Church. The significance which the anti-Semitic movement has since acquired for our emotional life later helped to fix the thoughts and feelings of that earlier period.' Rome comes to stand for the Viennese medical establishment and the Hapsburg political regime at large. Freud offers a studio portrait of himself as a Hannibal who might storm the citadel of his chosen profession but still be denied the ultimate prize: a professorship and recognition. 'Like Hannibal, I had been fated not to see Rome' (V.B.).

The narrative doors of *The Interpretation of Dreams* open in sequence, and the Hannibal comparison leads to the sudden recovery of the childhood scene that inaugurated Freud's Rome obsession. He recalls his father explaining, when he was ten or twelve years old, how the triumph of mid-century liberalism had ushered in a better world in which to be a Jew, and how formerly he himself had once been humiliated by a passer-by ('Jew! Get off the pavement!') At which the child's filial curiosity is aroused – 'What did you do?' – and he is disappointed to learn that his father submitted unheroically to the insult: 'I compared this episode, by which I was not impressed, with another more suited to my feelings: the scene (in Livy) where Hannibal's father makes his son swear before the household altar to take vengeance on the Romans. From that time on, Hannibal had a place in my fantasies.'

In adulthood, for Freud to take vengeance on the Romans means to affirm the liberal ideals that his father had momentarily failed to defend decades earlier, to resist the present crisis of liberalism – and the resurgence of institutional anti-Semitism in the 1890s – which threaten to destroy those principles. Freud travelled repeatedly to Italy during this decade, but each time failed to reach – found reasons for not reaching – Rome. But he succeeded in 1901, the year in which *Everyday Life* was published (five years after his father's death) – and he succeeded symbolically in the following year, when the long-awaited professorship was secured.

Freud often quoted Goethe on Lichtenberg: 'When he makes a joke, a problem lies concealed.' The light-heartedness of the *aliquis* example – told with a brio verging on triumphalism – is its autobiographical trace element. What is being played out, in diaologue form, is the retrospect of a struggle which Freud is aware of having all but come through. He looks forward to reaching Rome while looking *back* at his travelling companion, as at his own younger self. Two actors, one story. The young Austrian Jew appropriates Dido's cry and the older responds *qua* Hannibal, most particularly so since the latter goes unmentioned, or no longer needs to be mentioned. It has been suggested – the *aliquis* example attracts sceptical commentary – that the encounter with the young Austrian never occurred, that it was one of the fictions (true stories of a hidden self) which Freud smuggled in among his exhibits. At the least there is a symbolic working-through in this and other passages of *Everyday Life*, comparable to the way in which *The Interpretation of Dreams* contains a running frieze of personal history. One could say that in *Everyday Life*, as with an equally composite text like *Dora*, Freud 'provides us with the materials for understanding some things that have escaped his own understanding'.[16] A parapraxis might, after all, describe the arc of a life as well as a momentary episode.

'Oh, look, there's Herr L.'

A slip is, among other things, an act of pointing, a communication. It says: 'I want you to know that I am hiding something from myself,' as if it takes two to make a mistake. What makes the Freudian slipper example unconvincing is the lack of witness, the silence surrounding it, the absence of comedy, the atypical self-completion (no one enters the room just as the slipper is being thrown). A slip, like a crime, usually has witnesses: relatives, intimates, colleagues; the perpetrator is known to the victim. But, as we have seen, the message is a confused one, opaque to both parties. The slip resembles a seduction, neither more nor less real, factitious rather than fictitious. A slip is always a cancellation slip, a denial. As if to take one's keys with one is to have performed an act, but to forget them is to have not acted. The parapraxis opens a door into the unacted life of wishes fulfilled: I forget my keys, and the day acquires a subplot ('One's real life is so often the life one does not lead,' said Wilde).

The witness to a parapraxis could be pictured as an involved bystander. Whence the uncertainty of the proffered (but also the withdrawn) error. Freud makes us behold the everyday, whose self-absorption was formerly taken for granted, as something rescripted daily in front of others, whose presence modifies what occurs. Freud's absorption of the beholder into the mechanisms of the parapraxis (such as Manet made inescapable in art: *Le Déjeuner sur l'herbe* is the painting of a parapraxis) is so thoroughgoing as to go unmentioned. Just as one of the witnesses required is an internal other, because only a split subject can be described, by himself, as having made an error. One of Freud's specimens crystallizes this figure – 'the addressee necessarily implied by *every* articulation of the unconscious'[17] – in the person of an eavesdropping husband:

I was to read a certain lady a stern lecture at the request of her husband, who was listening on the other side of the door. At the end of my sermon, which obviously made an impression, I said, 'Well, goodbye then, *gnädiger Herr* [instead of *gnädige Frau*]!

The parapraxis in all its forms could also be said to take this form.

Coda

Freud avoids systematic reflection upon the language he employs. Or he worries at languge as a way of worrying about language. *The*

Psychopathology of Everyday Life is saturated in everyday usage – 'the insights that reflect our common experience' – and as a text it cuts its cloth from the same materials. It defers to ordinary language as its guide[18] so as to conduct a critique, a prising away of utterance from its uses in the world, and a giving back of new meanings to what has become occluded by habit – which hides everything under our noses – and by those actions (slips, dreams, jokes) that say what they have to say, but 'in other words'. Because the explanations are events in language, acts of translation, the focus is instructively sharpened, rather than diffused, by a consideration of how to find just equivalents in English. The question of how to translate Freud's text becomes as good a question as any to be asked of that text.

Ernest Jones's protective view was that Freud 'forged' his own terminology. One could equally say that he uses the same word in many different ways and contexts, so as to build up a 'picture' of its uses, and that it is by such means that his terms become instantiated. The standard English terminology was instantiated by James Strachey more by *fiat*, if only because Strachey's is the *Standard Edition*, and remains the only authorized translation to date. Revision is underway to accommodate the accumulated suggestion that Strachey and colleagues Englished at least some of Freud's German in doctrinaire, or retrospective, or over-systematic, or abstract, or Latinate, or unduly scientist ways.

Freud unites the main topics of *Everday Life* by choosing terms that share the same prefix, following the natural lead of the German language where the 'same word formation, with the prefix *ver-* [roughly, English 'mis-'], gives a linguistic indication of the internal similiary of most of these phenomena'. Thus *versprechen* ('to misspeak'; Strachey: 'slips of the tongue'), *vergreifen* ('to mishandle'; Strachey: 'bungled actions') and *vergessen* ('to forget). Cognate examples reinforce the decisions of language in respect of minor error: *verschreiben* ('to miswrite': Strachey: 'slips of the pen'), *verlesen* ('to misread'; Strachey: 'slips of reading'), *verlegen* ('to mislay'), *verlieren* ('to misplace', 'to lose'). Some of these are reflexive verbs (*sich verhoren*, 'to mishear', *sich versprechen*', 'to misspeak', *sich vergreifen*, 'to mishandle'), and in German many of Freud's uses hover on the verges of the vernacular, in and out of the lexically transparent – slightly stiffened uses of the usual, which create an air of alertness around themselves.

In addition to *ver-*, there is a complementary and overlapping cluster of German compounds for things going awry, which lead with the prefix *fehl-* ('wrong', 'false'). Thus *fehlen* ('to err', 'fail', 'mistake'), *Fehlgriff* ('a mistake') from *Griff* ('a grip', 'a handle') and *greifen* ('to grasp', 'to handle') – which leads in a circle back to Freud's *ver–greifen* ('to misgrasp', 'to mishandle'). There is even a verb *ver/fehlen* ('to miss' [a train], 'to choose wrongly' [a career]). When it came to finding a word to subsume all local strayings of the self in daily life, rather than employ existing usage Freud coined a new term from *fehl-*, namely *Fehl-leistung*. *Leistung* means 'act', 'performance', 'achievement': hence 'faulty performance'.

Strachey chose to render *Fehlleistung* as 'parapraxis', and in the *Standard Edition* the strange term appears for the first time in the editor's Introduction to *The Psychopathology of Everyday Life*, footnoted thus:

In German *Fehlleistung*, 'faulty function'. It is a curious fact that before Freud wrote this book the general concept seems not to have existed in psychology, and in English a new word had to be invented to cover it.

Neither of these assertons is quite valid (and faulty 'function' is already a running away with the bone). Freud's *Fehlleistung* may have been a new word, but its composite parts are thoroughly vernacular. Moreover, his employment of it in *Everyday Life* is not technical in the sense of proprietory or rigorously apodictic. *Fehlleistung* alludes to and is used by Freud alongside other extant terms – notably *Fehlhandlung* – as in *Fehl-und Zufallshandlungen*, for example, Englished by the *Standard edition* as 'parapraxes and chance actions'. *Handlung* means 'action', and *Fehlhandlung* – 'erroneous action' – has been in currency since Goethe.[19]

'Parapraxis' on the other hand is not English coin – it has the odd distinction of describing something we all do, while ensuring that none of us know what it means (in vain will you look up the word in the *Concise Oxford Dictionary*). It has held until now as the accepted translation,[20] but has found enemies along the way. Bruno Bettelheim pointed out that Freud's *Fehlleistung* simultaneously suggests achievement or accomplishment (*Leistung*) and failure, errance (*fehl-*):

When we think of a mistake we feel that something has gone wrong, and when we refer to an accomplishment we approve of it. In *Fehlleistung*, the two responses become somehow merged: we both approve and disapprove. *Fehlleistung* is much more than an abstract concept: it's a term that gives German readers an immediate, intuitive feeling of admiration for the cleverness and ingenuity of the unconscious processes, without the reader's losing sight of the fact that the end result of those processes is a mistake. For example, when we make an error in talking we frequently feel that what is said is right, though we also somehow know it is wrong. When we forget an appointment, we know that forgetting it was an error, but also feel that somehow we probably wanted to avoid keeping the appointment. Perhaps the best rendering of *Fehlleistung* would be 'faulty achievement'.[21]

'Faulty achievement' is not ideal, but it is alert to the problem, in translating Freud's words, of conveying their undertow of individual *agency*. Another example is *vergreifen*, literally 'mishandle'. This is not quite the same as Strachey's 'bungle', which suggests non-performance, or some such extenuation. The present translation prefers 'inadvertent actions' – since Freud's examples have often little to do with bungling *per se* (rather the dress unfastened 'with a conjuror's sleight of hand', the slipper aimed 'so well' at the statue, and so on). 'Bungled' suggests an action feebly intended and clumsily executed; Bettelheim suggests that in Freud's examples an action is not so much *intended* as carried out, and with perfect aplomb. But, in fact, a parapraxis is the site of a compromise (in Freud's words, 'a half-success and a half-failure for each of two intentions'). It is the chance meeting, on the operating table of the day, of a deflected and a deflecting intention – the former often the mere occasion for the latter. And the load-bearer of Freud's explanations is always the latter, the intervening counter-intention. The danger with the

English terms is that the two become equals. As a result, the Freudian slip gets understood as occasioned by something very like a banana peel in the self's path.

'Parapraxis' is usually decanted into plain English as [Freudian] 'slip', and this is the vernacular solution that has been adopted in the present translation. There are interesting difficulties with 'slip', its modern uses having elided precisely the earlier and germane associations of transgression, of error in conduct (*OED*: 'Adam's fatal slip', etc., from 1601 onwards). The modern sense of sheer 'inadvertence' or accident – *merely* a slip – suggests a cancelling passivity: it replaces the neutral clarity of agency with a warm muddle of intentionality. To adopt Austin's austerities, a 'slip' implies either justification ('I accept that it happened, but deny that it means anything') or excuse ('I accept that it means something, but deny that I meant it to happen'). From being something which merely occurred, there is a short exculpatory step to its becoming something which happened to me: the perpetrator as the victim of circumstance. At least 'parapraxis' suggests, albeit with decent obscurity, that the perpetration of an act is at issue. Freud's words weigh such feathers in their scales.[22]

'Slip' by now carries an inevitable [Freudian] cargo, which means that it is culturally too late to suggest a viable alternative (Bettelheim proposed 'lapse'). But by the same token it is impossible for 'a [Freudian] slip' to function non-tautologically within a translation of Freud's text. (The common German expression *eine [Freudsche] Fehlleistung* at least uses Freud's own word.) Likewise we need a *notional* term for both the generality of slips and the concept of 'slip' – since 'slip' clearly cannot serve as the class of which it is also a member.

Freud supplements ordinary usage – applies words in conflict with their uses – and sometimes supplants it with the unusual and therefore exact word. German meets this need halfway because it allows the coining of technical terms within a strong vernacular habitat, and neologism is not unilaterally inhibiting of common speech, whereas in English it is a case of either/or. In the present Introduction, however, 'parapraxis' has been retained to subsume the generality of slips, and to suggest something of the abstraction (if not the concretion) of *Fehlleistung*. 'Slip' has also been used, to refer to speech acts and suchlike, but inconsistently so, in that – as Freud might be the first to allow, given his profoundly rhetorical procedures – it must find its own level of sound and sense inside the accident of a sentence.

Paul Keegan, 2002

Notes

1. See pp. xxxviiff.
2. Carl Schorske remarks that, in the years immediately preceding the writing of *Everyday Life*, when academic promotions of Jews in the Viennese medical faculty became more difficult, Freud 'actually stepped down the social ladder, from the upper medical and academic intelligentsia . . . to a simpler stratum of ordinary Jewish doctors and businessman'. *Fin-de-Siècle Vienna: Politics and Culture* (Cambridge, 1981), pp. 185–6.
3. Cf. an entry for May 1900 in Alma Mahler-Werfel's *Diaries 1898–1902* (London, 2000), describing a walk to the Ringstrasse with Karl Kraus:

As we reached the Karlsplatz, I realized to my dismay that my right stocking was falling down. I walked on as far as the tram shelters. There, stammering helplessly, I stopped. He gloated at my predicament.

Can't you keep walking while we're talking?

I can't.

After making a series of stupid remarks, such as 'If you weren't so young', etc., I told him that my stocking was torn. Meanwhile the stocking had worked its way down into my shoe. I rushed off to the ladies' room. I re-emerged, blushing for shame. He said:

Why so petty, Fräulein? It can happen to anyone.

4. Sebastian Timpanaro, *The Freudian Slip* (London, 1974).
5. Timpanaro (ibid.) suggests that Freud's original audience – both the original readership (*The Psychopathology of Everyday Life* was very favourably received) and the interlocutors within the text – accede to the notion of the slip 'because they grasp that psychoanalysis does not demystify

bourgeois values in order to destroy them, but to reinstate and consolidate them'. Thus as psychoanalysis gradually ceased to be a moral scandal and became a vogue, so too the explanation of slips became a 'polite pastime'.

6. James Joyce, *Poems and Shorter Writings*, ed. Richard Ellmann and A. Walton Litz (London, 1991).

7. Henri Bergson, 'Memory of the Present and False Recognition' (1908).

8. Walter Benjamin, 'A Short History of Photography' in *One Way Street* (London, 1979).

9. Walter Benjamin, 'The Work of Art in an Age of Mechanical Reproduction' in *Illuminations* (London, 1968).

10. Samuel Weber, *The Legend of Freud* (Minnesota, 1982), p. 64.

11. Theodor W. Adorno, *Prisms*, trs. Samuel and Shierry Weber (London, 1981), p. 55.

12. Sigmund Freud, 'Some Neurotic Mechanisms in Jealousy, Paranaoia and Homosexuality' (Vienna, 1922).

13. As Freud wrote elsewhere: 'My self-analysis is still interrupted. I have now seen why. I can only embrace myself with objectively acquired knowledge (as if I were a stranger); self-analysis is really impossible, otherwise there would be no neurotic illness.'

14. Samuel Beckett, *Proust* (London, 1931).

15. In *Introductory Lectures* Freud was to reverse the procedure: beginning with easy examples and leading on to more complex cases, or at least more complex explanations.

16. Stephen Marcus, *Freud and the Culture of Psychoanalysis* (London, 1984), p. 78.

17. Samuel Weber, *The Legend of Freud*, p. 148.

18. In contrast to William James, for example, who considered the reliance of the language of psychology upon everyday speech to be parasitical, and one of its greatest sources of error, and whose call for a distinct discipline of psychology was a call for a distinct language. By which was meant not only a recourse to neologism but also an epic reinvigoration of the existing descriptive registers of language so as to capture nuances of consciousness. Thus his celebrated description of 'forgetting a name', *Principles of Psychology* (1890).

19. Jeremy Adler points out that Goethe coined *Fehlhandlung*, at the end of *Elective Affinites* (1807–9), to define Ottilie's action in 'inadvertently' drowning her baby – a moment in the novel at which Freud, a close reader of Goethe, would have been all ears.

20. Its coinage predates Strachey, and predates even A. A. Brill's 1914 translation of *The Psychopathology of Everyday Life*. (*OED*: *parapraxia*, 'a

condition in which there is a defective performance of certain purposive acts', 1912.) Brill preferred to render *Fehlleistungen* as 'faulty actions'.

21. Bruno Bettelheim, *Freud and Man's Soul* (London, 1983), pp. 85ff.

22. 'By imagining cases with vividness and fullness we should be able to decide in which precise terms to describe, say, Miss Plimsoll's action in writing, so carefully, 'DAIRY' on her fine new book: we should be able to distinguish between sheer, mere, pure and simple mistake or inadvertence' (J. L. Austin, 'A Plea for Excuses' in *Philosophical Papers* (Oxford, 1961).

Translator's Preface

Translators are always trying to get inside the minds of the authors on whom they are working. When the author in question is Sigmund Freud, the task is rather daunting, but fascinating. The experience of translating *The Psychopathology of Everyday Life* has left me with a great admiration for the man, a closer knowledge of his time, and a sense of finding him far more approachable than I did before.

Translation is an interpretative craft, often compared to acting, except that the translator of prose does not have the freedom of an actor or director to produce a startlingly individual version (poetry is a different matter, for very considerable freedom can produce what amounts to a new poem in its own right; Ted Hughes translating Ovid is a case in point). But in general the translator has a double duty: to the author, whose work is to be rendered as faithfully as possible, with the proviso that it may be more important to preserve the spirit than the letter of the original; and to the reader, who in my view should be able to read the text as easily as if it had been written in the language of translation in the first place. Today there is an interesting discussion among translators, some of whom believe that the foreignness of the original text ought to be preserved. I have seen them described as 'visible translators', while others attempt to be 'invisible translators'. There is a strong case to be made out for the first camp, but my own instinctive preferences place me in the second, among those who hope, ideally, to achieve invisibility.

In the case of Freud one could claim that there is a strongly 'foreign' element present anyway, first because of our distance from the period when he wrote his early titles. Working through *The*

Psychopathology of Everyday Life (several times, as one does in the course of translation), I have felt as if I were walking the streets of Vienna a century ago, or visiting those holiday resorts favoured by Freud, his patients, friends, colleagues and correspondents. It was a world where well-to-do ladies seldom worked for a living; where one gets the general impression that they were bent on marriage, while their suitors or lovers would rather avoid it. Second, certain attitudes taken for granted in that world have become foreign to us. Although some of Freud's subjects, as he recounts in this book, may have betrayed a reluctance to pay their medical bills through an inadvertent slip of word or deed, these were prosperous people used to employing domestic staff (who often figure in the anecdotal material of this title). Our ideas have undergone considerable change since Freud claimed that the servant classes were unable to appreciate art unless they could identify with it, in a proprietorial manner, out of loyalty to their employers, or (in a footnote) that a woman who is raped must really have wanted it in part of her mind, or she would have put up more resistance. Here one simply has to adjust one's ideas to those of upper middle-class society in the late nineteenth and early twentieth centuries. Freud wins the modern reader's strong sympathy, however, for his awareness of the latent anti-Semitism just below the surface of his world, and he was right to fear it, for it would eventually drive him into exile in London when he was old and approaching death. All the little case histories in this book – some of them only a few lines long – build up into a social history of their time and place.

The Psychopathology of Everyday Life is famous in the English-speaking world for giving the language the phrase 'Freudian slip'. From the layman's point of view, it is one of the more cheerful of Freud's works, since it is about the slips of speech, writing, reading, remembering and acting that normal people make, although he often uncovers disturbing motives behind these little incidents. He was scrupulously conscientious in trying to illustrate them not from the case histories of his neurotic patients, but from examples he had noted in himself, or instances contributed from their own experience by his medical colleagues. And indeed we all frequently make such slips, and it is entertaining to work out why; I kept catching myself out in them during my work on this title, and trying rather more consciously than usual to discover how they had arisen. One almost wanted to pick up the telephone and ring back to the year 1901, offering another specimen for the collection.

But although 'Freudian slip' has entered the English language to mean, broadly speaking, something said or done that betrays the existence of a subtext or a subliminal motive, of course it is not a term which could be *used* in the translation of this book. The terminology of the new science of Freudian psychoanalysis was, obviously, coined in Freud's native tongue of German, a good language for the purpose with its ability to alter the connotations of a word by the addition of a small prefix such as *ver-* or *zer-*. All of us working on the New Penguin Freud translations will have had our special problems, and we were not required to draw up a list of standard translations of Freudian terminology and stick to it. A set of specialist terms in English does exist, but on the whole they are not in *plain* English, but in a coinage either producing terms for use in the sphere of psychoanalysis alone ('unpleasure', 'affect' as a noun), or derived from ancient Greek ('cathexis', 'parapraxis', both dated in the *Shorter Oxford Dictionary* as first found in the early twentieth century, in fact specifically to render Freud's German terms).

In a work of this nature it is inevitable that many of the slips of the tongue or pen recounted by Freud himself or his informants must be given in German, and then translated and/or explained in English. My translations/explanations are contained in square brackets. I have also added, in square brackets, translations of those passages from French that Freud gave in the original text only. Parentheses in round brackets are of course Freud's own (as are the footnotes from the Fischer Psychologie edition I have used, itself from the *Gesammelte Werke* edition and therefore later than the very first publication of this title in 1901; the reader will find several comments by Freud referring back to that first publication and indicating that he made later additions to the material). But the necessary presence of so many quotations in German made me particularly anxious to avoid placing a heavy weight of specialist terminology on the rest of the book, in the passages that can go straight into plain English.

My own special problem has naturally been the translation of the word *Fehlleistung*, the Freudian slip itself, in German denoting a failure to achieve or embody some intended purpose. The specialist English term that has been coined for it is 'parapraxis'. I decided from the first not to use it if I could possibly avoid doing so; these new translations are for people like me who have no psychoanalytical training and do not find 'parapraxis' an instantly familiar term. Depending on context, I have therefore translated *Fehlleistung* sometimes as plain 'slip', sometimes as 'slip of the memory', 'slip of the mind', 'slip of the tongue', 'slip of the pen'. *Unlust* occurs only very occasionally in this particular title, and the literal English 'unpleasure' is, as the *Penguin Dictionary of Psychoanalysis* concedes, a clumsy word but useful as the antithesis of 'pleasure'. I might have had to use it if it had occurred more frequently in my text; as it was, in those contexts where the word was used in German I felt I could employ 'aversion' or 'sense of aversion' instead. Most of the time I have avoided 'affect' as a noun, for one thing because, as I found several times in going back over an earlier draft of the translation, it makes it difficult to use the verb 'to affect [something or someone]' in the usual way in English. I did use it as a noun, however, in the account of Professor N.'s lecture delivered in Switzerland in section V, where the whole point of the story depends on slang or jargon terms, and in that context it seemed appropriate.

Even more difficult than the *Fehlleistung*, however, was the problem of English terminology for the various actions that Freud describes mainly in sections VIII and IX of this book, as well as the final section. He sometimes speaks of such an action in general as a *Fehlhandlung* – an action which goes wrong in one way or another. But he then further divides them up into *Das Vergreifen* (the subject of section VIII), and *Symptom- und Zufallshandlungen* (the subject of section IX). The latter section heading translates easily enough, as *Symptomatic and Fortuitous Actions*, and when Freud comes to consider these he concludes that they are really one and the same thing. My major difficulty was with *Das Vergreifen*. None of the dictionary definitions of this word (from the verb *vergreifen*, here used as a verbal noun) will quite do in this Freudian context. I tried 'inappropriate/unsuitable actions', but did not want to import any suggestion, however slight, of sexual misconduct, although as the reader will find there is certainly a sexual undercurrent to some of the actions Freud describes in these chapters. I tried 'erroneous/mistaken/failed actions', and did not really care for them. 'Blunders' is perhaps closer to the sense of the German than any of those terms, but seemed to me too general. Since one of the chief meanings of the verb *vergreifen* is musical, 'to strike the wrong note', I tried 'off-key' or 'out-of-key' actions. I thought back to what Freud was actually talking about, and came up with 'actions that miss their mark': descriptive but clumsy. I contemplated using the phrase in conjunction with an occasional 'off-key', but ultimately felt it would be better to employ a single term throughout. In the end I settled upon 'inadvertent actions'. I then wondered whether the phrase was too close to the 'fortuitous actions' of Freud's second category, but since the English dictionary definition of 'inadvertent' in the context of an action is 'unintentional', I took comfort from Freud's own remarks in the opening paragraphs of section VIII: 'I have drawn up two groups of cases here: those in which the essential factor seems to be the effect of failure itself – the departure from an intention [*Intention* in German] – I have described as "inadvertent actions" [*Vergreifen*], and those in which, by contrast, the entire action appears inappropriate I call "symptomatic and fortuitous actions". However,' adds Freud, sensibly, 'no clear-cut distinction can be drawn; one has to acknowledge that all the categories mentioned in this work have only a descriptive significance.'

The translator's task often consists of such thinking around words in two languages like this, and in the end something has to go down on the printed page, even if one can never be sure of having found the best solution. But the experience, if sometimes tortuous, is always enjoyable. Translators generally would rather not read translations; they are so hungry to get at the words in the original that they inadvertently qualify themselves to *be* translators. Perhaps just because I had therefore never read Freud in anything but German, I have found the attempt to supply an English version of one of his works particularly fascinating.

Anthea Bell, 2001

The Psychopathology of Everyday Life

On Forgetfulness, Slips of the Tongue, Inadvertent Actions, Superstitions and Mistakes

So many ghostly beings haunt the air
That none can tell how to avoid them there.

Faust, Part II, Act V

I

Forgetting Proper Names

In the *Monatschrift für Psychiatrie und Neurologie* for 1898, I published a brief article entitled 'On the Psychic Mechanism of Forgetfulness', and I will summarize its content here as my point of departure for further discussion of the subject. In that article, I subjected the frequent occurrence of temporary inability to remember proper names to psychological analysis, using a telling example drawn from my own self-observation, and I came to the conclusion that this common, and in practice not very significant, case of the failure of a psychic function – the function of memory – casts light on matters going far beyond evaluation of the phenomenon itself.

Unless I am much mistaken a psychologist, asked to explain why we so often fail to remember names which we think we know, would content himself with saying that it is easier to forget proper names than the rest of what our memory contains. He would give plausible reasons explaining the special position occupied by proper names, but he would not suspect that the process had any wider relevance.

My own observation of certain details, which may not be present in all cases but can be clearly identified in some, led me to make a thorough study of the phenomenon of the temporary forgetting of names. In such cases the person concerned does not merely *forget*, but also *remembers incorrectly*. As he tries to remember the names that elude him other names – *substitute* names – come into his mind, and although they are immediately recognized as incorrect they persist in forcing themselves upon him. The process that ought to lead to the correct reproduction of the name he is looking for has, so to speak, become *displaced*, thus leading to the incorrect substitute. The basis of my argument is that in psychological terms this displacement is not merely arbitrary, but follows regular and predictable paths. In other words, I assume that the substitute name or names will relate to the name sought in a way that can be traced, and I hope that if I can succeed in proving this relationship I shall also cast some light on the process which makes us forget names.

In the example that I chose to analyse in 1898, I was trying in vain to remember the name of the Old Master who painted the magnificent frescos of the 'Four Last Things' in Orvieto Cathedral. Instead of the name I wanted – *Signorelli* – the names of two other painters, *Botticelli* and *Boltraffio*, sprang to mind, and were immediately and firmly rejected by my judgement as wrong. When I learned the correct name from another source I recognized it instantly and without any hesitation. My study of the influences and associations that had displaced my ability to reproduce the name in this way – taking me from *Signorelli* to *Botticelli* and *Boltraffio* – led me to the following conclusions:

a) The reason for my forgetting the name *Signorelli* is not to be sought in any special feature of the name itself, or in the psychological nature of the context in which it occurred. The name I had forgotten was just as familiar to me as one of the substitute names – Botticelli – and far more familiar than the other substitute name, Boltraffio, since I could have said hardly anything about the man who bore it except that he belonged to the Milanese school of painting. As for the circumstances in which I forgot the name, they appear to me innocuous, and cast no further light on the matter: I was travelling by carriage from Ragusa in Dalmatia, with a stranger, to a destination in Herzegovina, on the way we began talking about visits we had paid to Italy, and I asked my travelling companion whether he had ever been to Orvieto and seen the famous frescos by °°° there.

b) My forgetting the name is explained only when I remember the subject we were discussing immediately before I put this question, and it may be seen as a case of *disturbance of the new subject by its predecessor*. Just before I asked my travelling companion whether he had ever been to Orvieto, we had been speaking of the customs of the Turks who live in Bosnia and Herzegovina. I had told him something I had heard from a colleague who practised medicine among these people, and who said that they usually show both complete confidence in their doctors and a total resignation to fate. If you have to tell them that nothing can be done for a sick patient, they will reply: '*Herr* [Sir], what can I say? I know that if he could have lived, then you would have saved him!' And in these remarks the place-names *Bosnia* and *Herzegovina* and the word *Herr* occurred, setting off a series of associations between *Signorelli* and *Botticelli* or *Boltraffio*.

c) I assume that the train of thought leading from the customs of the Bosnian Turks and so forth could disturb my next idea because before that train of thought reached its end, I had withdrawn my attention from it. I remember that I had been about to tell a second story closely associated in my mind with the first. These Bosnian Turks set a very high value on sexual pleasure, and if anything impairs their sexual faculties they fall into despair, a despair which is in curious contrast to their resignation in the face of death. One of my colleague's patients once said to him: 'Well, you know, *Herr*, without all that, life's not worth living.' But I refrained from mentioning this characteristic of the Turks because it was not a subject I thought suitable for a conversation with a stranger. And I did more: I also distracted my attention from continuing my train of thought along those lines, lines that could have led to the subject of 'death and sexuality' in my mind. At the time I was feeling the after-effect of some news I had heard a few weeks earlier, during a brief visit to *Trafoi*: a patient over whom I had taken a great deal of trouble had committed suicide because of an incurable sexual disorder. I am perfectly sure that I did not consciously remember this sad event or anything connected with it on that journey to Herzegovina. But the similarity of the names *Trafoi* and *Boltraffio* obliges me to assume that at the time, and although I was intentionally distracting my attention from it, this memory was activated in my mind.

d) I can no longer regard the fact that I forgot the name of *Signorelli* as mere chance. I have to recognize the influence of a *motive* in the procedure. I had motives for interrupting myself as I was about to impart my ideas (about the customs of the Turks and so forth) to my companion, and those motives also caused me to block the ideas connected with them, which would have led on to the news I heard in Trafoi, out of my conscious mind. I therefore wanted to forget something; I had *repressed* something. What I wanted to forget was not in fact the name of the painter of the masterpiece in Orvieto, but the other subject, the one I did want to forget, contrived to associate itself with his name, so that my act of volition failed to find its target, and I *unintentionally* forgot one idea while I *intentionally* meant to forget the other. My aversion for remembering was directed against the content of one idea; my inability to remember emerged in another context. Obviously this case would have been simpler if the contexts of my aversion and my inability to remember had been the same. But the substitute names no longer seem to me so entirely unjustified as they were before the context was elucidated; in the manner of a compromise, they remind me of both what I wanted to forget and what I wanted to remember, showing that my intentional forgetfulness was neither wholly successful nor entirely unsuccessful.

e) The way in which I made a connection between the name I sought and the subject I had repressed (death and sexuality, etc., with mention of the names of Bosnia, Herzegovina and Trafoi) is very striking. The diagram I give here, taken from my 1898 article, attempts to illustrate this connection.

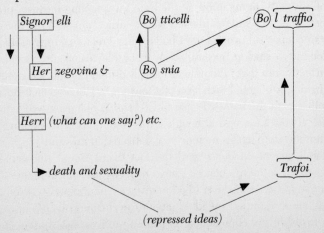

8

The name *Signorelli* has been divided into two. One pair of syllables (*elli*) also occurs unchanged in the substitute name; the other, if we translate *Signor* into *Herr*, has a number of different connections with the names belonging to the repressed subject, but because of those connections it eludes reproduction. The substitution occurred as if there had been a displacement of meaning through the linked names of 'Herzegovina and Bosnia', but disregarding the sense and the acoustic demarcation of the syllables. In the process, therefore, the names have been treated like the written characters of a sentence that is to be turned into a rebus or pictorial puzzle. No understanding entered my conscious mind of the way in which the substitute names replaced the name of *Signorelli. At first* it seems impossible to trace any connection – deriving from the recurrence of the same syllables (or rather sets of characters) – between the subject in which the name of *Signorelli* occurred and the subject that I had repressed just before broaching it.

It may not be superfluous to point out that the conditions assumed by psychologists to affect correct reproduction and forgetfulness, which we should seek in certain relationships and predispositions, are not invalidated by the explanation I have given above. Only in some cases can a *motive* be added to the recognized factors that may lead to our forgetting a name, thus also explaining the mechanism of false memory. In the case we are studying here, these predispositions are essential to allow the repressed element to associate itself with the name being sought, and then to repress that name too. The same thing might not have happened with another name, in conditions more favourable to its reproduction. In fact it is likely that a suppressed element is always trying to make itself felt somewhere else, but will succeed in doing so only where it finds suitable conditions. On other occasions, suppression may occur without any disturbance of the functions or, as we might accurately say, without showing any *symptoms*.

To sum up the conditions for forgetting a name and remembering it incorrectly, therefore, they comprise: 1) a certain predisposition to forget that name, 2) a process of suppression which has taken place shortly before, 3) the possibility of establishing an *external* association between the name concerned and the recently suppressed element. The last-named condition need not necessarily be considered very important, since the establishment of some association or other is so easy that it would probably be possible to find one in most cases. However, another question, and one that goes deeper, is whether such an external association can really be sufficient to make the repressed element prevent reproduction of the name being sought, or whether there must not necessarily be some closer connection between the two subjects. At first sight one would be inclined to reject this last requirement and say that the temporal proximity of a subject with an entirely different content is enough. On closer examination, however, it becomes increasingly frequent to find that the two elements (the repressed element and the new one), while linked by an external association, also have some connection of content, and such a connection can indeed be shown to exist in my example of *Signorelli*.

The value of the insight acquired through analysis of the *Signorelli* example of course depends on whether one wants to explain the case as typical or as an isolated instance. I can only say that it is extremely usual for a name to be forgotten and incorrectly remembered in the same way as in the *Signorelli* case which I have set out here. Almost every time I have observed the phenomenon in myself, I have also been able to explain it as being motivated by repression in the way described above. I must also state another point supporting the likelihood that this analysis was typical. I believe that in principle there are no grounds for drawing a distinction between cases in which names are forgotten and incorrectly remembered, and those in which no incorrect substitute names come to mind. Such substitute names occur spontaneously in a number of cases; in certain other cases, where they do not occur spontaneously, they can be made to do so by intense concentration, and they will then show the same connections between the repressed element and the name being sought as they would if they actually had been spontaneous. There seem to be two main factors in the emergence of a substitute name into the conscious mind: first, the effort of concentration, and second, an internal context associated with the psychic material. I might trace the latter to the comparative ease or difficulty of establishing the necessary external association between the two elements. A good many of the cases in which a name is forgotten but no false name is remembered may thus be classed with those cases in which substitute names are produced, as described in the mechanism of the *Signorelli* example. I will not, however, be so bold as to claim that all cases of forgetting proper names can be classified under this heading. There are undoubtedly cases where names are forgotten for much simpler reasons. We shall probably have defined the facts cautiously enough if we say that *while proper names are sometimes forgotten for simple reasons, they are also sometimes forgotten for reasons motivated by repression.*

II

Forgetting Foreign Words

The familiar vocabulary of one's native language, within the range of normal functioning, seems to be proof against being forgotten. As we all know, it is not the same with words in a foreign tongue. There is a predisposition to forget all parts of speech in another language, and the first degree of functional disturbance appears in the irregularity with which foreign words are available to us, depending on our state of health in general and how tired we happen to be. In a number of cases this kind of forgetfulness operates by the same mechanism as we found in the example of the name *Signorelli*. As evidence, I will cite a single analysis, but one which is notable for demonstrating some valuable features, and which concerns the forgetting of a word – not in this case a noun – in a Latin quotation. I hope I may be allowed to describe this little incident clearly and at some length.

Last summer – again while I was away on holiday – I renewed my acquaintance with a young man who had an academic education and, as I soon realized, was familiar with several of my psychological publications. I no longer remember how we broached the subject, but we were talking about the social standing of the race to which we both belong, and he, being an ambitious man, was deploring the fact that his generation, as he put it, was condemned to waste away unable to develop its talents or satisfy its needs. He concluded his passionately felt remarks with that famous line of Virgil in which the unfortunate Dido urges posterity to avenge her on Aeneas: *Exoriare* ... or rather that was how he meant to conclude, for he could not finish the quotation, and sought to conceal an obvious gap in his memory by rearranging the words: *Exoriar(e) ex nostris ossibus ultor!* At last he said, in some annoyance: 'Please don't smile in that ironic way as if you were relishing my difficulty – you might help me instead. There's something the matter with that line. How does the whole thing really go?'

'I'll be happy to tell you,' I replied, and quoted the line as it really runs: *Exoriar(e) aliquis nostris ex ossibus ultor!* [May someone rise, an avenger, from my bones!]

'How stupid of me to forget a word like that. But you're always saying that people don't forget things for no reason at all. Can you tell me how I came to forget the impersonal pronoun *aliquis*?'

I readily accepted this challenge, hoping for a contribution to my collection, so I said, 'We can get to the root of it at once if you'll tell me everything that occurs to you when you concentrate on the word you forgot, without any definite intention in mind but *honestly* and exercising no *critical judgement*.'[1]

'All right, I think of the ridiculous idea of dividing the word into two parts, like this: *a* and *liquis*.'

'What does that suggest to you?' 'I've no idea.' 'So what else occurs to you?' 'Well, it goes on like this: *relics – liquidation – liquidity – fluid* [German: *Reliquien – Liquidation – Flüssigkeit – Fluid*]. Does that tell you any more?'

'No, not by a long way. But go on.'

'Well,' he continued with a sarcastic laugh, 'I think of *Simone of Trento*, whose relics I saw a couple of years ago in a church in that city. I think of the accusations of ritual sacrifice once again being levelled against the Jews these days, and I think of the work by *Kleinpaul*, who sees all the alleged victims as incarnations of the Saviour, new editions of him, so to speak.'

'That idea isn't entirely unconnected with the subject we were discussing before you forgot the Latin word.'

'You're right. And then I think of a piece I read recently in an Italian newspaper. I think the headline was: *The Opinions of Saint Augustine on Women*. What do you make of that?'

'I'm still waiting to see.'

'Well, now I come to something that quite certainly has no connection with our subject.'

'I did ask you to abstain from any critical judgement – '

'All right, I know. Well, I remember a fine-looking old gentleman whom I met on my travels last week. A real *original* [German: *ein wahres Original*] who looks like a great bird of prey. His name is *Benedikt*, in case that's of any interest.'

'At least we now have a whole series of saints and church fathers: St *Simon*, St *Augustine*, St *Benedict*. And I believe one of the church fathers was called *Origen*. What's more, three of those names are first names, like *Paul*, part of the surname Kleinpaul.'

'Next I think of St Januarius and the miracle of his blood – but I imagine all this is just mechanical association.'

'Never mind that; St Januarius and St Augustine are both connected with the calendar. Can you remind me of the miracle of the saint's blood?'

'Oh, surely you know that! There's a phial of the blood of St Januarius which is kept in a Neapolitan church and miraculously *liquefies* on a certain feast-day. The people think highly of this miracle and get very upset if it is late to occur, as it once was under French occupation. At the time the commanding general – or am I wrong there? Was it Garibaldi? – well, he took the priest aside and let him know, indicating the soldiers posted outside in a very meaningful manner, that he very much hoped the miracle would soon take place. And sure enough, so it did . . .'

'Well, go on. Why do you hesitate?'

'I've just thought of something . . . but it's too private to tell you . . . anyway, I can't see any connection, so there's no need to mention it.'

'Leave me to make the connections. I can't force you to tell me something if you'd rather not, but in that case you can't ask me to tell you how you came to forget the word *aliquis* either.'

'Really? You think not? Very well, I suddenly thought of a lady who might soon be giving me news that would be very unwelcome to both of us.'

'You mean she's missed her period?'

'How on earth did you guess that?'

'It's not so difficult. You gave me plenty of background information. Remember the *calendar saints, the liquefaction of the blood on a certain day, the agitation when it failed to occur, the overt threat to the effect that the miracle must happen, or else . . .* The fact is that you reworked the miracle of St Januarius to make it an ingenious reference to the lady's period.'

'I had no idea. Do you really think I couldn't come up with that little word *aliquis* just because I'm waiting anxiously for news?'

'I'm sure of it. Remember the way you separated it into *a-liquis*, and then the associations with *relics, liquidation, fluid*. And need I point out how St Simon the child martyr, of whom the relics reminded you, fits into this context?'

'I'd rather you didn't. I hope you won't take these ideas of mine seriously – that is, if I ever really had them. In return I'll confess that the lady is Italian, and I went to Naples with her. But couldn't it all be coincidence?'

'I must leave it to your own judgement to decide whether you can explain away all these connections by assuming coincidence. But I can tell you that any similar case, if you care to offer it for analysis, will lead you to equally remarkable "coincidences".'[2]

I have several reasons to value this little analysis, and I owe my travelling companion of that time thanks for providing it. First, because in this case I was able to draw on a source not commonly available to me. I am usually obliged to take those examples of the psychic disturbance of functioning in everyday life that I am collecting in this work from my self-observations. I try to avoid the far greater wealth of material offered by my neurotic patients because I have to face the potential objection that the phenomena in question are the outcome and expression of neurosis. Consequently it is particularly valuable for my purposes when someone else, a person in good mental health, presents himself as the subject of such an investigation. This analysis is also valuable to me in another way, because it casts light on a case of forgetting a word *without* the substitution of another word by the memory, confirming my statement above that the emergence of incorrect substitute memories, or their failure to emerge, does not constitute grounds for any essential distinction.[3]

The main value of the *aliquis* example, however, lies in another of its differences from the *Signorelli* case. In that example, the reproduction of the name was impaired by the influence of a train of thought on which I had just embarked, then breaking it off, but the content of which stood in no clear relation to the new subject containing the name of Signorelli. Only a connection of temporal contiguity existed between the repressed subject and the forgotten name, but that was enough for me to connect the two by external association.[4] In the *aliquis* example, on the other hand, there is no trace of any such independent repressed subject occupying my acquaintance's conscious mind just before the incident and making itself felt as disturbance. The disturbed reproduction of the line of verse here arose from the subject on which it touched, producing unconscious opposition to the wishful thinking expressed in the quotation. One must reconstruct the process thus: the speaker was lamenting the fact that the rights of the present generation of his people are restricted; a new generation, he foretells, like Dido, will be avenged on its oppressors. So he has expressed a wish for off-spring. At the same moment a contradictory idea enters his mind. 'Do you really want children so much? Surely not. It would be very difficult for you to receive news at this point that you may in fact expect to have offspring by a certain person of your acquaintance. No, you do not want offspring – however useful they might be in the matter of revenge.' This contradiction makes itself felt by creating an external association between one of its conceptual elements, and an element in the wish that was rejected, and this time it does so very forcefully, through what appears to be an artificial and circuitous associative route. A second significant similarity to the *Signorelli* example derives from the fact that the contradiction arises from repressed sources and sets out from ideas which would divert the attention. – So much, then, for the difference and the internal relationship between these two paradigmatic examples of forgetting a name. We have become acquainted with a second mechanism for forgetting something: the disturbance of an idea by an inner contradiction arising from something repressed. This process strikes me as the more easily comprehensible, and we shall come across it again several times in the course of this work.

Notes

1. This is the usual way of bringing concealed ideas into the conscious mind. Cf. my *Interpretation of Dreams* [II] (*Gesammelte Werke*, 8th edition, p. 71).

2. This little analysis has aroused much attention in the professional literature on the subject, giving rise to lively discussion. E. Bleuler has tried to record the credence to be placed on psychoanalytical interpretation in mathematical terms by using this very example, and has concluded that such interpretation has a greater degree of probability than thousands of undisputed 'medical findings', occupying its present anomalous position only because we are not yet used to reckoning on psychological probabilities in science. (*Das autistisch-undisziplinierte Denken in der Medizin und seine Überwindung* [*Autistically Undisciplined Thinking in Medicine and Overcoming It*], Berlin 1919.)

3. Further observation tends to moderate the difference between the substitute memories in the *Signorelli* analysis and the *aliquis* case, for in both the forgetting seems to have been accompanied by a substitute formation. When I asked my interlocutor later whether some substitute had not occurred to him in his efforts to remember the missing word, he told me that initially he had been tempted to add an *ab* to the line: *nostris ab ossibus* (perhaps derived from the disconnected part of *a-liquis*), and that then the word *exoriare* had forced its way into his mind with particular clarity and persistence. Taking the sceptical approach, he added that this was obviously because it was the first word of the line. But when I asked him to think about the associations of *exoriare*, he gave me the word 'exorcism'. I can well imagine that the emphasis on *exoriare* in his recital of the line represented the force of such a substitute formation. It would have come about through the association of *exorcism* with the names of the *saints*. However, these are details upon which one need not dwell too much. (On the other hand P. Wilson, 'The Imperceptible Obvious', *Revista de Psiquitria*, Lima, January 1922, insists that the emphasis added to *exoriare* is very enlightening, since exorcism would have been the best symbolical substitute for the repressed idea of an abortion to get rid of the unwanted child. I am happy to accept this correction, which does not invalidate the force of the analysis.) It does, however, seem possible that the appearance of some kind of substitute memory is a constant, if perhaps only a characteristic and revealing, feature of tendentious forgetfulness motivated by repression. This substitute formation may also occur where no incorrect substitute names have emerged, by emphasizing an element closely related to the forgotten subject. In the *Signorelli* case, for instance, while the name of the painter eluded me, my visual memory of the cycle of frescos and his self-portrait in the corner of one of the pictures was *extremely clear*, or at least far more intense than my traces of visual memory usually are. In another case, also mentioned in my article of 1898, I had entirely forgotten the street name in an address in a strange town which I did not much want to visit, but as if to mock me the house number came into my mind with the utmost clarity, although I usually have the greatest difficulty in remembering numbers.

4. I would not like to say I am fully convinced that there was no internal connection at all between the two trains of thought in the *Signorelli* case. Careful study of my repressed thoughts on the subject of death and sexuality does produce an idea that comes close to the subject of the Orvieto frescos.

III

Forgetting Names and Sequences of Words

Experiences like the one just described, accounting for the way in which a sequence of words from a quotation in a foreign language can be forgotten, make one curious to know whether forgetting sequences of words in the speaker's mother tongue requires some fundamentally different explanation. People are not usually surprised to find that, after a certain lapse of time, they can reproduce a form of words or a poem learnt by heart only inaccurately, making changes and leaving gaps. However, as this forgetfulness is not uniform in the way it affects something learnt in a coherent context, but once again seems to dislodge only parts of it from the mind, it may be worth bringing analytical investigation to bear on some examples of this kind of inaccurate reproduction.

In conversation with me, a younger colleague said he thought that forgetting poems in one's mother tongue could well be motivated in the same way as forgetting parts of a sequence of words in a foreign language, and offered himself as a subject for study. I asked him to say what poem he would like as the test piece, and he chose Goethe's ballad 'Die Braut von Korinth' ['The Bride of Corinth'], a poem of which he said he was very fond, and he thought that he knew it by heart, or at least several verses of it. As he began reciting it he had a moment of really striking uncertainty. 'Does it go: "From Corinth to Athens there came", or: "To Corinth from Athens there came"?' he asked. I hesitated for some time myself, but then pointed out, with a smile, that the title of the poem, 'The Bride of Corinth', left us in no doubt of which way the youth was going. His recitation of the first verse then went smoothly, or at least without any notable inaccuracy. After the first line of the second verse, my colleague seemed to be searching for words, but he soon continued, and recited:

> *Aber wird er auch willkommen scheinen,*
> *Jetzt, wo jeder Tag was neues bringt?*
> *Denn er ist noch Heide mit den Seinen*
> *Und sie sind Christen und – getauft.*

[But will he still be welcome now that every day brings something new? For he and his kin are heathen, and they are Christians and – baptized.]

I had already been listening with a sense that something had gone wrong, and after the end of the second line we both agreed that there had been some distortion. As we could not think just what it was, however, we hurried off to the library to look up Goethe's poem, and found to our surprise that the wording of the second line of this verse was nothing like what my colleague had quoted, but had been, so to speak, rejected by his memory and replaced by something quite different. The lines really ran:

> *Aber wird er auch willkommen scheinen,*
> *Wenn er teuer nicht die Gunst erkauft?*

[But will he still be welcome if he does not buy favours dear?]

Getauft [baptized] rhymed with *erkauft* [buys], and I thought it odd that the combined ideas of 'heathen', 'Christian' and 'baptized' had not been more helpful to him in his reproduction of the text.

'Can you explain,' I asked my colleague, 'how you came to forget a whole line in a poem that you say you know very well, and do you have any idea where you found what you substituted for it?'

He was in fact able to offer an explanation, although he obviously did not like doing so. 'The line about "every day bringing something new" strikes me as familiar; I must have used those words recently in connection with my practice for, as you know, I'm very pleased with its flourishing state at the moment. But how did that sentence get into the poem? In fact I believe I can think of a connection. The reason why I obviously didn't care for the line about "buying favours dear" is to do with a lady to whom I recently proposed marriage. She turned me down, but now, in view of the great improvement in my financial situation, I am thinking of proposing again. I can't tell you any more, but of course if I am accepted this time, it won't be pleasant for me to remember that a certain amount of calculation was involved on both occasions.'

This seemed to me plausible enough without my needing to know the circumstances in any more detail. However, I went on to ask: 'But how did you come to insert yourself and your private relationships into the text of "The Bride of Corinth"? Are there perhaps differences of religious faith involved in your own case – differences of the kind that become significant in the poem?'

> *Keimt ein Glaube neu,*
> *Wird oft Lieb' und Treu*
> *Wie ein böses Unkraut ausgerauft.*

[When a new faith begins to burgeon, love and constancy are often rooted out like weeds.]

As it happened, I had not guessed right, but it was remarkable to see how this one penetrating question suddenly enlightened my colleague, enabling him to give me an answer which I am sure he had not known himself until that moment. He looked at me with a rather troubled and reluctant expression, and murmured a later quotation from the poem under his breath:

> *Sieh sie an genau!*
> *Morgen ist sie grau,*[1]

[Look closely at her! For tomorrow she'll be grey,]

adding briefly, 'The lady is a little older than me.' Here I broke off our investigation to spare him any more embarrassment. The explanation seemed to me adequate, although it was undoubtedly surprising to find that an attempt to trace a harmless slip of the memory back to its origins touched on such intimate and painful feelings in the subject I was studying, distant as they were from the poem.

Here, in the author's own words, I will quote from C. G. Jung,[2] who gives another example of a case in which words from a well-known poem were forgotten.

'A man was about to recite Heine's familiar poem "Ein Fichtenbaum steht einsam" ['A spruce tree stands alone']. In the line that says *Ihn schläfert* [It drowses] he became hopelessly stuck, having entirely forgotten the next words, *mit weißer Decke* [with a white covering]. It seemed to me odd for anyone to forget such a famous line, and I asked him to tell me what he thought of in connection with the phrase *mit weißer Decke*. He produced the following train of thought: "Well, a white covering suggests a shroud – the linen cloth covering a corpse – (pause) – and that makes me think of a close friend – a friend whose brother recently died quite suddenly – apparently it was a heart attack – and he was a very stout man – my friend is stout too, and it has occurred to me that he might go the same way – he probably doesn't take enough exercise – and when I heard of the death I suddenly feared the same thing might happen to me too, since our family is inclined to obesity anyway, and my grandfather died of a heart attack; I'm afraid I am overweight myself, so I have recently gone on a diet."

'Unconsciously, therefore, this gentleman identified with the spruce tree wrapped in its white shroud,' comments Jung.

The following example of forgetting a series of words, which I owe to my friend S. Ferenczi of Budapest, differs from those mentioned above in referring to something said in ordinary conversation, not a quotation from a poet. It will also illustrate the rather unusual kind of case in which we forget something for our own good, because our common sense threatens to be overcome by some passing fancy. The slip of the mind thus has a useful function. Once we are in a more sober mood again, we concur with those ideas that could previously express themselves only in failure – forgetting something, psychic impotence.

'At a party someone quoted the saying: *Tout comprendre c'est tout pardonner* [To understand all is to forgive all]. I said that the first part of the sentence was enough on its own; to speak of "pardoning" was arrogant, since forgiveness is best left to God and men of the cloth. Another man present thought this remark of mine very good, and I was emboldened – probably to heighten my kindly critic's good opinion of me – to say that I had recently thought of something better. But when I was about to repeat it, it refused to come back to my mind. I immediately withdrew and wrote down the ideas that had screened it out. First was the name of a friend of mine in Budapest and the street where he lives, which was where the idea I was trying to retrieve had come to me; then the name of another friend, *Max*, known to us as *Maxi*. This in turn led me to the word *maxim*, and I remembered that on that occasion (as in the case mentioned above) I was thinking about an alteration to a familiar maxim. Oddly enough, I then came up not with a maxim, but with the phrase *God created man in his own image*, and its reverse: *Man created God in his*. Thereupon the memory of what I was looking for immediately surfaced: that day in Andrássy Street my friend had said: *Nothing human is alien to me*, whereupon I – referring to psychoanalytical findings – said: *You should go further than that, you ought to confess that nothing animal is alien to you*.

'However, when I had finally remembered what I was trying to recall, I could not tell my story in the company where I happened to find myself. The party included the young wife of the friend to whom I had commented on the animal nature of the unconscious mind, and I was aware that she would not like such a distasteful notion. My forgetting the story had spared me a number of awkward questions from her and a discussion leading nowhere, and that must have been the reason for my "temporary amnesia".

'It is interesting that the substitute idea which occurred to me was a saying in which the deity is downgraded to the status of a human invention, while the comment I was really looking for referred to the animal element in human nature. What both sayings had in common was a *capitis diminutio*, the idea of demotion. The whole thing was obviously just the continuation of the train of thought about understanding and pardoning set off by our conversation.

'The fact that in this case I found what I was looking for so quickly may also owe something to the fact that I immediately withdrew from the party where I felt I could not tell such a story, and went into an empty room.'

Since then I have analysed many other cases of forgetting a phrase, or reproducing it inaccurately, and the general consensus of my findings in these studies makes me inclined to think that the mechanism of forgetting, as demonstrated in the *aliquis* and 'Bride of Corinth' examples, is almost universally valid. It is usually rather awkward to describe such analyses, since like those mentioned above they always lead to intimate subjects that are painful to the person who is the subject of analysis, so I will add no more such examples. Something in common to all these cases, regardless of their material, is that whatever has been forgotten or distorted is linked by association, in some way or other, with unconscious ideas which manifest themselves as forgetfulness.

I will now go back to the subject of forgetting names, since we have not yet thoroughly investigated either how or why such cases occur. Since this is a kind of slip that, on occasion, I am particularly apt to observe in myself, I am not at a loss for examples here. The slight migraines from which I still suffer usually announce themselves hours in advance by my inability to remember names, and when they are at their worst, although they do not force me to stop work, I often forget all proper names entirely. Now, cases like mine could raise an objection in principle to our analytical work. Should we not conclude from such observations that the reasons for forgetfulness, more particularly the forgetting of names, reside in circulatory and general functional disturbances of the cerebrum, and spare ourselves the attempt to find psychological explanations of these phenomena? I would not agree at all: that would mean confusing the mechanism of a process which is the same in every case with features encouraging it, which vary and are not necessarily present. Rather than engaging in a dispute, however, I will counter any such objection with a parable.

Let us suppose I have been incautious enough to go walking at night in a part of a city where there are few people around. I am attacked, and my watch and purse are stolen. I report the theft at the nearest police station, saying: I was in such and such a street, where *isolation* and *darkness* robbed me of my watch and purse. Although this account would not have been inaccurate, such a way of putting it would risk making the police think me not quite right in the head. I could describe the facts of the matter correctly only by saying that, aided by the isolation of the place and under cover of darkness, unknown criminals had stolen my valuables. The situation in which we forget names need not be different; encouraged by weariness, circulatory disturbance or intoxication, an unknown psychic power deprives me of access to the proper names in my memory, whereas in other cases the same power can cause the same failure of memory in someone enjoying his full health and strength.

When I analyse those instances of forgetting names that I observe in myself, I almost always find that the name which eludes me is related to some subject closely affecting my own person, and able to cause me strong and often painful feelings. According to the felicitous phraseology of the Zurich school (Bleuler, Jung and Riklin), which I recommend, the phenomenon can be expressed thus: the name eluding me has touched on some 'personal complex' of mine. The relation of the name to my person is unexpected and is usually conveyed by superficial association (double meanings, similarities of sound); in general, it can be described as a tangential relationship. A few simple examples are the best way to clarify its nature:

1) A patient asked me to recommend him a spa resort on the Riviera. I knew of such a place very near Genoa, I recollected the name of my German colleague who practises there, but although I believed I knew the place itself very well I could not remember its name. I had to ask my patient to wait while I went off in a hurry to consult the female members of my family. 'What's the name of that place near Genoa where Dr N. has his little clinic, the one where Frau so-and-so had treatment for so long?' 'Well, fancy you of all people forgetting the name! It's called *Nervi*.' And as a neurologist I do indeed have a great deal to do with *nerves*.

2) Another patient mentioned a nearby holiday resort, saying that it has not only two well-known inns but also a third, one which he remembered very well for a certain reason; give him a moment, he said, and he would tell me its name. I queried the existence of this third inn, pointing out that I had spent seven summer holidays running at the same resort, and must therefore know it better than he did. Annoyed by my contradicting him, however, my patient soon produced the name. The inn was called the *Hochwartner*. I had to admit that I was wrong, and indeed confess that during my seven summers at the resort I had stayed very close indeed to that same inn, although I had denied its existence. Why should I have forgotten both that fact and its name? I think it was because the name was uncomfortably like that of a Viennese colleague of mine, in this case touching on a 'professional' complex in me.

3) Another time, just as I was about to buy a train ticket at *Reichenhall* station, I could not remember the name of the next large railway station, although I had passed it very often, and it was usually perfectly familiar to me. I actually had to look for it on the timetable. It was *Rosenheim*, and then I immediately knew the association that had made me forget it. An hour earlier, I had been to see my sister who lives quite close to Reichenhall. My sister's name is Rosa, so I had been visiting a 'Rose Home'. The 'family complex' had removed the name of the place from my mind.

4) I can trace the positively predatory effects of the 'family complex' through a whole series of examples. One day a young man visited my consulting rooms. He was the younger brother of a woman patient of mine, I had met him on countless occasions, and I was used to referring to him by his first name. I was about to mention his visit when I discovered that I had forgotten that first name, not at all an unusual one, and there was no way I could call it to mind. I went out into the street to read the signboards over business premises, and recognized the name as soon as I encountered it. Analysis told me that I had seen a parallel between my visitor and my own brother which was trying to lead me to the repressed question of whether my brother would have acted in a similar way or an entirely different one in the same case. The external connection between the ideas of his family

and my own was established by the coincidence that both our mothers had the same first name: Amalia. In retrospect, I was then able to understand the substitute names, Daniel and Franz, which had come into my mind without throwing any light on my difficulty. Like Amalia, they are names of characters in Schiller's play *Die Räuber* [*The Robbers*], and in his essays on 'Walks in Vienna', the Viennese journalist Daniel Spitzer makes a humorous reference to these names.

5) On another occasion I could not remember a patient's name because of certain associations dating back to my youth. My analysis took a long and circuitous path around the subject before coming up with the name I wanted. My patient had expressed a fear of going blind, which reminded me of a young man who had in fact been blinded by a shotgun; this memory was associated with the thought of another young man who had shot himself and whose surname was the same as the first patient's, although they were not related. However, I hit upon the name only after realizing that I had transferred a sense of anxious expectation from these two cases involving young people to a member of my own family.

There is thus a constant stream of 'self-referentiality' going through my mind. I am not usually aware of it, but it betrays itself when I forget names in this way. It is as if I were obliged to relate everything I hear about other people to myself: as if my personal complexes were aroused by my perception of others. This cannot possibly be a quality peculiar to myself alone; instead, it must contain some indication of the way in which we perceive 'otherness'. I have reason to suppose that exactly the same thing happens in other people's minds as in mine.

My best example of this kind was told me, as an experience of his own, by one Herr *Lederer*. On his honeymoon in Venice, he met a gentleman whom he knew slightly and whom he therefore felt he should introduce to his young wife. But as he had forgotten the stranger's name, he got over the difficulty on this first occasion by murmuring something indistinct. When he met the man again, as he was bound to do in Venice, he took him aside and asked him to remind him of his surname, which he, Herr Lederer, was sorry to say he had forgotten. The stranger's answer showed great understanding of human nature: 'I can easily believe that you didn't remember my name. It's *Lederer*, like yours!' One cannot help feeling slightly uncomfortable on discovering that a stranger has the same name, as I realized very clearly not long ago, when a Herr S. Freud called during my consulting hours. (However, I must mention here the assurance of one of my critics that his reaction to such an eventuality is the opposite of mine.)

6) The effectiveness of self-referentiality is also evident in the following example, cited by Jung:[3]

'A certain Herr Y. fell in love with a lady who did not return his affection, and soon afterwards married another man, Herr X. Although Herr Y. had known Herr X. for some time and even had business dealings with him, he was constantly forgetting the man's name, and on several occasions when he wanted to correspond with Herr X. he had to ask other people what it was.'

In this case the motivation for his forgetting the name is clearer than in the previous one, which was governed by self-referentiality. Here the forgetfulness seemed to derive directly from Herr Y.'s dislike of his more successful rival; he did not want to know anything about him; 'let him be expunged from memory [*Nicht gedacht soll seiner werden*: a line from the poet Heine]'.

7) There can also be a subtler motive for forgetting a name, something that might be called 'sublimated' resentment of its bearer. For instance, a lady called Fräulein I. von K. writes, from Budapest:

'I have a little theory. I have noticed that people with a talent for painting do not generally have any feeling for music, and vice versa. Not long ago I was talking to someone about my theory, and said, "So far I have found that my observation always holds good, with just a single exception." But when I tried to remember the name of that one exceptional person it was lost from my mind without trace, although I knew that the man concerned was one of my closest acquaintances. When I heard someone mention him by chance a few days later, of course I realized at once that this was the name of the man who invalidated my theory. My unconscious resentment of him was expressed in my forgetting his name, which I usually knew perfectly well.'

8) Self-referentiality led to a name's being forgotten in a rather different way in the following case, recorded by Ferenczi. Its analysis is particularly useful because of the light it casts on substitute ideas (as in my substitution of Botticelli-Boltraffio for Signorelli).

'A lady who had heard something about psychoanalysis could not remember the name of the psychiatrist Jung.

'Instead, she came up with the following ideas: "Kl. (a name) – Wilde – Nietzsche – Hauptmann."

'I did not tell her Jung's name, but asked her to try free association on each of the ideas that had occurred to her.

'Taking Kl., she immediately thought of *Frau Kl.*, saying she was an affected lady but good-looking for her *age*. "She never seems to grow *old*." She mentioned "*mental illness*" as something in common to both *Wilde* and *Nietzsche*, and said ironically: "You *Freudians* will go on looking for the causes of mental illnesses until you fall mentally ill yourselves." Then she added: "I can't bear *Wilde* and *Nietzsche*. I just don't understand them. I've heard they were both homosexual, and Wilde went around with *young* men." (She had actually given the correct name in this sentence, Jung, although admittedly in Hungarian, but she still could not remember it.)

'When she came to *Hauptmann* she thought first of *Halbe*, and then of *Jugend* [Hauptmann and Halbe are the names of dramatists; *Jugend* – 'youth' – was the title of a play by Halbe]. Only now, when I drew her attention to the word "youth", did she realize that the name she was trying to remember was Jung [young].

'In fact this lady, who had lost her husband when she was thirty-nine and was unlikely to marry again, had sufficient reasons to avoid thinking of anything that would call *youth* and *age* to her mind. The striking factor is that her substitute ideas were associated with the name she was looking for purely in terms of their content, and there were no associations of sound.'

9) Another and very subtly motivated example of the forgetting of a name was explained by the person concerned himself.

'When I was taking an examination in philosophy as a subsidiary subject, the examiner asked me about the doctrines of *Epicurus*, and then inquired whether I knew who had taken up his doctrines again in later centuries. I gave the name of *Pierre Gassendi*, whom I had heard mentioned in a café only a couple of days before as a disciple of *Epicurus*. When the examiner asked, in surprise, how I came to know that name, I boldly told him that I had long taken an interest in *Gassendi*. As a result I passed the examination *magna cum laude*, but later, I am sorry to say, I had a persistent tendency to forget Gassendi's name. I suspect I should blame my guilty conscience for my failure to keep that name in my mind now, however hard I try – I ought not really to have known it at the time.'

To appreciate the intensity of this informant's distaste for remembering that episode during his examination, one needs to know how highly he values his doctorate, which has to compensate for a great deal else in his life.

10) Here is another example of the name of a town being forgotten, perhaps not such a simple case as those cited above, although it will seem both convincing and valuable to anyone familiar with such investigations. The name of an Italian city could not be recalled because of its close similarity of sound to a woman's first name, which the subject associated with a number of deeply felt memories, not all of them, probably, exhaustively covered in the following account. S. Ferenczi of Budapest, who observed this case of forgetfulness in himself, treated it much as one might analyse a dream or a neurotic idea, and that was certainly the right approach.

'Today, when I was visiting a family with whom I am friendly, our conversation turned to certain cities in northern Italy. Someone said that they still betray traces of Austrian influence. The names of some of these cities were cited, and there was one that I wanted to mention myself, but I could not think of its name, although I do know that I passed two very pleasant days there, a fact which does not bear out Freud's theory of forgetfulness. Instead of the name of the city I was looking for the following ideas came into my mind: *Capua – Brescia – the Lion of Brescia*.

'I saw this "lion" vividly before me, as if it were really there in the shape of a *marble statue*, but I immediately noticed that it looked less like the lion on the monument to liberty in Brescia (which I have seen only in a picture) than another marble lion which I saw in Lucerne on the *monument to the Swiss Guards who fell at the Tuileries*. I have a miniature reproduction of it standing on my bookshelves. Then, at last, I remembered the name I was looking for: *Verona*.

'I also know at once whom to blame for this amnesia – none other than a woman who had once been employed by the family I was visiting at that moment. Her name was *Veronika*, or in Hungarian *Verona*, and I used to dislike her very much because of her unattractive face, her hoarse, raucous voice and her insufferably overbearing manner (which she felt was justified by her long period of service). Nor could I stand the tyrannical way in which she treated the children of the house. And now I knew the significance of my substitute ideas.

'I had immediately associated Capua with the phrase *caput mortuum*, and I had often compared Veronika's face to a *death's head*. The Hungarian word *kapzsi* (avaricious) must also have played a part in the displacement of my ideas. Of course I also hit upon the much more direct associations linking Capua and Verona, as geographical terms and as Italian words with the same rhythm.

'The same may be said of Brescia, but once again tortuous byways were involved in the association of ideas.

'My dislike of Veronika in the past had been so great that I found her actually nauseating, and expressed amazement, on several occasions, at the idea that she had a love life at all, or could ever be loved. "Surely," I said, "kissing her would make you feel sick [*Brechreiz*, 'nausea' in German, echoing the sound of *Brescia*".] And yet I had obviously associated her, long ago, with ideas of the dead Swiss Guards.

'*Brescia* is often mentioned, here in Hungary at least, in connection not with the lion but with another *wild beast*. The most hated name in this country and in northern Italy alike is that of General Haynau, known here simply as the Hyena of Brescia. So one train of thought led from the detested tyrant Haynau by way of Brescia to the city of Verona, and another led from that *grave-digging, raucous creature the hyena* (an idea connected in my mind with that of a funerary monument) to the death's head and the grating voice of Veronika, whom my unconscious mind had accused so harshly of being almost as tyrannical in this house in the past as the Austrian general was after the Hungarian and Italian freedom-fighting.

'And *Lucerne* was associated with thoughts of the summer spent by Veronika with her employers beside the Lake of Lucerne near that city; then again, the *Swiss Guard* reminded me of the way she used to tyrannize over not only the children but even the adult members of the family, since she liked to think of herself in the role of *Garde-Dame* or chaperone.

'I hasten to add that I long ago overcame this antipathy of mine towards V. – at least consciously. She has now changed very much for the better in both her outward appearance and her behaviour, and I can feel genuinely friendly to her when I meet her (not that I often do so). But as usual, my unconscious mind clings more tenaciously to old impressions, and is unforgiving in retrospect.

'The *Tuileries* referred to another person, an elderly French lady who really did act as a chaperone *guarding* the ladies of the family on many occasions, and who was respected – and probably to some extent feared – by one and all. For a time I was her *élève* for French conversation. And the word *élève* reminded me that when I was visiting my present host's brother-in-law in northern Bohemia, I couldn't help laughing at the way in which the local rustic people called the *élèves* [students] at the College of Forestry there *Löwen* ['lions', because of a similarity of sound between the French and German words]. This amusing memory may also have played a part in the displacement of my ideas from hyena to lion.'

11) The following example[4] is another that shows how a personal complex affecting someone at a certain time can induce him to forget a name very remote from it:

'Two men, one older and one younger, who had visited Sicily together six months earlier, were exchanging reminiscences of their pleasant and eventful holiday. "Now, what was the name of that place where we spent the night before going on our expedition to Selinunt?" asked the younger. "I think it was Calatafimi, wasn't it?" The elder man contradicted him. "No, I'm sure it wasn't, but I've forgotten the name too, although I remember every detail of our visit to the place very clearly. I only have to find that someone has forgotten a name in order to forget it myself. Let's try to remember the name – although the only thing that comes to my mind is Caltanisetta, and I'm sure that's not right." "No," agreed the younger man, "the name begins with a *w*, or there's a *w* in it somewhere." "There's no letter *w* in Italian," the elder man reminded him. "Well, I meant *v*. I only said *w* because that's what I'm used to in my native German." But the older man would have none of the *v*. "In fact," he said, "I think I've forgotten quite a number of those Sicilian names; it's about time I tried remembering them. For instance, what's the name of that place at high altitude which the ancients called Enna? Oh, now I remember: *Castrogiovanni*," Next moment the younger man remembered the name he had forgotten too. "*Castelvetrano*," he cried, pleased to find that the name did in fact contain the *v* he had claimed for it. For some time the older man still did not feel that the name was familiar, but once he had accepted it he had to try explaining why it had eluded him. "Obviously because the second half of the name, *vetrano*, sounds like *veteran*," he said. "I know I don't like to think of growing old, and I react oddly when I'm reminded of the subject. For instance, not long ago I told a friend whom I esteem highly, in rather a strange phrase, that he was "well past his youthful years", because once he himself, although making various flattering remarks about me, had said that I was not a young man any more. The fact that the first sound in the name *Castelvetrano* also occurs in my substitute name *Caltanisetta* shows that it was the second half of the place name I didn't like." "What about the name *Caltanisetta* itself?" asked the younger man. "It has always sounded to me like a pet name for a young woman," the elder man admitted.

'And a little later he added: "The name I gave *Enna* was a substitute name too, and now I realize that the name *Castrogiovanni*, which rationalized its way into my mind, suggests *giovane* – young – just as the name I could not remember, *Castelvetrano*, suggested the word *veteran* – old."

'The elder man thought he had accounted for his forgetting the name in this way, but they did not stop to wonder why the younger man had forgotten it too.'

The mechanism of the phenomenon whereby names are forgotten

deserves our interest, as well as the motives for forgetting them. In a great many cases a name is forgotten not because it evokes such motives in itself, but because some similarity of sound suggests another name which we do have good reason to forget. It will be obvious that this broader application of the factors causing the phenomenon helps it to occur very much more easily, as the following examples will show:

12) From Dr E. Hitschmann: 'Herr N. wanted to give someone the name of the booksellers Gilhofer & Ranschburg, but however hard he racked his brains he could remember only the name of Ranschburg, although he was very familiar with the firm. Coming home with a sense of slight dissatisfaction, he felt the matter was important enough for him to ask his brother, who seemed to have fallen asleep, for the first half of the firm's name. The brother supplied it at once. Thereupon Herr N. immediately associated the name "Gallhof" with "Gilhofer". A few months earlier, he had taken a walk which he remembered with pleasure to the Gallhof in the company of an attractive girl, who gave him a souvenir inscribed with the words: "In memory of our delightful hours at the Gallhof" [*Gallhofer Stunden*]. A day or so before he forgot the name of Gilhofer, this item, which it seems was rather fragile, was damaged when N. closed a drawer too rapidly and, being familiar with the significance of symptomatic actions, he registered the fact with a certain feeling of guilt. His attitude to the lady was rather ambivalent at the time; he loved her, but he hesitated to fall in with her wish to get married' (*Internationale Zeitschrift für Psychoanalyse* I, 1913).

13) From Dr Hanns Sachs: 'While he was talking about Genoa and its immediate surroundings, a young man wanted to mention a place called *Pegli*, but he had to think hard before he could remember the name. On the way home he thought about the embarrassing way in which this usually familiar name had eluded him, and his mind led him to the word *Peli*, which sounds very like *Pegli*. He knew that there was a South Sea island of that name, and that its inhabitants have retained some curious customs, of which he had recently read in an ethnological work. At the time, he decided to use the information for a hypothesis of his own. Then it struck him

that Peli was also the setting of a novel that he had read with interest and pleasure, Laurids Bruun's *Van Zantens glücklichste Zeit* [*The Happiest Time of Van Zanten's Life*]. The ideas that had occupied him almost all that day were connected with a letter which he had received that morning from a lady who was very dear to him, and which made him fear that a rendezvous they had arranged would fall through. Having spent the whole day in a very bad temper, he had set out in the evening intending to shake off his distressing thoughts and enjoy the party he was going to as whole-heartedly as possible, for he had been looking forward to it a great deal. Obviously the word *Pegli* was a severe threat to this good resolution, since it sounds so much like *Peli*, while *Peli*, which had associated itself with his own ego because of its ethnological interest for him, stood for not only the "happiest time" of Van Zanten's life but also of his own, and consequently for the fears and anxieties he had felt all day. It is typical of the phenomenon that he could make this simple interpretation only after a second letter had transformed his doubts into the happy certainty of seeing the lady again soon.'

If, in thinking of this example, we remember that other and very similar case in which it proved impossible for me to recollect the place name Nervi (example 1), we shall see how the double meaning of a single word can be replaced by assonance between two words.

14) When war with Italy broke out in 1915, I found from my self-observations that a considerable number of Italian place names which I usually knew perfectly well had suddenly vanished from my memory. Like so many others of German origin, I had fallen into the habit of spending part of my holidays on Italian soil, and I could not doubt that my forgetting these names *en masse* expressed the understandable sense of hostility to Italy which had replaced my old liking for the country. This directly motivated forgetfulness of names, however, went together with an indirect version of the phenomenon that could be traced back to the same influence. I was also inclined to forget non-Italian place names, and in studying these cases I found that some distant similarity of sound connected those words with the enemy place names which I now felt were taboo. For instance, I was racking my brains one day to remember the name of

the Moravian town of *Bisenz*. When it finally came into my mind I knew at once that I could blame my forgetting it on the Palazzo *Bisenzi* in Orvieto, in which the Hotel Belle Arti, where I had stayed on all my visits to Orvieto, is situated. Naturally, my fondest memories were those that had suffered most damage from my change of emotional attitude.

It will also be useful to cite some examples reminding us of the various different purposes that can be served by the slip of the mind which makes us forget names.

15) A. J. Storfer ('Forgetting Names to Ensure that an Idea is Forgotten'): 'A lady living in Basel was told one morning that Selma X. from Berlin, a friend of her youth now on honeymoon, was passing through that city. This friend from Berlin would be in Basel for only a single day, so the lady who lived there made haste to her hotel. When the two friends parted they arranged to meet again that afternoon, intending to spend the rest of the time until the lady from Berlin had to leave together. That afternoon the lady living in Basel *forgot* to keep the appointment. I do not know just why she forgot, but in this kind of situation (a meeting with a friend of her youth who was just married) there are several typical sets of circumstances that might have set up resistance against the second meeting. But the really interesting aspect of this case is *another* slip unconsciously reinforcing the first. At the time when she should have been with her friend from Berlin again, the lady living in Basel was in company elsewhere. The conversation turned to the recent marriage of the Viennese opera singer Kurz. The lady from Basel expressed some criticism (!) of this marriage, but when she was about to mention the singer's full name she found, much to her embarrassment, that she could not remember her first name. (As we all know, when someone's surname is monosyllabic we tend to mention that person by his or her first name too.) The lady living in Basel was particularly annoyed by her poor memory because she had often heard Kurz sing, and she usually knew her full name perfectly well. Before anyone else could mention the elusive first name, the conversation took another turn. On the evening of the same day, however, our resident of Basel happened to be in company with some of the

people who had also been with her that afternoon. By chance, the conversation again turned to the marriage of the Viennese singer, and the lady gave her full name of *"Selma Kurz"* without any difficulty, exclaiming immediately afterwards: "Oh dear, I've just remembered that I quite forgot I had an appointment with my friend *Selma* this afternoon." But a glance at the time showed that her friend from Berlin would have left by now' (*Internationale Zeitschrift für Psychoanalyse* II, 1914).

We may not yet be prepared to do justice to every aspect of this interesting example. The following case is simpler, although it concerns not a forgotten name, but a foreign word forgotten for a motive arising from the situation. (It will be observed that the procedure is the same whether it relates to proper names, first names, foreign words or sequences of words.) In this example a young man forgot the English word for *Gold*, which in fact is identical with the word in German, to give himself a reason for something he wanted to do.

16) From Dr Hanns Sachs: 'A young man staying in a mixed boarding house met an Englishwoman and was attracted to her. On the evening of their first meeting he was talking to her in her native language, having a reasonably good command of it, and he wanted to use the English word for "gold" but could not remember it, however hard he tried. Instead, substitute words come into his mind – French *or*, Latin *aureum*, Greek *chrysos* – so persistently that he had difficulty in rejecting them, although he knew perfectly well that they were not related at all to the word he wanted. Finally, the only way he could make himself understood was to touch a gold ring which the lady was wearing on her finger; he was abashed to discover from her that the word for "gold" he had been seeking for so long is exactly the same in English as in German. The significance of the physical contact motivated by his forgetfulness lies not merely in the inoffensive satisfaction of his wish to hold or touch her, a satisfaction that can be fully exploited by lovers on various other occasions, but rather in the light it cast on the prospects for his courtship. The lady's unconscious mind, particularly when it was well disposed to her interlocutor, would have guessed at the erotic purpose concealed

behind the harmless disguise of a forgotten word; her acceptance of the touch and the motive behind it could thus be a means of coming to an understanding on the prospects of this new flirtation – a very significant one even when neither party was conscious of it.

17) I will also add, from J. Stärcke, an interesting observation of the forgetting and subsequent recollection of a proper name, notable for the fact that the forgetting of the name is linked, as it was in the example of 'The Bride of Corinth', with the distortion of a sequence of words from a poem.

'An old lawyer and linguistic scholar, Z., said in company that when he was studying in Germany he knew a remarkably stupid student, claiming that he could tell many tales of this student's lack of intelligence. However, he could not remember the student's name; he said he thought it began with W, but then changed his mind. He did remember that the stupid student later became a *wine merchant*. Then he told another anecdote about the stupidity of this same student, marvelled once more at his inability to remember the name, and said: "He was such an ass that I can still hardly understand how, by dint of sheer repetition, I was able to get some Latin into his head." A moment later he remembered that the name he was looking for ended in . . . *man*. We asked whether he could think of another name ending in the same way, to which he replied: "*Erdmann*." "So who was he?" "Oh, another student I knew at the time." His daughter, however, pointed out that there was also a Professor Erdmann. On further inquiry, it turned out that this Professor Erdmann, as editor of a journal, had recently printed a paper submitted by Z., but only in abbreviated form, because he was not entirely in agreement with it, etc., and that Z. had taken this badly. (I also learned later that in the past Z. was probably a candidate for a professorial chair in the faculty where Professor E. was now lecturing, so the name may have touched him on the raw for that reason too.)

'But now he suddenly remembered the name of the stupid student: *Lindeman*! He had already remembered that the name ended in . . . *man*, but the element *Linde* was repressed for longer. When asked what ideas he associated with *Linde* [lime tree] he said at first, "None at all." But when I insisted that the word must convey some kind of idea to him, he said, looking up and airily waving a hand: "Well, the lime is a handsome tree." However, nothing else occurred to him. The company fell silent, and we all went on with our reading or whatever else we had been doing until a few moments later, in an abstracted tone of voice, Z. quoted the following lines:

> *Steht er mit festen*
> *Gefügigen Knochen*
> *Auf der* Erde,
> *So reicht er nicht auf,*
> *Nur mit der* Linde
> *Oder der* Rebe
> *Sich zu vergleichen.*

[Though he may stand with firm and compliant bones upon the *earth*, he cannot rise so far as to compare himself even to the *lime tree* or the *vine*.]

'I uttered a cry of triumph. "There we are, there's your Erdmann," I said. "The man who "stands upon the earth" is the "earth man" or *Erdmann*, and cannot compare himself with the lime tree [*Linde*], *Lindeman*, or the *Rebe* [vine], the wine merchant. In other words: Lindeman, the stupid student who later became a wine merchant, was an ass, but Erdmann is a much worse ass and doesn't even compare with this Lindeman." For the unconscious to produce such an expression of contempt is very usual, and it seemed to me that we had now discovered the main reason why Z. had forgotten the name.

'I then asked from what poem the lines came. Z. said they were from a poem by Goethe, and he thought it began:

> *Edel sei der Mensch,*
> *Hilfreich und gut!*

[May mankind be noble, helpful and good!]

'and went on a little later:

Und hebt er sich aufwärts,
So spielen mit ihm die Winde.

[And if he rises upwards, the winds will play with him.]

'Next day I looked up this poem by Goethe, and the case turned out to be even more interesting (and more complicated) than it had seemed at first.

a) the first lines quoted (cf. above) really run:

Steht er mit festen
Markigen *Knochen* . . .

[Though he may stand with firm, *powerful* bones . . .]

'"*Compliant* bones" would have been rather an odd construction, but I will leave that aside.

b) The following lines of the verse (cf. above) run:

Auf der wohlbegründeten
Dauernden *Erde,*
Reicht er nicht auf,
Nur mit der Eiche
Oder der Rebe
Sich zu vergleichen.

[On the *well-founded*, *enduring* earth, he cannot rise so far as to compare himself even to the *oak tree* or the vine.]

'So there is no lime tree at all in the whole poem! The change of oak to lime was made (in Z.'s unconscious mind) purely to allow a play on words between "earth – lime – vine".

c) The poem is called 'Grenzen der Menschheit' ['Limitations of Mankind'] and compares the omnipotence of the gods with the feeble powers of man. The poem, which actually does begin:

Edel sei der Mensch,
Hilfreich und gut!

is another one and comes a few pages further on. It is called 'Das Göttliche' ['The Divine'], and it too contains the poet's ideas about gods and men. Since we did not go into the matter any further, I can only suspect that ideas about life and death, the temporal and eternal, man's own weakness and the approach of death played a part in the background to this case.'[5]

In many of these examples all the subtleties of psychoanalytical technique have been employed to explain why a name was forgotten. I would suggest that anyone wishing to discover more about such work should read a paper by E. Jones of London which has been translated from the English.[6]

18) Ferenczi has pointed out that forgetting names can also be a symptom of hysteria, when it operates by means of a mechanism very far from the inadvertent slip. I quote his own account to show the meaning of this distinction:

'At the moment I am treating a patient, an elderly spinster lady, who cannot recall the most common proper names, even those she knows well, although in other respects she has a good memory. During analysis it turned out that this symptom was intended to illustrate her lack of schooling. Her demonstrative display of ignorance was really a reproach to her parents for denying her any higher education. Her painful compulsion to do housework ("housewife psychosis") also derived in part from the same source. In effect, she was saying: you have made me into a domestic servant.'

I could multiply such examples of forgetting names, and discuss them at much greater length, but at this point I would like to avoid mentioning many, indeed almost all, of the points to be considered under later headings. However, I will permit myself to sum up briefly the findings of the analyses described here:

The mechanism of the forgetting of names (or, rather, the way they elude the mind in temporary forgetfulness) consists in the fact that an alien train of thought, which is not consciously perceived at the time, disturbs the intended reproduction of the name. Either there is an established connection between the name disturbed and the complex that disturbs it, or else such a connection has occurred through superficial (external) associations, often by what may seem a tortuous route.

Among the complexes disturbing the memory those of a private nature (personal, family or professional) turn out to be the most influential.

A name belonging to several cycles of ideas (or complexes), as a result of some ambiguity of meaning, is often forgotten in connection with a certain train of thought because it belongs to another, stronger complex.

A wish to avoid arousing unpleasant feelings through the agency of memory is a very strong motive for such disturbances.

In general we can distinguish between two main categories of cases in which names are forgotten: in one the name itself refers to something distressing, in the other it is linked with another that has a similar effect, and consequently the reproduction of names can be disrupted because of the names themselves or because of their immediate or more remote associations.

A survey of these general remarks shows that temporarily forgetting names is one of the most frequently observed of all slips of the mind.

19) However, we are a long way from having described all the features of this phenomenon. I will add that forgetting names is extremely infectious. In a conversation between two people, it is often enough for one of them to say he has forgotten some name or other for the other to forget it too. Where forgetfulness is thus induced, however, it is easier to recollect the forgotten name again. This 'collective' forgetfulness, strictly speaking a phenomenon of mass psychology, is a subject that has not yet been analytically studied. T. Reik provides a good explanation of this remarkable occurrence in a single but particularly good case.[7]

'In a small social gathering of academics, which included two women students of philosophy, the conversation turned to the many questions posed in cultural history and theology by the origin of Christianity. One of the young ladies taking part in the discussion remembered finding an interesting picture of the many religious currents influencing the history of that period in an English novel she had recently read. She added that the novel described the whole life of Christ, from his birth to his death, but she could not remember the name of the work (although she had a very clear visual memory of the cover of the book and the typographical appearance of the title). Three of the men present said that they knew the same novel, and added that, oddly enough, they could not remember its title either . . .'

Alone among the four of them, the young lady underwent analysis to find out why she had forgotten the title. It was *Ben Hur*, by Lewis Wallace. Her first substitute ideas had been: *Ecce homo – homo sum – quo vadis?* The girl herself realized that she had forgotten the name 'because it contains an expression that neither I nor any other young girl would wish to employ, particularly in front of young men' [Ben Hur – *Hure*: 'whore' in German], an explanation which acquired a further dimension through this very interesting analysis. In the context on which she had touched, the translation of *homo*, 'man' in the sense of human being, can also have a risqué meaning. Reik concludes that the young lady treated the word as if, by simply mentioning the suspect title of the book in front of young men, she would have been admitting to desires that she rejected as both unseemly and out of tune with her character. In short, she unconsciously equated uttering the title of *Ben Hur* out loud with offering sexual favours ['Ich bin Hure' – I am a whore'], and consequently her inability to remember it amounted to rejecting any unconscious temptation of that kind. There are reasons to suppose that the young men's inability to remember it was caused by similar unconscious processes. Their unconscious minds picked up the real reason why the girl forgot the title and, as it were, interpreted it so that their own forgetting it shows deference to her attitude of repudiation. It is as if, through her sudden lapse of memory, their interlocutor had given them a clear signal, which they unconsciously understood very well.

Names may also continue to be forgotten in such a way that whole series of them elude the memory. If a name escapes us, and we seek other and closely connected names in order to retrieve it, these other names, sought as points of reference, quite often escape us too. Forgetfulness thus moves on from one name to another, as if to demonstrate the existence of an obstacle that cannot easily be removed.

Notes

1. My colleague in fact slightly changed both the wording and the application of this fine passage in the poem. The ghostly girl really tells her bridegroom:

> *Meine Kette hab' ich dir gegeben;*
> *Deine Locke nehm' ich mit mir fort.*
> *Sieh sie an genau!*
> *Morgen bist du grau,*
> *Und nur braun erscheinst du wieder dort.*

[I have given you my necklace; I will take your lock of hair. Look closely at it! Tomorrow you'll be grey, and only in this lock will your hair still be brown.]

2. C. G. Jung, *Über die Psychologie der Dementia praecox*, 1907, p. 64.

3. *Dementia praecox*, p. 52.

4. *Zentralblatt für Psychoanalyse* I, 9, 1911.

5. From the Dutch edition of this book, entitled *De invloed van ons onbewuste in ons dagelijke leven* [*The Influence of Our Unconscious on Our Daily Life*], Amsterdam 1916, published in German by the *Internationale Zeitschrift für Psychoanalyse* IV, 1916.

6. 'Analyse eines Falles von Namenvergessen' ['Analysis of a Case of Forgetfulness'], *Zentralblatt für Psychoanalyse* II, 1911.

7. 'Über kollektives Vergessen' ['On Collective Forgetfulness'], *Internationale Zeitschrift für Psychoanalyse* VI, 1920. (Also in Reik, *Der eigene und der fremde Gott* [*Our Own God and the God of Others*], 1923.)

IV

On Childhood Memories and Screen Memories

In a second article (published in 1899 in the *Monatschrift für Psychiatrie und Neurologie*) I was able to demonstrate the tendentious nature of human memory in an unexpected area. I started out from the striking fact that a person's earliest childhood memories frequently seem to be of trivial and unimportant matters, while often (although not always) no trace of major, impressive events with a strong emotional content remains in the adult memory. Since it is well known that the memory selects among the impressions it receives, one might think it likely that in childhood this selection functions according to principles quite different from those in operation at the age of intellectual maturity. Close investigation, however, shows that it is unnecessary to make such an assumption. The neutral memories of childhood owe their existence to a process of displacement; as reproduced, they are substitutes for other, genuinely significant impressions, the memory of which can be elicited by psychic analysis although resistance prevents their direct reproduction. Since they owe their retention in the mind not to their own content but to its associative connection with another, repressed subject, they have a good claim to be described, in the term I have adopted for them, as 'screen memories'.

I did not by any means give an exhaustive account of the full diversity of the associations between screen memories and their significance in the article mentioned above. In the example that I analysed there in detail, I laid particular emphasis on a special feature of the *temporal* relation between the screen memory and the subject it has screened out. The content of the screen memory in that example derived from a very early stage of childhood, while the thought processes represented by it in the subject's memory, which had remained almost unconscious, occurred in his later years. I described this kind of displacement as *retrospective* or *retrograde*. It is perhaps even more frequent to come upon the opposite relationship, in which a neutral impression recently received establishes itself in the mind as a screen memory, owing that distinction only to its connection with an earlier experience which resists direct reproduction. These might be described as *advanced* or *anticipatory* screen memories. In such a case the essential matter on the subject's mind occurred later in time than the screen memory. Finally, there is a third possibility: the screen memory may be linked with the impression it screens out not only in content but in temporal contiguity as well, and is thus a *simultaneous* or *contingent* screen memory.

In my article I did not go into the question of how much of our stock of memories belongs to the screen memory category, or of the part screen memories play in various neurotic thought processes, nor shall I study it here. My aim is simply to emphasize the similarity between the forgetting or faulty reproduction of proper names and the construction of screen memories.

At first glance the differences between the two phenomena are much more striking than any potential similarities. In the first case proper names are forgotten, in the second complete impressions – experiences that either really took place or occurred in the mind; the first phenomenon concerns an obvious failure of the function of memory, the second an operation of the memory which seems disconcerting. The first is a brief slip of the mind – for the name that has just been forgotten may have been spoken correctly a hundred times before and will be correctly spoken again tomorrow – the second is a permanent and unremitting condition, since it seems that neutral childhood memories can accompany us through a great part of our lives. The riddle appears to be of a diametrically different nature in the two cases. In the first, scientific curiosity is aroused by what has been forgotten, in the second by what is remembered. Further study of the question, however, makes it clear that despite the differences in the psychic material and duration of the two phenomena, the similarities by far predominate. Both involve a failure of memory, which does not reproduce what it should correctly, but instead substitutes something else. When we forget names the memory is still at work, but forms substitute names. When we construct screen memories, we substitute them for other and more important impressions which have been forgotten. In both cases we feel a certain intellectual impression that memory has been disturbed, but in different ways. In forgetting names we *know* that the substitute names are incorrect; in reproducing screen memories we are *surprised* to find that we have them at all. While psychological analysis shows that the construction of substitutes has occurred in the same way in both cases, through displacement by way of some superficial association, it is the difference of material, duration and focal interest in the two phenomena which contributes to heightening our sense that we have come upon something important and generally valid. This general validity would imply that the failure and misdirection of the function of memory indicates, more frequently than we suppose, that a partisan factor has intervened, a *tendency* which favours one memory while it works against another.

The theme of childhood memories appears to me so significant and interesting that I would like to add a few more remarks, going further than the views I have put forward so far. How far back into childhood do memories go? I know of certain studies of this question, for instance by *V.* and *C. Henri*[1] and *Potwin.*[2] These show great individual differences between the subjects studied, some of whom dated their first memories back to the age of six months, while others could remember nothing before the end of their sixth or even eighth year of life. But what are these differences in the retention of childhood memories connected with, and what is their significance? Obviously, the simple accumulation of material relating to such questions is not enough; the information must be studied further with the help of the person who provided it.

I believe we are far too ready to accept the fact of infantile amnesia, the obliteration from our memory of the first few years of life, failing to notice a curiously puzzling factor. We forget the high intellectual achievement and complex emotions of which a child of about four is capable, whereas we should feel surprised that, as a rule, later memory has retained so few of these mental processes, all the more so since there is every reason to assume that those same forgotten childhood achievements have not, so to speak, been eliminated from someone's development leaving no trace, but have exerted an influence that will affect the whole of the rest of his life. Yet in spite of this unprecedented degree of efficacy they have been forgotten! This fact indicates the very special way in which the memory (the conscious memory, that is) is conditioned, something which has so far eluded perception. It is perfectly possible that the forgetting of events in childhood can give us the key to understanding amnesia of the kind which, according to the latest findings, lies at the heart of the construction of all neurotic symptoms.

Of the childhood memories we do retain, some appear easy to understand, others strange or incomprehensible. It is not difficult to correct certain errors affecting both kinds. If a person's retained memories are analytically investigated, one can easily see that there is no guarantee of their accuracy. Some remembered images are certainly falsified, incomplete, or temporally and spatially displaced. Statements by the subjects of such studies to the effect that, for instance, their first memory dates from the age of two, are obviously unreliable. It is also quite easy to find reasons accounting for the distortion and displacement of an experience, but also showing that such slips cannot be put down simply to faulty memory. Strong forces from later periods of a subject's life have affected his ability to remember childhood experiences, probably the same forces that are responsible for the fact of our having removed ourselves, in general, so far from an understanding of our childhood years.

Adult memory is well known to operate on the basis of various kinds of psychic material. Some people remember in visual images and have good visual memories; others can hardly reproduce the faintest visual memory of something they have seen. In Charcot's classification such people are called *auditifs* and *moteurs*, as distinct from the first category, the *visuels*. These differences disappear in dreams; we all dream mainly in visual images. But this development works in reverse on childhood memories; they are realistically visual even in those whose later memories lack the visual element. Visual memory thus preserves typical infant memory. My own earliest childhood memories are the only visual memories I have, and they are positively three-dimensional, scenes that I can compare only to a stage performance. Whether such childhood scenes turn out to be accurate or misremembered, we regularly see our own childish selves in them, complete with our clothing. This is surprising, for even adults with good visual memories do not visualize themselves in their memories of later events.[3] It runs counter to all we know to suppose that a child's attention is directed to himself rather than entirely to the outside impressions he is receiving from his experiences, so for various reasons we must assume that our so-called earliest childhood memories preserve not the real trace of memory but a later revision of it, one which may have undergone the influence of many later psychic forces. 'Childhood memories' in general thus take on the significance of 'screen memories', and in this are remarkably analogous to early racial or national memories as recorded in myths and legends.

Anyone who has studied a number of minds using psychoanalytical methods will have assembled a wealth of examples of screen memories during his work. Communicating these examples, however, is greatly complicated by the nature of the relationship of childhood memories to later life; if a childhood memory is to be identified as a screen memory, the subject's whole life story would often have to be recounted first. It is rarely possible – as it is in the following fine example – to take a single childhood memory out of context and communicate it.

A man of twenty-four had retained the following memory from his fifth year. He was sitting on a little chair in the garden of a holiday house, next to an aunt who was trying to teach him his alphabet. He had difficulty in distinguishing between *m* and *n*, and asked his aunt to show him how to tell them apart. The aunt pointed out that when compared with *n*, *m* has a whole extra part to it, a third stroke. There was no reason to query the accuracy of this childhood recollection, but it acquired its true significance only later, when it could stand symbolically for something else the boy wanted to know. Just as he had been anxious to be able to tell *m* and *n* apart in the past, later he was trying to discover the difference between boys and girls, and one senses that he would have been happy to get the information from the same aunt. And the differences, as he discovered, were of a similar nature: by comparison with a girl, a boy has a whole extra part to him. It was when he found out this that his memory of his childish thirst for knowledge revived.

Another example comes from later childhood: a man of over forty, who suffered from severe inhibitions in his sexual life, was the eldest of nine children. When the ninth and youngest was born he was fifteen, but he insisted that he had never noticed any of his mother's pregnancies. Challenged by my disbelief, he did remember that once, when he was eleven or twelve, he had seen his mother rapidly undoing her skirt in front of the looking-glass. He now added, quite casually, that she had just come in from the street and unexpectedly found that she had gone into labour. Her undoing [German: *Aufbinden*] of her skirt had become a screen memory for her delivery [German: *Entbindung*]. We shall find such 'verbal bridges' used again in other cases.

I would like to cite one more example illustrating the significance that an apparently random childhood memory can acquire through analytical study. In my forty-third year, when I became interested in the remnants of my own childhood memories, I recollected a scene which had come into my mind now and then over a long period – for ever, as it seemed to me – and there were reliable indications that it must date from before the end of my third year of life. I saw myself standing in tears in front of a wardrobe [in Austrian usage: *Kasten*] and demanding something, while my half-brother, twenty years older than me, was holding its door open, and then my mother suddenly came in, beautiful and slender, as if just coming home from a walk through the streets. I had used these words to describe the three-dimensional scene, but I could take it no further. I had no idea whether my brother was going to open or close the wardrobe – in the first translation of the image into words I called it a *Schrank* ['wardrobe' in standard German] – or why I was crying, or what my mother's arrival had to do with it; I was tempted to explain it to myself as a memory of my older brother's teasing me and being interrupted by our mother. Such misinterpretations of a remembered childhood scene are not at all unusual; we remember a situation, but it is unfocused, and we do not know exactly where the psychic emphasis lies. My analytical investigations led me to an entirely unexpected interpretation of this image. I had been missing my mother, and began to suspect that she might be shut up in the wardrobe – the *Schrank* or *Kasten* – so I asked my brother to open it. When he did, and I could see that my mother was not inside, I began screaming; that was the part I remembered, along with my mother's appearance immediately afterwards, which calmed my fears and longings. But what made me, as a child, think of looking for my absent mother in the wardrobe? Some of my dreams from the same period relate vaguely to a nursemaid of whom I had certain other memories, for instance that she consistently used to make me hand over to her the small change people gave me as presents, a detail which itself could claim to figure as a screen memory for later events. This time, I decided to facilitate the task of interpretation, and I asked my now elderly mother, about the nursemaid. I learned a good deal, including the fact that this clever but dishonest character had stolen from the household on a large scale while my mother was lying in, and my half-brother had insisted on bringing legal charges against her. This information, casting a sudden bright light on my childhood memory, helped me to understand it. The nursemaid's sudden disappearance had affected me quite deeply, and in fact I had turned to that same brother to ask where she was, probably because I had noticed that he had something to do with her removal from the household. Evasively playing on words, as he commonly did, he had told me that she was 'in the clink [German: *eingekastelt*, a colloquial expression for 'in jail']'. I understood this answer in a purely childish way [as meaning 'in the wardrobe' – *Kasten*] and asked no more questions, since there seemed no more to learn. When my mother went out a little later I was anxious, fearing that my bad brother had shut her up too, just like the nursemaid, and I made him open the wardrobe for me. And now I also understand why my mother's slender figure, which seemed to have been just restored, featured so prominently in my visual version of this childhood scene; I am two and a half years older than my sister, who was born at this time, and when I was three years old my half-brother left our household.[4]

Notes

1. 'Enquête sur les premiers souvenirs de l'enfance' ['An Inquiry into Early Childhood Memories'], *L'année psychologique* III, 1897.
2. 'Study of Early Memories', *Psychological Review*, 1901.
3. I state this on the basis of several inquiries I have made.
4. Anyone with an interest in the mental processes of childhood will easily understand the deeper conditioning of my demand to my big brother. At the age of not quite three, I realized that my recently born sister had grown in my mother's uterus. I was not at all pleased about the new baby and suspected, gloomily, that my mother's body might be harbouring yet more children. The wardrobe symbolized the maternal womb to me; I therefore demanded to see inside the cupboard, and to that end I applied to my big brother. As other material shows, an older brother can replace a father as a little boy's rival. Apart from my well-founded suspicion that this brother was responsible for putting the absent nursemaid in prison, I also feared that he had somehow implanted the new-born child in my mother's body. My sense of disappointment when the wardrobe proved empty arose from the superficial motivation of my childish demand, and was misplaced in relation to my deeper level of feeling. On the other hand, my great satisfaction at noting my mother's slender figure on her return is fully comprehensible only on that deeper level.

V

Slips of the Tongue

While our everyday vocabulary in our mother tongue seems immune to being forgotten, it is all the more prone to another disturbance, familiar to us as a 'slip of the tongue'. When observed in normal people, such slips give the impression of being a preliminary stage for the phenomenon known as 'paraphasia' that occurs under pathological conditions. Here, for once, I am in a position where I can pay tribute to an earlier work. In 1895, Meringer and C. Mayer published a study on 'Slips of the Tongue and Slips in Reading', approaching the subject from a standpoint very far from my own. One of the authors, who wrote the major part of the text, is a philological scholar and was led by his linguistic interests to study the rules governing slips of the tongue. He hoped that they would enable him to conclude that there is 'a certain intellectual mechanism [. . .] in which the sounds of a word or a sentence, and the words themselves, show typical connections and interrelationships' (p. 10).

The authors initially classify the examples of their collection of 'slips of the tongue' from a purely descriptive viewpoint: as *reversals* (for instance, the Milo of Venus instead of the Venus of Milo); *anticipations* or *anticipated sounds* (for instance, 'Es war mir auf der Schwest . . . auf der Brust so schwer ['I felt it weigh heavy on my breast' but with *Brust* replaced by *Schwest*, echoing *schwer* and also suggesting *Schwester*, 'sister'])'; *echoes* or *resonances* (for instance, 'Ich fordere Sie auf, auf das Wohl unseres Chefs aufzustossen' instead of *anstossen* ['I will ask you to belch to the health of our leader' instead of 'drink a toast to the health of our leader']); *contaminations* (for instance, 'Er setzt sich auf den Hinterkopf', from 'Er setzt sich einen Kopf auf' combined with 'Er stellt sich auf die Hinterbeine' ['He stands up on the back of his head', from 'He is headstrong' combined with 'He gets up on his hind legs']); and substitutions (for instance, 'Ich gebe die Präparate in den Briefkasten' for *Brütkasten* ['I will put the specimens in the letterbox' for 'incubator']), adding to these main categories some that are less important or less significant for our purposes here. It makes no difference to this system of classification whether the distortion, transposition, disfigurement, amalgamation or any other slip affects the separate sounds in a word, or syllables, or whole words of the intended sentence.

In order to explain the slips of the tongue he has observed, Meringer suggests that spoken sounds have different psychic strengths. If we give innervation to the first sound of a word or the first word of a sentence, that stimulatory process immediately affects subsequent sounds and words, and in so far as these innervations are simultaneous they can modify each other. Stimulation of the psychically more intense sound anticipates or echoes other sounds, thus disturbing the weaker process of innervation. It is then a question of determining which sounds in a word are the strongest. Meringer thinks that: 'If we want to know which is the most intense sound in a word, we should observe ourselves trying to remember a forgotten word, for instance a name. Whatever comes back to the conscious mind first had the greatest intensity before it was forgotten' (p. 160). 'Sounds of high value are therefore the initial sound of the root syllable, the initial sound of the word, and the stressed vowel or vowels' (p. 162).

Here I cannot help disagreeing. Whether the initial sound of a name is one of the strongest elements in the word or not, it is certainly wrong to claim that it will be the first sound of a forgotten word to be recalled to mind, so the rule Meringer gives above will not hold good. When we observe ourselves trying to remember a forgotten name we are relatively often convinced that it begins with a certain letter, but as often as not there turns out to be no basis for that conviction. Indeed, I would even say that we claim the wrong initial letter for the name in the majority of cases. In my own example of *Signorelli* the initial sound and the most important syllables were lost in the substitute name; only the weaker couple of syllables, *elli*, came back to my mind in the substitute name *Botticelli*. The following case may serve to show how few substitute names respect the initial sound of the forgotten name:

One day I could not remember the name of the small country whose capital is *Monte Carlo*. The substitutes I thought of were:

Piedmont, Albania, Montevideo, Colico.

I soon replaced *Albania* by *Montenegro*, and it then struck me that the syllable *mont* (pronounced *mon*) occurred in all my substitute names except the last. That made it easier for me to make my way from the name of Prince Albert to the name of the country I had forgotten, *Monaco*. *Colico* more or less follows the syllabic sequence and rhythm of the forgotten name.

Assuming that a mechanism similar to the mechanism already demonstrated in the forgetting of names may also operate to some extent in causing slips of the tongue, one is led to assess such phenomena on a more firmly established basis. Verbal disturbance in the form of a slip of the tongue can be caused, first, by the influence of another component in the same word or set of words – through an anticipation or echo of sound – or by another version within the sentence or its context that we intend to express (all the examples cited above from Meringer and Mayer belong in this category). Second, however, the disturbance can be caused, in a way analogous to the process in the *Signorelli* case, by influences outside the word, the sentence or the context, deriving from elements that we do not intend to express, and only the disturbance itself makes us aware of their arousal. The common factor in the mechanisms causing these two kinds of slips of the tongue would lie in the simultaneity of the arousal, and the distinguishing factor would be in its position within or outside the same sentence or context. At first the difference does not seem to be very great, deriving as it does from certain deductions drawn from the symptomatology of slips of the tongue. However, it is clear that only in the first instance is there any prospect that such slips of the tongue will allow us to draw conclusions from them about a mechanism linking sounds and words so that they will influence each other – conclusions, that is to say, such as a linguistic scholar would hope to gain from studying the phenomenon. In the case of disturbance by influences outside the same sentence or linguistic context, discovering the disturbing elements would be the main concern, and we would then have to look at the question of whether the mechanism of this disturbance can, in itself, tell us anything about the laws of linguistic construction that we may assume to be operating.

It cannot be said that Meringer and Mayer have overlooked the possibility that speech disturbance may arise from 'complex psychic influences', elements outside the word, the sentence or the sequence of words themselves. They could hardly help noticing that their theory of the psychic imbalance of strength between sounds is adequate, strictly speaking, only to elucidate disturbances of sound, anticipations of sound and echoes of sound. Where verbal disturbances cannot be reduced to disturbances of sound, for instance in substituted and contaminated words, they themselves, without a second thought, have looked for the cause of a slip of the tongue *outside* its intended context, demonstrating their point with some good examples. I quote the following passages:

(p. 62) 'Ru. was describing certain things that he privately called *Schweinereien* [obscenities, filthiness, from *Schwein*, 'pig']. However, trying to find a milder way of putting it, he said, "Dann aber sind Tatsachen zum *Vorschwein* gekommen [meaning to say *Vorschein*: 'But then facts came to light']." Mayer and I were present, and Ru. admitted that he had indeed been thinking of *Schweinereien*. The similarity of sound is enough to explain the way in which the presence of this word in his mind suddenly betrayed itself through another word, which ought to have been *Vorschein*.'

(p. 73) ' "Hovering" or "wandering" verbal structures play a considerable part in substitutions as well as contaminations, and probably to an even greater degree. Although they may be subliminal they are in operative proximity, and can easily be brought to light by some similarity to the intended spoken complex, producing a slip or disarranging the verbal construction. Such "hovering" or "wandering" verbal structures are often, as we have pointed out, resonances or echoes of something recently said.'

(p. 97) 'A slip may also be made possible by similarity, when another and similar word lies just beneath the threshold of consciousness *but the speaker has no intention of uttering it*. This is how substitutions occur. I hope that examination of my rules will confirm their validity. But if they are to be examined (and if someone else is speaking) *we have to be clear about everything the speaker was thinking*.[1] I add an instructive case. We heard a schoolteacher called Herr Li. saying: "Die Frau würde mir Furcht ein*l*agen ['That woman would give me a fright', but with an incorrect *l* in the intended verb *einjagen*]." I was baffled, since I could not explain the *l* to myself, and was emboldened to point out the substitution of "ein*l*agen" for "ein*j*agen" to the speaker, whereupon he immediately replied: "Oh, that's because I was thinking: *Ich wäre nicht in der Lage* [I would not be in a position (to)], etc."

'In another case, I asked R. von Schid. how his sick horse was doing. He replied: "Ja, das draut . . . dauert vielleicht noch einen Monat ['Well, it may last another month', but with an intrusive *r* in the verb *dauert*]." I could make nothing of the *r* in *draut*, since it could hardly have been caused by the *r* towards the end of *dauert*. I pointed this out to R. von S., who explained that he had been thinking, "Das ist eine *traurige* Geschichte [It's a *sad* story]." The speaker had two answers in mind, and they had mingled.'

It will be obvious that study of the 'wandering' verbal but subliminal structures which were not meant to be uttered, together with a demand to know what the speaker was thinking about, approximate to the conditions of my own 'analyses'. I too am in search of unconscious material, and indeed I go about it in the same way, except that, using a complex series of associations, I have to trace a longer route from the ideas of the person I am questioning to the discovery of the disruptive element.

I will dwell briefly on another interesting procedure demonstrated in Meringer's examples. According to the author himself, it is some similarity of a word in the intended sentence with another word, one not meant to be spoken, which allows the latter to enter the conscious mind by causing a distortion, a mixed construction, or a structural compromise (contamination):

jagen, dauert, Vorschein
lagen, traurig, . . . schwein.

In my work on *The Interpretation of Dreams*[2] I showed what part *compression* played in creating what may be called the manifest content of the dream out of the latent dream ideas. Some similarity of objects or verbal ideas between two elements in the unconscious material causes the creation of a third composite or compromise idea, one representing both components in the content of the dream, and it is because of this origin that the new idea frequently tends to pull in two different directions. The formation of substitutions and contaminations in slips of the tongue is thus the first stage in that process of compression which is most active in the construction of dreams.

In a small article meant for a wide public (*Neue Freie Presse* of 23 August 1900: 'How slips of the tongue occur'), Meringer claimed that there is a particular practical significance in certain cases of verbal confusions, those in which a word is mentally replaced by its opposite. 'You will probably remember the words of the President of the Austrian Parliament when, some time ago, he *opened* a session by announcing: "Members of this House! I confirm the presence of such-and-such a number of gentlemen, and hereby declare this session *closed*." Only the general mirth made him realize what he had said, whereupon he corrected his mistake. In this case the explanation may well have been that the President *wished* he was already in a position to close the session, since nothing very productive could be expected to come of it, but – and this is a frequent phenomenon – his underlying idea made its influence felt, at least in part, and as a result he said the opposite of what he meant to say: "closed" and not "open". However, many and various observations have taught me that verbal opposites are very often interchanged; they are associated with each other in our verbal awareness, they lie close together, and the wrong word can easily be summoned up by mistake.'

In instances of interchanged words, it is not always as easy as it was in the case of the Austrian President to make it seem likely that a slip of the tongue arose from opposition to the intended remark in the speaker's mind. I found a similar mechanism operating in my analysis of the *aliquis* case, where internal opposition was expressed by the speaker's forgetting a word rather than replacing it by its opposite. To level out that difference, however, let me note that the little word *aliquis* cannot really suggest a contradiction of the kind arising from the ideas of 'to close' and 'to open', and that the verb 'to open', as a common part of everyday vocabulary, is proof against being forgotten.

If these last examples from Meringer and Mayer show us that speech disturbance can equally well originate in the influence of sounds and words intended to be spoken, anticipating or echoing others within the same sentence, or in the influence of words outside the intended sentence, *which would not otherwise have given away the fact that they suggested themselves*, we shall want to start by finding out whether we can draw any clear distinction between these two categories of slips of the tongue, and how we can tell the two apart. At this point, however, I must mention the comments of Wundt, who discusses instances of slips of the tongue in his comprehensive work on the development of language (*Völkerpsychologie*, vol. I, part 1, pp. 371ff., 1900). A constant characteristic of these and related instances, according to Wundt, is the presence of certain psychic influences. 'First, as a positive requirement, is the uninhibited flow of *verbal and tonal associations* aroused by the sounds uttered. This is accompanied, as a negative factor, by the suspension or remission of those operations of the will which inhibit that flow, and of the careful attention which is also a function of the will. Whether the play of association is expressed in anticipation of a coming sound or reproduction of the sound that has just been uttered, or in the insertion of what is usually a very familiar sound among others, or finally whether it is expressed in entirely different words that have an associative relationship with the spoken sounds and bring influence to bear on them – all this merely describes differences in the tendency and above all in the scope of the associations entering the mind, not in their general nature. In many cases, moreover, it is hard to decide in which category a certain disturbance belongs, and perhaps it would have been more correct to derive it from a combination of several reasons, *on the principle of the complexity of causes*[3] (pp. 380 and 381).

I think these remarks by Wundt are thoroughly justified and very instructive. Perhaps one might lay a little more emphasis than he does on the way in which the positive factor encouraging slips of the tongue – the uninhibited flow of associations – and the negative factor – the suspension of the attention that would inhibit them – regularly operate together, the two factors being only different aspects of the same process. With the suspension of the attention that would inhibit it, the uninhibited flow of associations is activated and may be said, even more definitely, to do so *through* that suspension.

Among the examples of slips of the tongue that I have collected myself I can scarcely find any where I have had to derive the verbal disturbance solely from what Wundt calls the 'contact effect of sounds'. Almost always, I discover that there is also a disruptive influence from something *outside* the intended utterance, and that this disruptive element is either a single idea that has remained unconscious, makes itself felt in the slip of the tongue, and can often be brought into the conscious mind only after thorough analysis, or it is a more general psychic motive directed against the intended utterance as a whole.

1) My daughter bit into an apple and pulled a nasty face; I was going to quote the lines:

> *Der Affe gar possierlich ist,*
> *Zumal wenn er vom Apfel frisst.*

[The monkey is very funny, particularly when he's eating an apple.]

Instead, I began to say: 'Der Apfe . . .' This seems to be a contamination of *Affe* by *Apfel* (a compromise structure), or alternatively it may be seen as anticipation of the word *Apfel* which I was about to utter. The fact is, however, that I had already begun on the quotation once, and I made no mistake the first time. My slip of the tongue was made only when I repeated it, as I had to because my daughter's attention was elsewhere when I first quoted her the lines, and she was not listening. This repetition, and my impatience to get my quotation of the lines over and done with, must be included as part of the motivation for my slip of the tongue, which represents a case of compression.

2) My daughter told me: 'I'm writing to Frau *Schres*inger.' In fact the lady's name was *Schles*inger. This slip was probably connected with a tendency to make articulation easier, since it is difficult to say the letter *l* after a repetition of *r*. However, I must add that my daughter's slip of the tongue came a few minutes after I had said *Apfe* instead of *Affe*. Slips of the tongue are very infectious, in the same way as the forgetting of names, as noted by Meringer and Mayer. However, I can give no reason for this psychic tendency to contagion.

3) 'Ich klappe zusammen wie ein Tassenmescher – Taschen-messer ['I'm folding up like a – penknife', with *Taschenmesser* mispronounced as *Tassenmescher*],' a woman patient told me at the beginning of her session of treatment, and, again, this could be put down to the difficulty of articulation (as in tongue-twisters such as *Wiener Weiber Wäscherinnen waschen weisse Wäsche* [Viennese washerwomen wash white washing] and *Fischflosse* [fish fin]). When I pointed out her slip of the tongue she immediately replied: 'Yes, but that was only because you said *Ernscht* today.' Sure enough, I actually had greeted her by saying: '*Heute wird es also Ernst* [We're in earnest today, then],' because it was to be our last session before the holiday, and I had jokingly drawn out the pronunciation of *Ernst* to make it *Ernscht*. However, she kept making more slips of the tongue, and at last I realized that she was not just imitating me but had a particular reason to linger on the word *ernst* [earnest] in her unconscious mind, since it can also be a proper name, *Ernst* [Ernest].[4]

4) 'Ich bin so verschnupft, ich kann nicht durch die Ase natmen – Nase atmen ['I have such a bad cold I can't breathe through my nose', with *Nase atmen* mispronounced as *Ase natmen*, in a spoonerism],' said the same patient on another occasion. She immediately realized how she had come to make that slip of the

tongue. 'I catch the tram every day in Hasenauerstrasse, and this morning, as I was waiting for it, I thought that if I were a French-woman I would call the street *Asenauerstrasse*, because the French never pronounce an initial *H*.' She then embarked on a series of reminiscences about French people she had met, and after going a long way round the subject she came up with a memory of herself at the age of fourteen, when she took the part of Picarde, in which she had to speak broken German, in the little play *Kurmärker und Picarde*. By a coincidence, there was a guest from Paris in her lodgings at present, a fact that had aroused this whole series of memories. The transposition of the sounds was therefore the result of disturbance by an unconscious idea in an entirely different context.

5) I observed a slip of the tongue operating similarly in another woman patient, whose power of recollection forsook her while she was telling me about a long-forgotten event in her childhood. Her memory refused to tell her what part of her body it was that a certain intrusive and lustful hand had touched. Directly afterwards she visited a woman friend, and was discussing summer holiday cottages with her. Asked about the location of her cottage in M. she said: *an der Berglende* [on the loin of the mountain] instead of *Berglehne* [on the side of the mountain].

6) When I asked another patient at the end of her session how her uncle was, she replied: 'I don't know; these days I see him only *in flagranti*.' Next day she began: 'I felt really ashamed of myself, giving you such a silly answer. You must have thought me a very uneducated person, always getting foreign words mixed up. What I meant to say was *en passant*.' At this point we did not know where she had found the incorrectly used foreign phrase. In the same session, however, and going on from what we had been discussing the day before, she came up with a reminiscence to which being caught *in flagranti* was central. The previous day's slip of the tongue, therefore, anticipated the memory of which she was not yet consciously thinking.

7) With another patient, a point in her analysis came where I had to express my suspicion that at the time we were discussing she felt

ashamed of her family, and had blamed her father for something, we were not yet sure what. She did not remember this, and said that anyway it was unlikely. However, she went on to talk about her family: 'You have to say one thing for them; they're not part of the common herd, they're all well known for their *Geiz* [avarice] – I meant to say *Geist* [intellect, wit].' So now we knew the real accusation that her memory had suppressed. It is quite common for the idea one is trying to keep at bay to emerge in a slip of the tongue (cf. Meringer's case of *zum Vorschwein gekommen*). The only difference is that in Meringer's example the subject was trying to suppress something he knew, whereas my patient did not know what she was suppressing, or one might say that she did not know either that she was keeping any idea at bay, or what idea it was.

8) The following example of a slip of the tongue was also the result of an intentional suppression of an idea. One day in the Dolomites I meet two ladies in walking dress. I accompanied them for a little way, and we talked about the pleasures and pains of a walking holiday. One of the ladies admitted that there were a number of disadvantages to a day spent out walking. 'The fact is,' she said, 'it's not at all comfortable to be out in the sun all day until your blouse and under-vest are drenched in sweat.' At one point in bringing out this sentence she had to overcome a small hesitation. Then she went on: 'But when you get *nach Hose* [*Hose*, 'knickers', substituted for *nach Hause*, 'home'] and you can change your clothes . . .' I imagine that this slip of the tongue hardly needs much study to explain it. The lady had obviously begun by intending to enumerate her items of underwear in full, 'blouse, under-vest and knickers', but for reasons of decorum refrained from naming the third garment. However, in the next sentence, which was quite independent in content, the suppressed word *Hose* involuntarily emerged as a distortion of the similar phrase *nach Hause*.

9) 'If you want to buy carpets, try Kaufmann in Matthäusgasse. I think I can safely recommend you to go there,' a lady told me. I repeated what she had said: 'Oh, so you really think I should try Matthäus . . . I mean Kaufmann.' My giving one name instead of another looks like the result of mere inattention, and the lady's

remark had in fact distracted me, turning my attention to something else, of far more importance to me than carpets. As it happens, the building where my wife lived before we were married was in Matthäusgasse, but its main entrance was in another street, and I realized that I had forgotten the name of that street and could only recall it to my mind by a circuitous train of thought. The name Matthäus on which I dwelt was thus a substitute for the forgotten name of the street, and a more suitable one than the name Kaufmann, since Matthäus is exclusively a personal name, but Kaufmann is not [it is not only a surname but also means 'merchant', 'dealer'], and in fact the street I had forgotten also bears a personal name, *Radetzky*.

10) I could equally well include the following case among the 'Errors' to be discussed later, but I will cite it here because the phonetic relationships accounting for the compensatory word are particularly clear. A woman patient told me her dream: she dreamed that a child had decided to kill itself by snakebite, and did so. She watched the child writhing in pain, and so forth. I now wanted her to locate what had happened during the day that was connected with her dream. She remembered at once that she had been to hear a popular lecture that evening, on first aid in cases of snakebite. If an adult and a child have been bitten at the same time, the audience was told, the child's injury must be treated first, and she also remembered the lecturer's instructions for treatment. It all depended, he had said, on which species of snake bit you. Here I interrupted, asking her: 'Didn't he tell you that we have very few poisonous snakes in this country, and which the most dangerous species are?' 'Yes, he particularly mentioned the *Klapperschlange* [rattlesnake].' My laughter made her realize that she had slipped up. However, instead of simply correcting the name, she returned to her statement. 'Oh no, of course we don't have rattlesnakes here; it was the viper he mentioned. However did I come to say rattlesnake?' I suspected it was through confusing the ideas concealed by her dream. Suicide by snakebite can hardly be anything but a reference to the beautiful *Kleopatra* [the German spelling of Cleopatra]. The considerable similarity of sound between the two

words in German, the coincidence of the letters *Kl . . . p . . . r*, appearing in that order, and the emphasis on the vowel *a* cannot be overlooked. The strong connection between the noun *Klappersch-lange* and the name of *Kleopatra* caused her to suspend her judgement for a moment, and as a result she found nothing odd about the idea of the lecturer's instructing his Viennese audience on the treatment of rattlesnake bites. She normally knows as well as I do that rattlesnakes are not among our native fauna. Nor should she be blamed for so glibly transferring the rattlesnake to Egypt, since we commonly put everything non-European and exotic into the same category in our minds, and I had to stop and think for a moment myself before saying that rattlesnakes are found only in the New World.

More confirmation came to light in the further course of her analysis. The day before, the dreamer had seen Strasser's statuary group of Mark Antony, which is near her home, for the first time. This was the second cause of her dream (the first being the snakebite lecture). In the later part of the dream she was cradling a child in her arms, and this scene brought Gretchen [of the Faust legend and Goethe's drama] to mind. Other ideas produced reminiscences of *Arria und Messalina* [by the dramatist Adolf Wilbrandt]. The emergence in her dream of so many names from stage plays had already made me suspect that in the past the dreamer had cherished a secret wish to be a professional actress. The beginning of the dream, in which a child decided to commit suicide by snakebite, really meant simply that, as a child, she was determined to be a famous actress some day. Finally, the train of thought leading to the subject at the heart of her dream derived from the name *Messalina*. Certain recent incidents had made her anxious about her only brother, who might be about to contract an unsuitable marriage with a non-*Aryan* woman – and if he did it would be a *mésalliance*.

11) I will now describe a perfectly innocuous example, or perhaps one with motives only inadequately clear to us, because it illustrates an obvious mechanism:

A German travelling in Italy needed a strap to secure his suitcase, which had been damaged. Looking up the German word for strap,

Riemen, in the dictionary, he found the Italian version *coreggia*. I shall remember that easily enough, he told himself, if I think of the painter Correggio. But when he went into a shop he asked for *una ribera*.

Evidently he had not quite managed to replace the German word by its Italian equivalent in his mind, but his efforts had not been entirely unsuccessful. He knew it was a painter's name that would serve as his *aide-mémoire*, so he came up not with the name of the painter resembling the Italian word, but with another painter's name that resembles the German word *Riemen*. Of course I could just as well have put this example among the instances of forgetting names as in this section on slips of the tongue.

When I was collecting examples of slips of the tongue for the first edition of this work, I subjected all cases I had observed to analysis, including the less impressive of them. Since then many other people have amused themselves by taking the trouble to collect and analyse such slips, thus allowing me to select from a greater wealth of material.

12) A young man said to his sister: 'I've broken off my acquaintance with the D. family, I don't even pass the time of day with them now.' She replied: 'Oh, what a *Lippschaft* they are!' She meant to say *Sippschaft* ['clan', or in this context with the pejorative meaning of 'gang'], but her slip of the tongue combined two ideas: first, her brother himself had once embarked on a flirtatious relationship with the daughter of this family, and, second, it was said of the same girl that she had recently entered into a serious and illicit *Liebschaft* [love affair].

13) A young man addressed a lady in the street, saying: 'If you will allow me, Fräulein, I would like to *begleit-digen* you.' He was clearly thinking he would like to accompany her (*begleiten*), but feared that the offer might insult her (*beleidigen*). The expression of these two contradictory ideas in a single word – his slip of the tongue – shows that the young man's real intentions were certainly not as pure as they might have been, and even to himself might seem insulting to the lady. But while he was trying to conceal this from her, his unconscious mind tricked him into betraying his real

purpose, also and conversely making him anticipate her conventional answer: 'What on earth do you take me for? How can you insult [*beleidigen*] me so?' (Communicated to me by O. Rank.)

I take a number of examples from an article by W. Stekel in the *Berliner Tageblatt* of 4 January 1904, entitled 'Unconscious Confessions'.

14) 'The following example reveals a distasteful side to my unconscious thinking. I should begin by saying that as a doctor I have never been concerned for material gain, and have concentrated solely on the interests of the patient, which of course is only natural. I had a woman patient whom I was treating during her convalescence from a severe illness; we had passed some trying days and nights together. I was pleased to find her better one day, painted a picture of the pleasure she would derive from a visit to Abbazia, and added, "That is if, as I hope, you do *not* leave your bed soon." Obviously the "not" arose from a selfish wish on the part of my unconscious that I could go on treating this prosperous patient longer, an idea entirely alien to my conscious mind and one which I would reject with horror.'

15) Another example (from W. Stekel). 'My wife was interviewing a Frenchwoman whom she was thinking of employing in the afternoons, and once they had agreed on terms said she would like to keep her references. But the Frenchwoman wanted them back, giving as her reason: "Je cherche encore pour les après-midis, pardon, pour les avant-midis [I am still looking for work in the afternoons – oh, I beg your pardon, in the mornings]." She obviously intended to look elsewhere and perhaps get better terms – and in fact that was just what happened.'

16) Another example from Dr Stekel: 'I was to read a certain lady a stern lecture at the request of her husband, who was listening on the other side of the door. At the end of my sermon, which obviously made an impression, I said, "Well, goodbye then, *gnädiger Herr* [instead of *gnädige Frau*]!" In doing so I had given away, to anyone who knew the circumstances, the fact that what I had said was on behalf of the husband and was really addressed to him.'

17) Dr Stekel tells us how he himself was once treating two

patients from Trieste whom he always used to greet by the wrong names. 'I would say "Good morning, Herr Peloni," to Askoli, and: "Good morning, Herr Askoli," to Peloni.' At first he was inclined to ascribe no very profound motivation to this switch of their names, and explained it by the fact that the two gentlemen had several things in common. However, he was easily able to convince himself that his confusing the names was really a kind of boastfulness, enabling him to let each of his Italian patients know that he, the patient, was not the only person to have come from Trieste to Vienna to seek Stekel's medical advice.

18) Dr Stekel himself, in a heated general meeting, announced: 'Wir *streiten* (in error for *schreiten*) nun zu Punkt 4 der Tagesordnung [We will now *quarrel* (in error for *proceed*) to point 4 of the agenda].'

19) A professor said, in his inaugural lecture: 'Ich bin nicht *geneigt* (for *geeignet*), die Verdienste meines sehr geschätzten Vorgängers zu schildern [I am not *inclined* (for *qualified*) to say anything about the merits of my highly esteemed predecessor].'

20) Dr Stekel said to a lady who, he suspected, might have Basedow's disease: 'Sie sind um einen *Kropf* (in error for *Kopf*) grösser als Ihre Schwester [You are a *goitre* (in error for *head*) taller than your sister].'

21) Another incident reported by Dr Stekel concerns a man trying to describe the relationship of two friends, one of whom was Jewish. ' "They lived together," he said, "like Castor and Pollak [substituting the Jewish surname Pollak for the name Pollux, one of the Dioscuri in classical myth]." This was not meant as a joke; the speaker failed to notice his own slip of the tongue, and became aware of it only when I pointed it out.'

22) 'Sometimes a slip of the tongue paints the picture of an entire character. A young lady who wore the trousers in her marriage told me that her husband, who was unwell, had been to the doctor and asked what diet would be best for him. The doctor, however, said diet had nothing to do with it. "He can eat and drink what I like," said the wife.'

The following two examples, taken from T. Reik (*Internationale Zeitschrift für Psychoanalyse* III, 1915), arise from situations where it is particularly easy for a slip of the tongue to occur, because in such cases more must be withheld than can be openly said.

23) A gentleman was condoling with a young lady whose husband had recently died, and added: 'Sie werden Trost finden, indem Sie sich völlig Ihren Kindern widwen ['You will find comfort in devoting yourself entirely to your children', but using the slip *widwen*, echoing *Witwe*, 'widow', in error for *widmen*, 'devote'].' The suppressed idea is of another kind of comfort: a beautiful young widow would soon be likely to enjoy sexual pleasure again.

24) The same gentleman was talking to the same lady at an evening party about the large-scale Easter preparations being made in Berlin, and asked: 'Have you seen the display in Wertheim's windows today? It is all *dekolletiert* [in error for *dekoriert*].' He had not been able to express his admiration for the beautiful woman's décolletage explicitly, but the taboo idea surfaced when he referred not to the *decoration* of a store window but to a *décolletage*, unconsciously using the word *Auslage* [display, put on show] with a double meaning.

The same circumstances applied to an observation of which Dr Hanns Sachs has done his best to supply a full account:

25) 'A lady told me that when she last saw a common acquaintance of ours he was as elegantly dressed as ever, and in particular he was wearing remarkably handsome brown flat-heeled shoes (*Halbschuhe*). When I ask where they had met she said: "Oh, he rang my doorbell, and I saw him through the roller blinds, which were pulled down. However, I didn't open the door or give any other sign of life, because I didn't want him to know I was back in town." Listening, I suspected that she was hiding something from me, and very likely she didn't open the door because she was not alone and was improperly dressed to receive visitors. I asked, with some irony: "Oh, so you could admire his *Hausschuhe* [slippers] – his *Halbschuhe* through the drawn blinds?' The idea of her *Hauskleid* [dressing gown], which I had refrained from expressing, emerged in the word *Hausschuhe*. I may also have tried not to say *Halb* [half] because it contained the answer I would not let myself give: "You are telling me only *half* the truth; you forget to say that you were

only *half* dressed." The slip of the tongue was also encouraged by the fact that immediately before we had been discussing the conjugal life of the gentleman in question and his *häusliches Glück* [domestic happiness], a term that probably helped to determine the displacement to his own person. Finally, I must admit that perhaps my own envy played a part in my making this elegant gentleman stand in the street in his slippers, since I myself had recently bought some low-heeled brown shoes which were by no means "remarkably handsome" any more.'

Times of war like the present give rise to a number of slips of the tongue that are readily comprehensible.

26) 'What is your son's regiment?' a lady was asked. She replied: 'The 42nd *Mörder* ['murderers', in error for *Mörser*, 'mortars'].'

27) Lieutenant Henrik Haiman wrote from the front: 'I was torn away from reading a fascinating book to deputize briefly for the reconnaissance telephonist. When the gun emplacement rang to test the line I reacted by saying: All correct, *Ruhe* [shut up]. It ought really to have been: All correct, *Schluss* [over and out]. My lapse can be explained by my annoyance at being disturbed in reading my book' (*Internationale Zeitschrift für Psychoanalyse* IV, 1916/17).

28) A sergeant told his men to send their addresses home accurately so that the *Gespeckstücke* [a word suggesting 'pieces of bacon', *Speck*, for *Gepäckstücke*, 'packages'] would not go astray.

29) I owe the following outstandingly fine example, significant for its very unfortunate background, to Dr L. Czeszer, who made this observation while he was in neutral Switzerland during the war and analysed it at length. I reproduce his own account with a few minor cuts:

'Let me permit myself to describe a case of a "slip of the tongue" made by Professor M. N. in O., during one of the lectures he was delivering during the last summer semester on the psychology of the emotions. I must state first that these lectures were held in the great hall of the university, and were well attended by interned French prisoners of war as well as the French-speaking Swiss students, most of whom were very much in favour of the Entente. In O., as in France itself, the word *boche* is now generally and exclusively used as a term for Germans. In public announcements, how-ever, and in lectures and so forth, senior civil servants, professors and other responsible people try to avoid this unfortunate word for reasons of neutrality.

'Professor N. was in the middle of describing the practical signifi-cance of affects, and he intended to quote an example of the inten-tional exploitation of an affect in order to endow intrinsically uninteresting physical labour with pleasurable feelings, thus inten-sifying its structure. He therefore told the story, in French of course, that at the time had just been reprinted from a German journal in the local Swiss papers, about a German schoolmaster who made his pupils work in the garden, and to encourage them to work harder told them to imagine that instead of every clod of earth they dug they were smashing a French skull. Whenever he mentioned Germans in telling his story of course N. said, quite correctly, *allemand*, not *boche*. However, when he reached the point of the story he rendered the schoolmaster's remarks as follows: *Imaginez-vous qu'en chaque moche vous écrasez le crâne d'un Français*. He had turned *motte* [a clod of earth] into *moche*!

'Here we can actually see the impeccable scholar taking care, from the very beginning of his story, not to give way to the usual habit, and perhaps the temptation, of allowing the taboo word (which in fact had been expressly banned by a Swiss decree) to be uttered from the lectern of the university hall! And just as he had successfully pronounced the phrase *instituteur allemand* for the last time, per-fectly correctly, and was making haste, with an inward sigh of relief, towards the inoffensive conclusion of the story, the word he had so laboriously suppressed fastened on the similarity of sound in the word *motte* – and the mischief was done. Fear of political tact-lessness, perhaps a suppressed wish to use the common and indeed expected word after all, and the distaste of a man who had been a republican and democrat from birth for any constraint on freedom of expression all interfered with his main intention of giving a correct account of his example. The speaker was aware of the interfering tendency, and we may well suppose that he was thinking of it directly before his slip of the tongue.

'Professor N. did not notice his slip, or at least he did not correct it, as people usually do quite automatically. On the other hand, his lapse was noted with real satisfaction by most of the French in his audience, and had just the same effect as an intentional play on words. Personally, I followed this apparently innocuous process with a genuine sense of internal excitement. Although for obvious reasons I could not ask the professor the questions forcibly suggested by psychoanalytic method, I still saw his slip of the tongue as striking evidence for the accuracy of your theory of the determination of such slips, and the profound analogies and relationships between slips of the tongue and jokes.'

30) It was also under the depressing influence of wartime impressions that an Austrian officer, First Lieutenant T., made a slip of the tongue that he described on his return home:

'For several months while I was a prisoner of war in Italy our group of 200 officers was billeted in cramped accommodation in a villa. During this time one of us died of influenza. The impression that this incident made on us was naturally profound, for our present circumstances, the lack of medical aid, and our powerlessness at the time made an epidemic more than likely. We had laid the dead man out in a room in the basement. In the evening, when I went out to walk around the house with a friend, we both thought we would like to look at the corpse. I went first, and when I entered the cellar I saw a sight that greatly alarmed me, since I had not been prepared to find the bier so close to the door or to have to see the face, which seemed to be moving in the flickering candlelight, at such close quarters. Still under the influence of this image, we went on with our walk. At a place where we had a view of the park bathed in full moonlight, and of a brightly illuminated meadow with faint drifts of mist beyond, I expressed the idea it suggested to me, that one could imagine elves dancing among the pines surrounding this place. Next afternoon we buried our dead comrade. We found the way from our prison to the graveyard of the little village near by both bitter and humiliating, since half-grown, yelling lads, mocking, contemptuous locals and people shouting vulgarities at the top of their voices had seized on this occasion to give open expression to their emotions of mingled curiosity and hatred. A sense of inevitable resentment, even in this defenceless situation, and my distaste for such rough behaviour preyed upon my mind until evening. Then, at the same time as the day before and with the same companion, I set out on the gravel path round the villa again, and on passing the grille in front of the cellar behind which the corpse had been lying I was overcome by the memory of the impression the sight had made on me. At the place from which I had seen a view of the moonlit park, and by the light of the same full moon, I stopped and said to my companion: "We could sit down here in the *Grab* [grave] – I mean *Gras* [grass], and *sinken* ['sink', in error for *singen*, 'sing'] a serenade." Only when I made my second slip of the tongue did I realize what I had said; the first time I had corrected myself without understanding the reason for my mistake. Now that I thought about it I connected the ideas of "sinking" and "into the grave". Then these images immediately came into my mind: elves dancing and hovering in the moonlight; our comrade on his bier; his face, apparently moving; various scenes from the funeral; my sense of distaste, the disruption of our mourning; the memory of certain remarks about the onset of an epidemic, expressions of alarm on the part of several of the officers. Later I remembered that it was the anniversary of my father's death on that day. I found this recollection striking, because I am usually very bad at remembering dates.

'On thinking it over later I noticed the way in which the external conditions matched each other on the two evenings: the same time of day, the same light, the same place and the same companion. I remembered my uneasiness when concern about the possible spread of influenza was discussed, but also my inner determination not to let fear get the better of me. I also saw the significance of my word order in saying that we could sink into the grave [German: *wir könnten ins Grab sinken*] and I realized that the first correction of "grave" to "grass", which had not been a very emphatic one, was the only reason for my second slip of turning "sing" into "sink", thus ensuring that the suppressed complex could finally come into the open.

'I will add that at this time I was suffering from anxious dreams in which I repeatedly saw a woman member of my immediate family lying ill, and once even dead. Just before I was taken prisoner, I had heard that the flu was raging particularly virulently in the place where this relation of mine lived, and I had told her of my alarm for her. We had been out of touch since then. Months later I heard that she had indeed fallen victim to the epidemic two weeks before the event I have described!'

31) The following example of a slip of the tongue casts a revealing light on one of those painful conflicts that doctors are always having to resolve. A man who was probably mortally sick, although his diagnosis was not yet certain, had come to Vienna to await the outcome of his problems, and had asked a friend of his youth, now a well-known doctor, to take on his case. The doctor, not without reluctance, finally agreed. The sick man had to stay somewhere where there was medical help on hand, and the doctor suggested the Hera Sanatorium. Oh no, objected the invalid, that's only for certain kinds of cases (it was a maternity hospital). No, indeed, the doctor protested: they can *umbringen* [kill] – I mean *unterbringen* [accommodate] any kind of patient in the Hera. He then vehemently protested against the obvious interpretation of this slip of the tongue. 'You surely don't believe I feel aggressive towards you?' Quarter of an hour later, the doctor told the lady who had agreed to look after the sick man and was seeing him out: 'I can't find anything very bad, and I still don't believe it will come to the worst, but if it does I'm in favour of a good dose of morphine, and then he'll be at rest.' It turned out that his friend had made him promise to cut short his suffering with drugs as soon as it was certain that no more could be done for him, so the doctor had in fact undertaken to kill [*umbringen*] the sick man.

32) I must include here a particularly instructive example of a slip of the tongue, although according to my informant it happened some 20 years ago. 'A lady once said in company – and the words themselves show that they were uttered with feeling and under the pressure of all kinds of concealed emotions: "Oh yes, a woman must be pretty if she is to please men. It's much easier for a man: so long as he has his *fünf geraden Glieder* [five straight limbs] that's all he

needs!" This example provides a good insight into the intimate mechanism at work when a slip of the tongue is caused by *compression* or *contamination* (cf. p. 53). It seems obvious that two rather similar expressions have been merged:

wenn er seine vier geraden Glieder hat [so long as he has his four straight limbs]

wenn er seine fünf Sinne beisammen hat [so long as he has the use of his five senses].

Alternatively, the word *gerade* [straight] may contain the element in common to two intended remarks, running:

wenn er nur seine geraden Glieder hat [so long as he has his straight limbs]

alle fünf gerade sein lassen ['to let all five be even (*gerade*) numbers', but also, colloquially, 'to stretch a point, turn a blind eye'].

There is nothing to prevent us from supposing that *both* expressions, one turning on the five senses and the other on even numbers, could have introduced into the sentence about straight limbs first a number and then the puzzling five instead of the expected four. However, it is unlikely that they would have merged if the construction arising from the slip of the tongue had not made perfectly good sense in itself, having a double meaning [taking *Glied* in its sense of male member, penis] which the speaker, being a woman, could not acknowledge openly. Finally, one must point out that the wording of the lady's remark could just as well have made it an excellent joke as an amusing slip of the tongue, depending on whether she said it intentionally or unintentionally. However, her manner in this case showed that her remarks were unintentional and not meant to be funny.'

The close approximation of a slip of the tongue to a joke can go quite a long way, as it does in this case described by O. Rank, where the lady who made the slip of the tongue eventually laughed at it herself:

33) 'A young husband whose wife, wishing to preserve her girlish looks, was reluctant to let him have frequent sexual intercourse, told me the following story, which in retrospect amused both of them very much: the morning after a night when, yet again, he had ignored

his wife's desire for sexual abstinence, he was shaving in the bedroom they shared, and used the *powder-puff* lying on his wife's bedside table, as he often did for the sake of convenience, while she was still in bed. The lady, who thought a great deal of her complexion, had asked him several times before not to do it, and now cried out in vexation: "Oh no, there you go powdering *me* again with *your* puff!" Alerted to her slip of the tongue by her husband's laughter (for she had meant to say: powdering *yourself* with *my* puff), she finally laughed heartily too. ("To powder" is an expression for sexual intercourse known to any Viennese, and a powder-puff is an obvious phallic symbol)' (*Internationale Zeitschrift für Psychoanalyse* I, 1913).

34) An intentional joke might also be suspected in the following case (from A. J. Storfer):

Frau B., who was suffering from an ailment of obviously psychogenic origin, was repeatedly urged to consult X. the psychoanalyst. She always refused, objecting that such treatment was never any use, and the doctor, mistakenly, was bound to say her trouble was all due to sexual causes. At last, however, she agreed to take this advice, and asked: 'Nun gut, wann *ordinärt* also dieser Dr X. ['When does this Dr X. have his consultations?', but confusing the verb *ordinieren*, 'to hold consultations', and the adjective *ordinär*, 'vulgar']?'

The relationship between a joke and a slip of the tongue is also obvious in the fact that the slip of the tongue is often simply a short cut:

35) A young girl left school and, in the contemporary fashion, registered to study medicine, but after a few semesters she changed from medicine to chemistry. A few years later she described the reason for her change by saying: 'I never felt squeamish about dissection in general, but once, when I had to remove the nails from the fingers of a corpse, I found I had entirely lost my enthusiasm for – *chemistry*.'

36) Here is another case of an easily interpreted slip of the tongue. 'A professor of anatomy was speaking about the nasal cavity, which is known to be a very difficult enterological subject. When he asked whether his audience had understood his explanation, there was

a general "Yes". At this the professor, a man notorious for his self-assurance, commented: I doubt whether, even in a city with a population of millions like Vienna, those who really understand the nasal cavity can be counted on *one finger* – I beg your pardon, I meant on the fingers of one hand.'

37) On another occasion the same anatomist said: 'The study of the female genitals, despite many *Versuchungen* [temptations] – I beg your pardon, *Versuche* [experiments] . . .'

38) I am grateful to Dr A. Robitsek of Vienna for drawing my attention to two cases of slips of the tongue noted by a French author of the past, which I quote in the original French. In the *Discours second* of his *Vies des Dames galantes*, Brantôme (1527–1614) writes: 'Si ay-je cogneu une très belle et honneste dame de par le monde, qui, devisant avec un honneste gentilhomme de la cour des affaires de la guerre durant ces civiles, elle luy dit: "J'ay ouy dire que le roy a faict rompre tous les c . . . de ce pays là." Elle voulait dire les ponts. Pensez que, venant de coucher d'avec son mary, ou songeant à son amant, elle avoit encor ce nom frais en la bouche; et le gentilhomme s'en eschauffa en amours d'elle pour ce mot [I knew a very beautiful and virtuous society lady who, discussing the war during this time of civil unrest with a gentleman of the court, told him: "I have heard that the king has mounted an assault on all the c . . . of that part of the country." She meant "all the bridges" [*ponts*, rhyming with *cons*, 'cunts']. Very likely, having just been to bed with her husband or else thinking of her lover, she still had that word on the tip of her tongue, and it inflamed the gentleman with love for her.'

'Une autre dame que j'ai cogneue, entretenant une autre grand dame plus qu'elle, et luy louant et exaltant ses beautez, elle luy di après: "Non, madame, ce que je vous en dis: ce n'est point pour vous adultérer;" voulant dire adulater, comme elle le rhabilla ainsi: pensez qu'elle songeoit à adultérer [Another lady I knew, speaking to a lady whose rank was higher than hers, praising her and complimenting her on her beauty, finished by remarking: "No, madame, I do not say these things to *adulterate* you." She meant to *adulate*, but the way she put it suggests that she was thinking of *adultery*].'

39) Of course more modern examples exist of sexual double meanings arising from slips of the tongue: Frau F. said, of her first lesson in a language course she was taking: 'It's really interesting; the tutor is a nice young Englishman. In the very first lesson he indicated to me *durch die Bluse* [through my blouse]' – and corrects herself: '*durch die Blume* [literally, 'through the flower' but colloquially 'with veiled hints'] – that he would rather give me private tuition' (Storfer).

In the psychotherapeutic methods that I use to resolve and eliminate neurotic symptoms, I very often have to track down the subject of a train of thought from the remarks and ideas which patients bring out as if by chance. They may try to conceal that subject, but cannot help revealing it unintentionally in many different ways. In such circumstances a slip of the tongue often proves very helpful indeed, as I could demonstrate by quoting some very odd but extremely cogent examples. Speaking of an aunt, for instance, patients may consistently call her 'my mother' without noticing the slip, or a woman patient may describe her husband as her 'brother'. This tells me that they are 'identifying' these people with each other and have arranged them in a manner which suggests that the same type of character recurs in their emotional lives. Again, a young man of 20 introduced himself to me when he came for a consultation by saying, 'You treated so and so; I'm his father. Oh, I'm sorry, I meant his brother. He's four years older than me.' I realize that his slip of the tongue was intended to convey that it was their father's fault if both he and his brother were ill, and like his brother he wanted to be cured, but it was their father who needed a cure most urgently. On other occasions an unusual verbal construction or what appears to be a stilted manner of expression is enough to reveal part of a repressed idea in the patient's differently motivated remarks.

I do not, therefore, think that those instances of obvious or subtler speech disturbances which can also be subsumed under 'slips of the tongue' are mainly due to the influence of phonetic contacts; I believe that such slips derive from ideas outside what the speaker intends to say, which are sufficient to explain the slip. I do not mean to imply any doubt of the phonetic laws causing sounds to modify each other, but they do not seem to me strong enough to impair correct speech by their own influence alone. In those cases that I have studied closely and of which I can claim some understanding, they merely represent an existing mechanism that can easily be used by a more remote psychic motive without its binding itself to the sphere of influence of those connections. *In a great many substitutions, a slip of the tongue occurs quite regardless of such laws of phonetics.* Here I am completely in agreement with Wundt, who like me assumes that conditions producing slips of the tongue are complex and go far beyond phonetic interaction. On the other hand, while I accept these 'more remote psychic influences', as Wundt calls them, I do not see why we should not also admit that when someone is speaking fast, and his attention is to some extent distracted, the conditions for a slip of the tongue can easily be restricted to those defined by Meringer and Mayer. But in some of the examples they collected it seems likely that there is in fact a more complex solution. Let me take the case already mentioned above [p. 53].

Es war mir auf der Schwest . . . Brust *so schwer*.

Was this really a simple instance of *Schwe* displacing *Bru*, a syllable of equal value, as the initial sound? It can hardly be denied that here the sound *Schwe* could also have superseded *Bru* because of a special relationship, none other than the associated ideas of *Schwester – Bruder* [sister – brother], and perhaps also *Brust der Schwester* [sister's breast], leading on to other trains of thought. These assistants, invisible backstage, lent the otherwise innocuous *Schwe* the force to express itself as a slip of the tongue.

In other slips of the tongue we may assume that an echo of indecent words or meanings is the really disruptive factor. The sole aim of the intentional distortion and misrepresentation of words and phrases, so popular among the vulgar-minded, is to take something harmless in itself as the occasion for referring to taboo subjects, and such plays on words are so common that it would hardly be surprising for them to emerge unintentionally and against the speaker's will. Examples that belong in this category probably include *Eischeissweibchen* [egg-shit-female] for *Eiweissscheibchen* [small slices of egg white], *Apopos Fritz* [*Popo*, bum] for *A propos Fritz*,

Lokuskapitäl [lavatory capital] for *Lotuskapitäl* [lotus capital], etc., and perhaps even the transposition of the vowels in St Mary Magdalene's *Alabasterbuchse* [alabaster casket] to create *Alabüster-bachse* [a coinage with the central element suggesting *Büste*, bosom].[5] The example quoted above [p. 53] – 'I will ask you to belch to the health of our leader' – is little more than an unintentional parody echoing what the speaker intended to say, and had I been the man to whose honours this lapse was contributed, I would probably have thought how wise the Romans were, when an emperor celebrated a triumph, to let the common soldiers express their private reservations about the great man in satirical songs. Meringer (p. 50) tells us that when the oldest man in a certain gathering was addressed by the familiar honorary title of 'Senexl' or 'altes Senexl ['old man', using Latin *senex* with the Austrian diminutive *l* added]', he himself had drunk a toast to him saying, 'Prost, Senex altesl!' His own slip shocked him, and perhaps we can understand why if we remember how close 'Altesl ['old fellow', again with the Austrian ending]' comes to insulting someone by calling him 'alter Esel [old donkey]'. There have always been strong inhibitions against failing to show the veneration due to age (or reduced to childhood ideas, respect for one's father).

I hope my readers will note the difference of value between those interpretations for which there is no evidence, and the examples I have collected myself and elucidated by analysis. If at heart, however, I still expect to find that even apparently simple cases of slips of the tongue will prove to derive from disruption by a partly suppressed idea from *outside* the intended context, then I am led to do so by a very interesting remark of Meringer's. As he says, it is worth noting that no one likes admitting to a slip of the tongue. There are some very clever and honest people whose feelings will be quite injured if they are told they have perpetrated one. I would not venture to make this statement as universal as Meringer's 'no one' suggests, but there is significance in the emotion we feel when faced with the evidence of our slips of the tongue, which is obviously in the nature of shame. It may be equated with our annoyance on being unable to remember a forgotten name and our surprise at the persistence of an apparently insignificant memory, and always indicates that there has been some reason for the disturbance.

The intentional distortion of names is taken as insulting, and in a considerable number of cases where it manifests itself as an unintentional slip of the tongue it may well have the same signifi- cance. The person who, according to Mayer (p. 38), once said *Freuder* instead of *Freud* because just before that he had mentioned the name of *Breuer*, and on another occasion spoke of a *Freuer- Breudian* method (p. 28), was no doubt a fellow professional who felt no great sympathy for that method. I will deal later, under the heading of slips of the pen, with a case of the distortion of a name which cannot be explained in any other way.[6]

In these cases, a criticism that has to be dismissed because just at that moment it does not correspond to the speaker's intention is the disturbing factor.

Conversely, the substitution of names, the appropriation of another name, and identification by a slip in the name must denote some kind of recognition that at the moment, for one reason or another, has to stay in the background. S. Ferenczi tells us of an experience of this kind from his schooldays:

'In my first year at grammar school, I was to recite a poem in public (that is, in front of the whole class) for the first time in my life. I was well prepared, and was dismayed to have my recitation disrupted by roars of laughter at the very beginning. The teacher explained this curious reception: I had given the title of the poem, "Aus der Ferne" ['From Afar'] perfectly correctly, but as its author I had named not the real poet – but myself. The poet's name is Alexander (Sándor) Petöfi. The fact that his first name was the same as mine encouraged the confusion, but its real cause was surely my identification at the time in my heart of hearts with that famous and heroic poet. I felt love and deep respect bordering on adoration for him even in my conscious mind, and of course there was also a whole lamentable ambition complex behind my slip.'

I heard of a similar case of identification through the switching of names from a young doctor, who hesitantly and reverently intro- duced himself to the famous *Virchow* in the words: Dr *Virchow*.

The professor turned to him in surprise and asked: 'Oh, is your name *Virchow* too?' I don't know how the ambitious young man justified himself for this slip of the tongue: whether he hit upon the engaging excuse that he had felt so insignificant beside the man who bore this great name that his own was bound to escape him, or whether he was brave enough to confess that he hoped to become as great a man as Virchow himself some day, and trusted that the professor would not despise him for that. One of those two ideas – or perhaps both of them at once – may have cast the young man into confusion when he introduced himself.

For very personal reasons, I must leave the question of whether a similar interpretation can be applied to the following case open. At the International Congress in Amsterdam in 1907, the theory of hysteria that I had put forward was the subject of lively discussion. In his vehement tirade against me, it appears that one of my most energetic adversaries repeatedly slipped up by putting himself in my place and speaking as if in my name. He said, for instance: 'As everyone knows, Breuer and I have shown . . .' whereas he must have meant to say: 'Breuer and Freud'. The name of this opponent of my theories is not in the least like my own. This example, and many other cases of names being switched by a slip of the tongue, remind us that such slips can dispense entirely with any resonance to help them come into being, and can emerge purely through concealed associations of content.

In other and much more significant cases a slip of the tongue, or indeed the replacement of an intended remark by its reverse, is caused by self-criticism and internal resistance to what one is saying. We are surprised to find the wording of a statement working against its intention, so that the linguistic slip reveals an internal insincerity.[7] Here the slip of the tongue acts as a mimic means of expression, although often, admittedly, the expression of something unintended; it is a means of giving oneself away. For instance, when a man who does not prefer what might be described as normal intercourse in his relations with women says in conversation, of a girl with a reputation as a coquette: 'If she had anything to do with me she'd soon stop her *Koëttieren*,' there is no doubt that he can only have meant the word *koitieren* [to have sexual intercourse], and its effect on the intended word *kokettieren* [to be coquettish] can be ascribed to this kind of modification. Or take the following case: 'An uncle of ours was greatly offended for months because we never visited him. When we moved house we took the chance of going to see him again after a long interval. He appeared to be delighted by our visit, and on parting said, with warm feeling: "Well, from now on I hope to see you *less frequently* than before." '

Favourable opportunities that the verbal material happens to offer frequently cause slips of the tongue to occur, with the startling effect of a revelation or the full comic effect of a joke.

For instance, take the following case, observed and reported by Dr Reitler: 'One lady said or intended to say admiringly to another: "I expect you trimmed that pretty new hat yourself?" but instead of *aufgeputzt* [trimmed] said *aufgepatzt* [echoing the word *Patzerei*, a clumsy job]. She could not go on praising the hat, as she meant to, since her unfortunate slip of the tongue had expressed her silent criticism of the trimming of the hat as "clumsily done" only too clearly, and no phrases of conventional admiration would now have carried conviction.'

Milder but still unmistakable is the criticism in the following example:

'A lady visiting an acquaintance felt very impatient and weary after listening to the other woman's verbose and long-winded remarks. At last she managed to bring the visit to an end and take her leave, but another torrent of words delayed her as her acquaintance accompanied her into the hall, and even on her way out she had to stand in the doorway and go on listening. At last she interrupted, asking: "Are you at home in the *Vorzimmer* [the hall]?" Only the other woman's surprised expression alerted her to her slip of the tongue. Tired of standing in the hall so long, she had intended to conclude the conversation by asking: "Are you at home *Vormittag* [in the morning]?", and had inadvertently given away her sense of impatience at being prevented yet again from leaving.'

The next example, recorded by Dr Max Graf, is a warning to us to think before we speak:

'At the general meeting of the Concordia journalists' association a young member who was always impecunious delivered a vehement speech of opposition, and in his agitation spoke of *Die Herren Vorschussmitglieder* (in error for *Vorstandsmitglieder* or *Ausschussmitglieder*) ['committee members', 'members of the board', whereas *Vorschuss* means 'a financial advance']. The committee was empowered to grant loans, and the young speaker had applied for one.'

The example of the word *Vorschwein* for *Vorschein* showed how easily a slip of the tongue can be made when we have been going to some trouble to suppress indecorous words. We then air our true feelings in this way:

A photographer who had resolved not to call his clumsy assistants any rude names referring to animals told an apprentice who was about to empty a large and very full dish, and of course tipped half the liquid on the floor: 'Oh, for goodness sake, *schöpsen Sie* [for *schöpfen Sie*, 'take out', but suggesting *Schöps*, an Austrian word for 'sheep'] some of it first!' And soon afterwards, when a woman assistant had carelessly endangered a dozen valuable plates and he was scolding her at length, he asked, 'Must you be so *hornverbrannt*' [for *hirnverbrannt*, 'crack-brained', but suggesting *Hornochse*, literally 'horned ox' but colloquially 'fool'] . . . ?'

The next example illustrates a serious case of a speaker's giving himself away by a slip of the tongue. Several accompanying circumstances justify its reproduction here in full from the account given by A. A. Brill in the *Zentralblatt für Psychoanalyse*, year II.[8]

'One evening, when Dr Frink and I went out walking, we were discussing several matters raised at the New York Psychoanalytical Society. We encountered a colleague, Dr R., whom I had not seen for years and of whose private life I knew nothing. We were very glad to meet again, and at my suggestion went to a coffee house where we spent two hours in lively conversation. He seemed to know a good deal about me, for after the usual greetings he asked how my small child was, and told me that he heard news of me now and then from a mutual friend, that he had read about my activities in the medical journals and took an interest in them. When I asked whether he was married himself he said no, and added: "Why would someone like me marry?"

'On leaving the coffee house he suddenly turned to me: "I wonder what you would do in the following situation? I know a nurse who was involved as the other woman in a divorce case. The wife was suing her husband, citing the nurse as co-respondent, and *he* got the divorce."[9] Here I interrupted him: "You mean *she* got the divorce." He corrected himself at once – "Of course, *she* got the divorce" – and went on to say that the nurse was so upset by the case and the scandal in general that she took to the bottle, lapsed into a very nervous state, and so forth. He wanted my advice on how he should treat her.

'Once I had corrected his mistake, I asked him to explain it, and received the usual rather surprised answers: surely everyone had a right to make a slip of the tongue now and then, it was only a coincidence, there was nothing behind it, etc. I replied that every slip of the tongue was made for some reason, and I would be tempted to believe that he himself had been the protagonist in the story if he hadn't already told me he was unmarried, since then the slip of the tongue would have been explained by his wish that his wife, not he, had lost the case, with the result that (in line with our laws on marriage) he would not have to pay alimony and could marry again here in New York. He firmly denied that there was anything in my assumption, but at the same time reinforced it by his strong emotional reaction, showing clear signs of agitation followed by laughter. When I asked him to tell me the truth in the interests of scientific research, he replied: "Well, if you don't want to hear a lie you'll simply have to take my word for it that I'm a bachelor, so your psychoanalytical explanation is completely wrong." He added that a man like me, meticulously studying every tiny detail, was positively dangerous, and then he suddenly recollected another appointment and left us.

'All the same, Dr Frink and I were both convinced that I had found the explanation for his slip of the tongue, and I decided to prove or disprove it by making inquiries. A few days later I visited a neighbour, an old friend of Dr R.'s, who was able to confirm the whole of my assumption. The case had been heard a few weeks earlier, the nurse being cited as co-respondent. Dr R. is now firmly convinced that the theory behind Freudian mechanisms is correct.'

In the following case, recounted by O. Rank, another slip of the tongue was an equally obvious self-revelation:

'A father who had no patriotic emotions at all, and intended to bring up his children free of what seemed to him such unnecessary feelings too, blamed his sons for taking part in a patriotic rally, and put their recruitment to the cause down to similar conduct on their uncle's part, saying: "There's no call for you to emulate him of all people; he's an *idiot*." The expression of surprise on the children's faces at the unusual tone their father had adopted made him aware of his slip of the tongue, and he added, apologetically: 'Of course, I meant to say *patriot*.' [In German, as in English, the terms are *Idiot* and *Patriot*.]

The woman in a conversation described by J. Stärcke (op. cit.) perpetrated a slip of the tongue that can also be interpreted as self-revelation. Stärcke adds a comment which is very relevant although it goes further than actual interpretation.

'A woman dentist had agreed to examine her sister's mouth and see if the contact between two of her molars was correct (that is to say, whether the sides of the molars touched in such a way that bits of food could not get stuck between them). Her sister complained of having to wait so long for the examination, and said, jokingly: "I dare say she's treating another woman now, some dental colleague of hers, while she keeps her own sister waiting." The dentist then examined her sister and did in fact find a small hole in one of her molars. "I didn't know it was as bad as that," she says. "I just thought you might have no *Kontant* [ready cash] . . . I mean *Kontakt* [contact between the teeth]." "There," cried her sister, laughing, "now do you agree that it was just your avarice that made you keep me waiting longer than your paying patients?"

'(I ought not, of course, to add ideas of my own to hers or draw conclusions from them, but on hearing about this slip of the tongue my mind flew straight to the fact that these two delightful and clever young women are unmarried and do not mix in company much with young men, and I wondered whether they would have more contact with young men if they did have more ready money.)'

The following slip of the tongue, communicated by T. Reik (op. cit.), is another case of self-revelation:

'A young girl was to be engaged to a young man whom she did not like. Hoping to bring the two young people closer, their parents arranged a party to be attended by the prospective fiancés. The girl had enough self-control not to let her suitor, who was very attentive to her, see that she did not care for him. But when her mother asked if she liked the young man, she replied politely: "Oh yes. He's very *liebenswidrig* ['adverse to love', in error for *liebenswürdig*, 'charming', literally 'worthy of love']." '

The same may be said of another case, which O. Rank describes as a 'comical slip of the tongue'.

'A young man told the following anecdote to a married woman who liked a good story, and was said to be not unwilling to entertain extra-marital advances if they came with suitable presents attached; he was seeking her favours himself. One of a couple of business acquaintances was trying to win the favour of his colleague's rather aloof wife, which she finally agreed to grant him in return for a present of a thousand gulden. When her husband was about to go away, his colleague borrowed a thousand gulden from him, promising to return them to his wife next day. He then, of course, gave that sum of money to the wife, allegedly in return for her love, and she thought all was discovered when her husband came home and asked for the thousand gulden, thereby adding insult to injury. When the young man telling this tale had reached the point where the seducer told his companion, "I'll return the money to your wife tomorrow," the lady interrupted him with a very significant remark "But haven't you *given it back to me* already? Oh, I'm sorry, I meant haven't you *told me that* already?" She could hardly have revealed her willingness to give herself to the storyteller more clearly without saying so straight out' (*Internationale Zeitschrift für Psychoanalyse* I, 1914).

A good case of self-revelation of this kind, but with an innocuous outcome, is recounted by V. Tausk under the title: 'The Faith of Our Fathers': 'Since my fiancée was Christian,' said Herr A., 'and did not want to convert to Judaism, I had to convert from Judaism to Christianity myself in order to marry. I changed my religion not without some inner reluctance, but the aim seemed to me to justify my conversion, particularly as I was not an observant Jew, and need not abandon any religious conviction, since I had none. None the less, I always acknowledged my Jewishness later, and few of my acquaintances know that I am baptized. The two sons of my marriage were baptized as Christians. When the boys had grown to a suitable age they were told of their Jewish descent, so that if they came under anti-Semitic influence at school they would not turn against their father for unnecessary reasons. A few years ago I and the children, who were then at primary school, were spending our summer holidays in D. with a teacher and his family. When we were eating a light meal with our very friendly hosts, the lady of the house, knowing nothing of the Jewish descent of her summer guests, made some very cutting remarks about Jews. I ought to have come straight out with the facts, thus setting my sons an example through the courage of my convictions, but I shrank from the unpleasant arguments that usually follow such a revelation. I was also afraid that if our hosts' attitude to us became less friendly because we were Jewish, we might have to leave the comfortable accommodation we had found, and that would spoil our holiday, which was short enough anyway. However, as I felt it quite likely that my boys would frankly and freely tell the truth, perhaps with serious consequences, if they went on listening to the conversation any longer, I thought I would send them into the garden to get them out of the present company. "Off you run into the garden, *Juden* [Jews]," I said, quickly correcting myself and saying "*Jungen* [boys]". In this case my slip of the tongue enabled me to express the courage of my convictions after all. Our hosts in fact drew no conclusions from my slip because they did not see it as significant, but I could not help drawing my own, to the effect that the "faith of our fathers" cannot be denied with impunity if one is a father's son and has sons of one's own' (*Internationale Zeitschrift für Psychoanalyse* IV, 1916).

The following case of a slip of the tongue was by no means innocuous, and I would not describe it had not the court official during the trial concerned noted it down himself for this collection:

A private soldier was accused of breaking and entering, and testified in court that: 'When it happened I hadn't yet been released from my military *Diebstellung* ['position as thief', in error for *Dienststellung*, 'military service']; I was still in the army at the time.'

A slip of the tongue can be amusing when it emerges in confirmation of something the speaker is denying, and may be very welcome to the doctor practising psychoanalytical methods. I was once interpreting a dream of one of my patients in which the name Jauner occurred. The dreamer did know someone of that name, but it was impossible to discover why that person should feature in the dream, so I ventured to suggest that it could be simply because the name Jauner resembles the pejorative term *Gauner* [rascal]. My patient instantly and energetically denied it, but his slip of the tongue as he did so confirmed my suggestion when he transposed the same initial letters a second time. He had told me, 'No, really, that's too *jewagt* [for *gewagt*, 'far-fetched'].' When I pointed out the slip, he accepted my interpretation. If a slip of the tongue that turns what the speaker intended to say into its opposite is made by one of the adversaries in a serious argument, it immediately puts him at a disadvantage, and his opponent seldom wastes any time in exploiting the advantage for his own ends.

It is clear, then, that in general people interpret slips of the tongue, like other slips, just as I do in this book, even if they do not theoretically support my ideas and are not themselves inclined to reject the toleration of slips as a convenient attitude. But the mirth and derision occasioned by such slips of the tongue at important moments militate against what is claimed to be the general consensus of opinion: that a slip of the tongue is merely a *lapsus linguae* with no psychological significance. It was none other than Prince Bülow, Chancellor of Germany, who tried to save the situation by making that claim when a slip of the tongue in the wording of his speech in defence of his Kaiser in November 1907 turned it into its opposite.

'Where the present is concerned, the new age of Kaiser Wilhelm II,' he said, 'I can only repeat my statement of a year ago: it would be neither right nor just to say that our Emperor was surrounded by a body of *responsible* advisers ... (loud cries of: *irresponsible*!) ... to say that our Emperor was surrounded by a circle of *irresponsible* advisers. Forgive my *lapsus linguae*.' (Laughter.)

However, the point of Prince Bülow's remark had to some extent been obscured by its accumulation of negatives, and sympathy for the speaker in his difficult situation prevented anyone from making any further use against him of this slip of the tongue. Another man fared worse in the same situation a year later, when he wanted to encourage his audience to demonstrate unreservedly in favour of the Kaiser, and in the process was reminded that other feelings resided in his loyal breast by a severe slip of the tongue.

'Lattmann (German Nationalist): As for the matter of the address, we take our stance on the orders of business of the Reichstag. According to those orders, the Reichstag has every right to offer such an address to the Kaiser. We believe that the united ideas and wishes of the German people are inclined to put forward such a unified demonstration on this point, and if we can do so in a form that pays due respect to our monarch's feelings then we should do so *rückgratlos* [without backbone]. (Riotous mirth, lasting several minutes.) Gentlemen, I meant *rückhaltlos* [without reservations], not *rückgratlos* (further laughter), and let us hope that such an unreserved expression of popular opinion will be accepted by our Kaiser in these difficult times.'

The journal *Vorwärts* of 12 November 1908 did not hesitate to point out the psychological significance of this slip of the tongue: 'It is likely that no member of any parliament ever before presented his own attitude towards the monarch, and that of the parliamentary majority, more accurately than the anti-Semitic Lattmann when, on the second day of the interpellation, he involuntarily made the solemn and emotional admission that he and his friends intended to tell the Kaiser what they thought *without backbone*. General merriment drowned the rest of the unfortunate man's remarks, and he thought it necessary to stammer out an explicit apology to the effect that he really mean *without reservations*.'

In another example, a slip of the tongue acquired the almost uncanny character of a prophecy: in the spring of 1923 it was a great sensation in the international world of finance when X., a very young banker, perhaps one of the newest of the *nouveaux riches* in W. and in any event both the richest and the youngest, acquired the majority shareholding in the °°° Bank after a brief contest. Consequently the former directors of that institution, financiers of the old stamp, were not re-elected at a remarkable general meeting, and young X. became chairman of the board of the bank. In the farewell speech made by a member of the board, Dr Y., on behalf of the old chairman who had failed to gain re-election, many of the audience noticed an unfortunate and repeated slip of the tongue on the part of the speaker. He kept speaking not of the *ausscheidend* [retiring] chairman but of the *dahinscheidend* [dying] chairman. As a matter of fact the old chairman, after failing to be re-elected, did die a few days after the meeting. However, he was over eighty years old at the time! (Storfer.)

A good example of a slip of the tongue that is as much a case of information for the audience as a revelation of the speaker's intentions comes in the second part of *Wallenstein* (*Die Piccolomini*, Act I, Scene 5), and shows us that Schiller must have understood the mechanism and purpose of slips of the tongue when he made use of one here. In the previous scene, Max Piccolomini has enthusiastically supported the duke's cause, and dwells on the blessings of peace revealed to him on his journey when he was escorting Wallenstein's daughter to the camp. He leaves his father and the court envoy, Questenberg, in a state of great dismay. The fifth scene continues like this [given here in Coleridge's translation]:

QUESTENBERG:
Alas, alas! and stands it so?
What friend! and do we let him go away
In this delusion – let him go away?
Not call him back immediately, not open
His eyes upon the spot?

OCTAVIO (*recovering himself out of a deep study*):
     He has now open'd mine
And I see more than pleases me.

91

QUESTENBERG:
> What is it?

OCTAVIO:
Curse on this journey!

QUESTENBERG:
> But why so? What is it?

OCTAVIO:
Come, come along, friend! I must follow up
The ominous track immediately. Mine eyes
Are open'd now, and I must use them. Come!
(*Draws Q. on with him*)

QUESTENBERG: What now? *Where* go you then?

OCTAVIO:
> To her herself.

QUESTENBERG:
To –

OCTAVIO (*correcting himself*):
To the Duke! Come let us go. (etc.)

This small slip of the tongue ('to her' instead of 'to him') is designed to tell us that the father understands his son's present partisanship, while the courtier Questenberg complains that he is speaking in riddles.

Otto Rank found another example of the poetic use of a slip of the tongue in Shakespeare. I quote Rank's comments from the *Zentralblatt für Psychoanalyse* I, 3: 'A poetically very subtle slip of the tongue, exploited with technical brilliance and showing us, like the slip in *Wallenstein* described by Freud, that dramatists both understand the mechanism and sense of such slips and assume that audiences will also understand them, occurs in Shakespeare's *Merchant of Venice* (Act III, Scene 2). Portia, forced by her father's wishes to choose a husband by lot, has hitherto been lucky enough to have escaped all her unwelcome suitors by chance. Now that she has finally found one whom she really likes in the person of Bassanio, she fears that he too will make the wrong choice. She would like to tell him that even so, he can be sure of her love, but her oath prevents her. Shakespeare gives her this speech, delivered to the suitor she favours in a state of inner turmoil [the italics are Freud's]:

> I pray you tarry; pause a day or two,
> Before you hazard: for, in choosing wrong,
> I lose your company; therefore, forbear awhile;
> There's something tells me (*but it is not love*)
> I would not lose you . . .
>   . . . I could teach you
> How to choose right, but then I am forsworn;
> So will I never be; so may you miss me;
> But if you do you'll make me wish a sin,
> That I have been forsworn. Beshrew your eyes,
> They have o'erlooked me, and divided me;
> *One half of me is yours, the other half yours –*
> *Mine own, I would say*; but if mine, then yours,
> And so all yours.

'With remarkable psychological subtlety, the poet makes Portia's slip of the tongue reveal the one thing she intended merely to convey in a slight hint, since she should not really have mentioned it at all – that even before Bassanio makes his choice she loves him and is all his. This device allays both her lover's intolerable uncertainty and the spectator's equally high suspense about the outcome of Bassanio's choice.'

Considering the interest that such support on the part of great writers supplies to my own ideas about slips of the tongue, I think I may be justified in giving a third such example, taken from E. Jones:[10]

'In a recently published article Otto Rank drew our attention to a pretty instance of how Shakespeare caused one of his characters, Portia, to make a slip of the tongue that revealed her secret thoughts to an attentive member of the audience. I propose to relate a similar example from the *Egoist*, the masterpiece of the greatest English novelist, George Meredith. The plot of the novel is, shortly, as follows: Sir Willoughby Patterne, an aristocrat greatly admired by his circle, becomes engaged to a Miss Constantia Durham. She discovers in him an intense egoism, which he skilfully conceals from the world, and to escape the marriage she elopes with a Captain Oxford. Some years later Patterne becomes engaged to a Miss Clara Middleton, and most of the book is taken up with a detailed description of the conflict that arises in her mind on also discovering his egoism. External circumstances, and her conception of honour, hold her to her pledge, while he becomes more and more distasteful in her eyes. She partly confides in his cousin and secretary, Vernon Whitford, the man whom she ultimately marries; but from loyalty to Patterne and other motives he stands aloof.

'In a soliloquy about her sorrow Clara speaks as follows: " 'If some noble gentleman could see me as I am and not disdain to aid me! Oh! to be caught out of this prison of thorns and brambles. I cannot tear my own way out. I am a coward. A beckoning of a finger[11] would change me, I believe. I could fly bleeding and through hootings to a comrade . . . Constantia met a soldier. Perhaps she prayed and her prayer was answered. She did ill. But, oh, how I love her for it! His name was Harry Oxford . . . She did not waver, she cut the links, she signed herself over. Oh, brave girl, what do you think of me? But I have no Harry Whitford; I am alone . . .' The sudden consciousness that she had put another name for Oxford struck her a buffet, drowning her in crimson."

'The fact that both men's names end in "ford" evidently renders the confounding of them more easy, and would by many be regarded as an adequate cause for this, but the real underlying motive for it is plainly indicated by the author. In another passage the same *lapsus* occurs, and is followed by the spontaneous hesitation and sudden change of subject that one is familiar with in psychoanalysis and in Jung's association experiments when a half-conscious complex is touched. Sir Willoughby patronizingly says of Whitford: " 'False alarm. The resolution to do anything unaccustomed is quite beyond poor old Vernon.' " Clara replies: " 'But if Mr Oxford – Whitford . . .

your swans, coming sailing up the lake, how beautiful they look when they are indignant. I was going to ask you, surely men witnessing a marked admiration for someone else will naturally be discouraged?' Sir Willoughby stiffened with sudden enlightenment."

'In still another passage, Clara by another *lapsus* betrays her secret wish that she was on a more intimate footing with Vernon Whitford. Speaking to a boyfriend, she says: "'Tell Mr Vernon – tell Mr Whitford'".'[12]

The theory of slips of the tongue proposed here will stand up to examination even in its minor details. I have often been able to show that the slightest and most apparently obvious cases of such slips make sense, and will admit the same kind of explanation as the more striking examples. A patient who was intent upon making a short excursion to Budapest, although I advised her against it, justified herself by saying she was going only for three days, but made a slip of the tongue and said: only for three *weeks*, thus revealing that, in defiance of my wishes, she would rather spend three weeks than three days in what I considered unsuitable company. One evening I had to apologize for failing to meet my wife when she came out of the theatre, and told her, 'But I was there at ten past ten.' She corrected me: 'You mean ten *to* ten.' Of course I had meant to say ten *to* ten; I could not have claimed that arriving *after* ten was any excuse, since I had been told that the posters advertising the play said the performance would be over before ten. When I reached the theatre, I found the foyer darkened and the building empty. The performance had already ended, and my wife had not waited for me to arrive. When I looked at my watch, it was only five to ten. However, I decided to put as good a face as possible on the matter at home, saying I had arrived while there were still ten minutes to go to the hour. Unfortunately, my slip of the tongue foiled my intentions, revealing my deception by making me confess to more than I really needed to admit.

This brings us to those disturbances of speech that cannot really be called slips of the tongue because they affect not merely a single word but the rhythm and mode of delivery of speech in general, for instance stammering and stuttering in embarrassment. But in both cases disturbed speech reveals an inner conflict. I do not really think that anyone would make a slip of the tongue in an audience with royalty, when seriously paying court to a lover, in a speech made in defence of his name and honour before a sworn jury, in short in all those cases where, as one may say, the mind is really concentrated on the matter in hand. Even when we are assessing an author's style we must, and habitually do, bear in mind the principle of elucidation so indispensable in tracking down the origin of various slips of the tongue. A clear, unambiguous written style tells us that the author is at ease with himself, but where we find forced, tortuous expressions, which can be rightly said to tend in more than one direction, we recognize the part played in them by a complex train of thought insufficiently worked out, or we hear the suppressed voice of the author's own criticism of himself.[13]

Since the first publication of this book, foreign friends and colleagues have taken to studying slips of the tongue that can be observed in the languages of their own countries. As one might expect, they have discovered that the laws of such slips are independent of the linguistic material itself, and have interpreted them in the same way as I have explained slips made by native German speakers here. I will cite just one example out of a countless number:

Dr A. A. Brill (New York) writes of himself: 'A friend described to me a nervous patient and wished to know whether I could benefit him. I remarked, I believe that in time I could remove all his symptoms by psycho-analysis because it is a *durable* case wishing to say *"curable"*!' ('A Contribution to the Psychopathology of Everyday Life', *Psychotherapy*, vol. III, no. 1, 1909).

Finally, for those readers who do not shrink from a certain amount of concentration and to whom psychoanalysis is not an entirely alien subject, I will add an example that shows how even the pursuit of a slip of the tongue can lead us into mental profundities.

Dr L. Jekels writes: 'On the eleventh of December I was addressed in Polish, rather imperiously and challengingly, by a lady whom I know and who demanded: "Now, do tell me why I said I had twelve fingers today!"

'At my request she gave a fuller account of the circumstances in which she made that remark. She and her daughter were getting ready to go out to pay a social call, and she had asked her daughter, a case of *dementia praecox* at present in remission, to change her blouse, which the girl did in the next room. When the daughter came back she found her mother busy cleaning her nails, and the following conversation took place:

Daughter: Oh, look, I'm ready but you aren't!

Mother: Well, you have only *one* blouse and I have *twelve* nails.

Daughter: What?

Mother (impatiently): Well, of course. I have *twelve fingers*, don't I?

'When a colleague who was also listening to this story asked what she associated with the number twelve, her answer was both prompt and decided: "*The twelfth of no month means anything very special to me.*"

'After a moment's hesitation, she associated *fingers* with the following reminiscence: "People in my husband's family tend to be born with six fingers on their feet." (There are no separate and distinct words for the digits "fingers" and "toes" in Polish.) "So when our children were born, they were examined at once in case they had six fingers." But for extraneous reasons we could not continue with the analysis that evening.

'Next morning, and it was the twelfth of December, the lady visited me and told me, visibly agitated: "Just think what's happened! For the last twenty years or so I've sent good wishes to my husband's old uncle on his birthday, which is today, so I always write to him on the eleventh. This year I forgot, and I've just had to telegraph him instead."

'I reminded myself and the lady how firmly she had waved aside my colleague's question about the number twelve, which might have been expected to remind her of the uncle's birthday, by saying that as a date the twelfth meant nothing special to her.

'She now confessed that this uncle of her husband's was rich, and she had always counted on a legacy from him, a particularly important factor in her present difficult financial situation.

'So he, or rather his death, had come straight into her mind when a woman friend told her fortune from the cards a few days earlier, and said she would be coming into a great deal of money. It immediately struck her that this uncle was the only person from whom she or her children stood to inherit money, and the scene reminded her instantly that the same uncle's wife had once promised to remember the narrator's children in her will. In fact the uncle's wife died intestate, but she might have given her husband instructions about a legacy.

'The lady's wish for her uncle by marriage to be dead must obviously have been very strong, since she had said to the friend who was telling her fortune: "Oh, you could really tempt a person to go out and kill someone!"

'In the four or five days between the fortune-telling incident and the uncle's birthday, she had kept looking at the death announcements in newspapers published in the part of the country where he lived.

'No wonder, then, that as she wished for his death with such intensity, her mind had suppressed the memory and date of his forthcoming birthday so strongly, inducing her not just to forget an occasion she had observed for years, but even to remain unaware of it after my colleague's question.

'In the *lapsus* "twelve fingers" the suppressed number twelve had emerged, and played a part in her slip of the tongue.

'I say "played a part", because the striking association she produced for "fingers" allows us to guess at other motivations, showing why the number twelve distorted the usually innocuous phrase about having ten fingers.

'The idea in itself ran: "Some children in my husband's family have been born with six digits on their feet."

'Six digits on hands or feet are signs of a certain abnormality, and thus six fingers mean *one* abnormal child, and twelve fingers *two* abnormal children, and that was indeed true in the lady's own case. She had married very young, and her husband, who had always been regarded as eccentric and abnormal, and who committed suicide after a brief period of married life, left her nothing but two children who had repeatedly been diagnosed by doctors as abnormal and with a severe handicap inherited from their father's side of the family. The elder daughter had recently come home after a serious catatonic attack, and soon afterwards the younger daughter, who had reached puberty, also fell ill with severe neurosis.

'Since in this case the children's abnormality was associated with their mother's death wish against the uncle, and merged with this far more firmly suppressed and psychically stronger element, we can assume that the second factor causing her slip of the tongue was a *death wish against her abnormal children*.

'The dominating significance of the number twelve as expressing a death wish, however, is suggested by the fact that in the narrator's mind the uncle's birthday was already very closely associated with ideas of death. For her husband had taken his life on the thirteenth, a day after the birthday of this same uncle, and the uncle's wife had told the young widow: "Only yesterday he was sending such kind, affectionate birthday wishes – and now this!"

'I will add that the lady had sufficient real reasons to wish her children dead. They gave her no joy, only sorrow, they severely limited her freedom of action, and she had given up any idea of happiness in love for their sake.

'As usual, she had been extremely anxious not to upset the daughter whom she was taking with her when she went visiting, and it is easy to imagine how much patience and self-denial that involves when someone is suffering from *dementia praecox*, and how many angry impulses must be suppressed.

'Consequently, the full meaning of the slip would run:

'I wish my husband's uncle would die, I wish my abnormal children would die (the whole abnormal family, so to speak), and I wish I could get some money out of them.

'To my mind, this slip has an unusual structure in several respects:

a) the presence of two determinants compressed into a single element.

b) the fact that the presence of the two determinants is reflected in the duplication of the slip of the tongue (twelve nails, twelve fingers).

c) the striking fact that one meaning of the number twelve, the twelve fingers expressing the children's abnormality, represents an indirect depiction; here, a psychic abnormality is illustrated by a physical abnormality, and the upper part of the body by the lower part.'[14]

Notes

1. My italics.
2. *Die Traumdeutung*, Leipzig and Vienna 1900, 8th edition, 1930.
3. My italics.
4. As it turned out, she was influenced by unconscious ideas of pregnancy and contraception. When she said she was 'folding up like a penknife', consciously using the expression as a complaint, she meant to describe the position of the foetus in the mother's uterus. The word *Ernst* in my greeting had reminded her of the name (S. Ernst) of a well-known Viennese firm with premises in Kärntnerstrasse, which used to advertise contraceptives for sale.
5. One of my patients went on making symptomatic slips of the tongue until we found that they derived from the childhood joke of saying *urinieren* [to urinate] instead of *ruinieren* [to ruin]. – Abraham's observations on slips 'with a tendency to over-compensate' (*Internationale Zeitschrift für Psychoanalyse* VIII, 1922) can be connected with the temptation to make free use of improper and taboo words by the artificial means of a slip of the tongue. A woman patient with a slight tendency to stammer and thus to duplicate the initial syllable of proper names spoke the name *Protagoras* as *Protragoras*. Just before this she had said *A-alexandros* instead of *Alexandros*. Inquiry showed that as a child she had been particularly fond of the naughty trick of repeating the initial syllables *a* and *po* [echoing nursery terms for 'faeces' and 'behind'], a game often known to induce stammering in children. She now felt there was a danger of leaving the *r* out of the first syllable of the name 'Protagoras' and saying 'Po-potagoras', so to avert the danger she clung firmly to the *r* and added another in the second syllable. Similarly, on other occasions, she distorted the words *parterre* [ground floor] and *Kondolenz* [condolence] into *partrerre* and *Kodolenz*, to avoid the words associated with them in her mind, *pater* [father] and *Kondom* [condom]. Another patient of Abraham's confessed to a tendency to say *angora* instead of *angina* on every occasion, very probably because he feared he might be tempted to replace *angina* by *vagina*. These slips of the tongue therefore occur because a tendency to deter prevails against a tendency to distort,

and Abraham correctly points out the analogy between this procedure and the development of symptoms in compulsive neuroses.

6. Another observation is that aristocrats are particularly apt to distort the names of doctors they have consulted, and we may conclude that in spite of their usual courteous manner towards these doctors they do not privately esteem them much. I will quote here some cogent remarks on the forgetting of names from the English discussion of our subject by Dr E. Jones, who at that time was in Toronto ('The Psychopathology of Everyday Life', *American Journal of Psychology*, October 1911):

'Few people can avoid feeling a twinge of resentment when they find that their name has been forgotten, particularly if it is by someone with whom they had hoped or expected it would be remembered. They instinctively realize that if they had made a greater impression on the person's mind he would certainly have remembered them again, for the name is an integral part of the personality. Similarly, few things are more flattering to most people than to find themselves addressed by name by a great personage where they could hardly have anticipated it. Napoleon, like most leaders of men, was a master of this art. In the midst of the disastrous Campaign of France, in 1814, he gave an amazing proof of his memory in this direction. When in a town near Craonne he recollected that he had met the mayor, De Bussy, over twenty years ago in the La Fère regiment; the delighted De Bussy at once threw himself into his service with extraordinary zeal. Conversely there is no surer way of affronting someone than by pretending to forget his name; the insinuation is thus conveyed that the person is so unimportant in our eyes that we cannot be bothered to remember his name. This device is often exploited in literature. In Turgenev's *Smoke* the following passage occurs. " 'So you still find Baden entertaining, M'sieu – Litvinov.' Ratmirov always uttered Litvinov's surname with hesitation, every time, as though he had forgotten it, and could not at once recall it. In this way, as well as by the lofty flourish of his hat in saluting him, he meant to insult his pride." The same author in his *Fathers and Sons* writes: "The Governor invited Kirsanov and Bazarov to his ball, and within a few minutes invited them a second time, regarding them as brothers, and calling them Kisarov." Here the forgetting that he had spoken to them, the mistake in the names, and the inability to distinguish between the two young men, constitute a culmination of disparagement. Falsification of a name has the same significance as forgetting it; it is only a step towards complete amnesia.'

7. B. Anzengruber used such slips of the tongue to characterize the hypo-critical legacy-hunter in his play *Der G'wissenswurm* [*The Worm of Conscience*].

8. Erroneously ascribed to E. Jones in the *Zentralblatt für Psychoanalyse*.

9. 'According to our (American) laws, whereby a divorce is granted only if there is proof that one party has committed adultery, and the divorce is granted only to the innocent party.'

10. 'An Example of the Literary Use of a Slip of the Tongue', *Zentralblatt für Psychoanalyse* I, 10.

11. The translator of this passage into German noted: 'At first I was going to translate the original "beckoning of a finger" by *leise Wink* [gentle hint], but then I realized that by leaving out the word "finger" I would deprive the sentence of a psychological subtlety.'

12. Further examples of slips of the tongue intended by the writer to be significant, mostly through self-revelation, occur in Shakespeare's *Richard II* (Act II, Scene 2) and Schiller's *Don Carlos* (Act II, Scene 8, a slip of the tongue by Princess Eboli). It would not be difficult to compile a more extensive list.

13.   *Ce qu'on conçoit bien*
     S'annonce clairement
     Et les mots pour le dire
     Arrivent aisément.

[What is well conceived is clearly expressed, and the words to say it come easily.]
Boileau, *Art poétique*.

14. *Internationale Zeitschrift für Psychoanalyse* I, 1913.

VI

Slips in Reading and Slips of the Pen

The same views and comments apply to mistakes in reading and writing as to slips of the tongue – not surprisingly, considering the close relationship between those functions. I shall confine myself here to an account of some carefully analysed examples, rather than making any attempt to describe these phenomena in their entirety.

A) *Slips in reading*

1) I was looking through a copy of the *Leipziger Illustrierte* in the coffee house, holding it at an angle in front of me, when I read the caption under a picture spread right across the page as: 'A Wedding *in der Odyssee* [in the Odyssey].' It caught my attention, and in some surprise I straightened out the page and read, correctly: 'A Wedding *an der Ostsee* [on the Baltic Sea].' How did I make this nonsensical mistake in reading the caption? My thoughts went at once to a book by Ruths, his *Experimentaluntersuchungen über Musikphantome*[1] [*Experimental Studies of Musical Phantoms*], which had been occupying my mind a great deal recently because it touches on matters close to the psychological problems with which I myself am concerned. Its author had said that he would soon be publishing a work entitled *Analyse und Grundgesetze der Traumphänomene* [*Analysis and Fundamental Laws of the Phenomena of Dreaming*]. No wonder that, as I had just published my own *Interpretation of Dreams*, I looked forward with keen anticipation to reading this book. In Ruths's previous work, on musical phantoms, I found an announcement, at the beginning of the contents list, of

extensive inductive evidence for the fact that the ancient Greek myths and legends were principally rooted in the phantoms of sleep and music, in dream phenomena and in states of delirium. I immediately looked up the text to see if the author was also aware that the scene in which *Odysseus* appears before *Nausicaä* can be traced back to the widespread dream of being naked. A friend had drawn my attention to the fine passage in Gottfried Keller's *Der Grüne Heinrich* that explains this episode in the *Odyssey* as an objective version of the dreams of a mariner wandering far from home, and I had added this reference to the account of exhibitionist dreams of nakedness in my book (8th edition, p. 170 [V.D]). But I found nothing on the subject in Ruths. In this case my mind was obviously occupied by ideas of priority.

2) How did I come to read in the paper one day: '*Im Fass* [In a tub] through Europe', instead of '*zu Fuss* [on foot] through Europe'? It took me quite a long time to find the answer. My first ideas suggested that I must have been thinking of Diogenes' tub, and I had recently been reading about art in the age of Alexander in a work of art history. It seemed obvious to think of Alexander's famous remark: 'If I were not Alexander I would wish to be Diogenes.' I also had a vague memory of a man called Hermann Zeitung [*Zeitung*, 'newspaper'] who went travelling packed up in a crate, but I could make no further connection, nor could I find the page in the history of art with the remark that had struck me. Only months later did I suddenly think of the puzzle again. I had put it out of my mind, but now it came back complete with its solution. I remembered a comment in a newspaper on the curious means of *transport* [German: *Beförderung*] some people now chose in order to go to the World Exhibition in Paris, and I believe the article also contained a facetious remark to the effect that some gentleman or other intended to get another man to roll him to Paris in a *tub*. Their sole motive, of course, was to attract attention through such silly pranks. Hermann Zeitung was indeed the name of the man who had first thought up this far-fetched method of transport. Next I remembered that I once treated a patient whose morbid fear of reading newspapers turned out to be a reaction against his morbid *ambition* to see himself

mentioned in print as a celebrity. Alexander of Macedonia was certainly one of the most ambitious men who ever lived, and indeed he complained that he could find no Homer to celebrate his great deeds. But how could I not have remembered another Alexander, much closer to me? Alexander is my own younger brother's name! I now immediately traced the unwelcome idea that I had wished to repress in relation to that Alexander, and the reason why it emerged now. My brother is an expert on tariffs and *transport*, and was to receive the title of professor in his work as a teacher at a commercial college. Several years ago, I myself had been proposed for the same *promotion* [in German, also *Beförderung*] to the title of professor at the university, but nothing came of it. At the time our mother expressed her surprise and dissatisfaction at the idea of her younger son's becoming a professor before his older brother. This had been the state of affairs at the time when I could find no reason for my slip in reading. But then my brother encountered difficulties of his own, and his chances of becoming a professor were now even less than mine. Suddenly the significance of my slip in reading was obvious: the turn taken for the worse in my brother's chances had removed an obstacle. It was as if I had been reading about his appointment in the newspaper and saying to myself: how strange to think a person can get into the papers (i.e., with the announcement of his appointment as professor) for something so stupid (as his profession). I then easily found the passage about Hellenistic art in the age of Alexander, and to my surprise realized that during my earlier search I had read the page on which it occurred several times, but as if I were under the influence of a negative hallucination I had skipped the relevant sentence on every occasion. In fact it contained nothing to enlighten me, nothing that I would have felt I would rather forget, and I think the symptom of my inability to find it in the book was designed merely to lead me astray. I was meant to continue with my train of thought where an obstacle had been placed in the path of my search, in some idea about Alexander of Macedonia, so that I would be better protected against thinking of my brother, that other Alexander. And the device had worked perfectly; I devoted all my efforts to looking for the lost passage in the history of art.

The double meaning of the German word *Beförderung*, in this case, was the associative bridge between the two complexes: the unimportant one evoked by the newspaper report, and the more interesting but unwelcome complex that emerged here in disrupting what I ought to have read. My example shows that it is not always easy to explain incidents such as this slip in reading, and finding the answer to the riddle sometimes has to be put off to a more favourable time. However, the more difficult it is to find that answer, the more certainly one may expect that the disruptive idea, once it is finally discovered, will be condemned by the conscious mind as strange and conflicting.

3) One day I received a letter from a place near Vienna containing bad news. I called for my wife at once, and asked her to sympathize with the fact that poor Wilhelm M. – whom I called, using the feminine article, *die arme Wilhelm M.* – was so ill that the doctors held out no hope for him. Something about the words in which I expressed my regret must have sounded wrong, for my wife seemed suspicious, asked to see the letter, and said she thought it couldn't say what I had claimed, since no one calls a wife by her husband's first name, and anyway our correspondent knew the first name of Wilhelm M.'s wife very well. I defended myself doggedly, mentioning the usual custom of visiting cards where a woman calls herself by her husband's first name – 'Frau Wilhelm M.' At last I had to bring out the letter again, and sure enough we read *der arme Wilhelm M.*, with the correct masculine article. In fact it even said, and this I had entirely overlooked, *der arme Dr W. M.* My misreading was therefore an almost convulsive reaction attempting to shift the sad news from husband to wife. The title of Dr between the article, the adjective and the name did not fit my insistence that the letter-writer must have meant the wife, and so I had simply overlooked it in reading the phrase. The reason for this slip in reading was not, however, because I liked the wife any less than the husband, but because the poor man's fate had aroused my anxieties about someone else who was very close to me, and who had what I knew was one of the medical symptoms also present in the case of Dr W. M.

4) A slip in reading that I perpetrate very often when I am on

holiday and walking down the street in a foreign town is both annoying and ridiculous: I read every shop sign that suggests the word in any way at all as *Antiques*. This must be an expression of my interests as a collector.

5) In his major work on *Affektivität, Suggestibilität, Paranoia* [*Affectivity, Suggestibility, Paranoia*] of 1906, p. 121, Bleuler writes: 'Once, when I was reading, my mind told me that I had seen my own name two lines further down. To my surprise, all I found was the word *Blutkörperchen* [blood corpuscles]. This is the most striking instance I know among thousands of cases of slips in reading in both peripheral and central vision. On other occasions when I thought I saw my name, the word suggesting it was usually much more like the real thing, and generally all the letters in my name had to be somewhere near each other before I could make such a mistake. In this case, however, the misconnection and the illusion could be easily established: I had been reading the conclusion of some remarks on a certain kind of bad style found in scientific works, and I did not feel entirely blameless myself.'

6) From H. Sachs: 'In his formality [*Steifleinenheit*, from *Steifleinen*, 'stiff linen', 'buckram'] he passes over what strikes other people.' The word *Steifleinenheit* caught my eye, and looking at it more closely I saw that it really said *Stilfeinheit* [stylistic subtlety]. This passage was in a piece by an author whom I admire, praising to the skies a historian whose work I do not like because it tends so much to stiff German academicism.'

7) In the *Zentralblatt für Psychoanalyse* I, 5/6, Dr Marcell Eibenschütz gives an account of a case of a slip in reading which he came upon in the course of his philological studies: 'I was working on the tradition behind the *Buch der Märtyrer* [*Book of Martyrs*], a Middle High German collection of legends, which I was to edit for the series of German medieval texts published by the Prussian Academy of Sciences. Very little was known about this work, which had never before been printed, and there was only a single critical account of it, by J. Haupt, "Über das mittelhochdeutsche Buch der Märtyrer" ['On the Middle High German Book of Martyrs'], *Wiener Sitzungsberichte*, 1867, vol. 70, pp. 101ff. Haupt's essay was based

not on an old manuscript but on a modern 19th-century copy of the main manuscript, Manuscript C (of Klosterneuburg), kept in the Hofbibliothek. The copy concludes with the following paragraph of attribution:

Anno Domini MDCCCL in vigilia exaltacionis sancte crucis ceptus est iste liber et in vigilia pasce anni subsequentis finitus cum adiutorio omnipotentis per me Hartmanum de Krasna tunc temporis ecclesie niwenburgensis custodem.

[I, Hartman of Krasna, began this book in the year MDCCCL [1850] on the eve of Holy Cross Day, and with the help of the Almighty finished it on Easter Eve in the next year, I being at that time sacrist of Klosterneuburg.]

'Haupt quotes this paragraph of attribution in his article, obviously believing that it was by the scribe who wrote Manuscript C itself, and suggests – consistently misreading the Roman numerals for the year 1850 – that C was written in 1350, although he had copied the paragraph of attribution down accurately and it is printed in his article perfectly correctly (with the Roman numerals MDCCCL).

'Haupt's account was the source of some difficulty for me. First, I was a mere beginner in the academic world and bound to respect Haupt's authority, and for a long time I too kept reading 1350 for 1850 in the accurate and correctly printed paragraph of attribution in front of me. But in the main Manuscript C, which I was using, there was no sign of any such paragraph, and moreover there turned out to have been no monk called Hartmann in Klosterneuburg throughout the whole of the 14th century. When light finally dawned on me I realized exactly what had happened, and further research confirmed my supposition: the much-quoted paragraph of attribution exists *only* in the copy used by Haupt and was by the copyist of the manuscript, Father Hartman Zeibig, born in Krasna in Moravia and choirmaster of Klosterneuburg, who also, as the monastery treasurer, copied Manuscript C in 1850, and mentions himself in the traditional way at the end of his copy. The medieval vocabulary and old orthography of the closing paragraph probably contributed to Haupt's *wish* to be able to give as many details as possible about the work he was studying, and thus to be able to *date Manuscript C*, and that was the reason for his constant misreading of 1350 instead of 1850.'

8) Lichtenberg's *Witzige und Satirische Einfälle* [*Witty and Satirical Notions*] contains a remark that must derive from observation and sums up almost the entire theory behind slips in reading: 'He had read Homer so often that he always read *angenommen* (assuming) as *Agamemnon.*'

In a majority of cases, the text is modified by the reader's readiness to see something in it that he is prepared to see, some subject that is occupying his mind at the time. The text itself has only to assist the slip in reading by showing some similarity of verbal structure which the reader can alter in his mind. A brief glance, particularly with an inattentive eye, undoubtedly makes such an illusion more likely, but is by no means an essential condition.

9) I believe that the war, giving us all a number of powerful and long-lasting preoccupations, encouraged misreadings more than any other kind of slip. I have had a great many such observations, but unfortunately I have recorded only a few of them. One day I was looking at one of the midday or evening papers, and thought I saw, printed in large letters: *Der Friede von Görz* [The Peace of Gorizia]. But no – what it said was only: *Die Feinde vor Görz* [The Enemy Outside Gorizia]. A man with two sons fighting in that theatre of war could easily misread such a headline. Someone else found mention in a certain context of an *alte Brotkarte* [old bread ration card], which on closer reading he had to reject in favour of *alte Brokate* [old brocades]. However, it is worth pointing out that he used to ingratiate himself with the lady of a house where he was often a welcome guest by bringing presents of bread ration cards. An engineer whose equipment never proved successful for long in preventing a tunnel under construction from becoming damp was surprised to see an advertisement apparently offering for sale items made of *Schundleder* [poor-quality leather]. But tradesmen are seldom so honest; the advertisement was really for goods made of *Seehundleder* [sealskin].

The reader's profession or present situation can also influence his slip in reading. A philologist who was at odds with his professional colleagues over his latest (and very fine) works read *Sprachstrategie* [linguistic strategy] for *Schachstrategie* [chess strategy]. A man walking in a strange city at around the time when, because of a course of medical treatment, he needed to open his bowels read the word *Klosetthaus* [lavatory] on a large sign over the first floor of a tall department store, although his pleasure at seeing it was mingled with some surprise at the unusual situation of this convenient place. Next moment he was less pleased to see that the signboard really read: *Korsetthaus* [corset-makers].

10) In another group of cases the part played by the text itself in a slip in reading is considerably greater. It contains something that the reader rejects, some information or supposition that is painful to him, and his slip therefore corrects it to bring it into line with his own rejection or with wish-fulfilment. Of course we have to assume that the text was initially correctly read and rejected before being altered, even though the conscious mind does not remain aware of that first reading. Example 3 above is of this kind: another very topical one I give as it is reported by Dr M. Eitingon, who was then in the field hospital in Igló (*Internationale Zeitschrift für Psychoanalyse* II, 1915):

'Lieutenant X., who was in our hospital with traumatic war neurosis, one day, and with obvious emotion, read aloud the last line of the last verse of a poem by Wilhelm Heymann,[2] who fell so young, as follows:

> *Wo aber steht's geschrieben, frag' ich, dass von allen*
> *Ich übrig bleiben soll, ein andrer für mich fallen?*
> *Wer immer von euch fällt, der stirbt gewiss für mich;*
> *Und ich soll übrig bleiben? warum denn nicht?*

[Where is it written then that of you all I should be left, another for me fall? Whoever falls dies certainly for me. Am I to live unscathed? But why not me?]

'Alerted by my surprise, he then, rather shamefacedly, read it correctly:

Und ich soll übrig bleiben? warum denn ich?

[Am I to live unscathed? How can that be?]

'I owe several analytical insights into the psychic material of such "traumatic war neuroses" to the case of X., and although conditions in a field hospital with many patients and few doctors are not very favourable to our working methods, I could see more in the "causes" of these cases than the terrifying sound of shells exploding.

'The same patient displayed the symptoms that at first glance lend a striking similarity to all bad cases of war neurosis: severe tremors, fearfulness, lachrymosity, an inclination to fits of fury accompanied by convulsive, infantile motor expressions, and a tendency to vomit ("for the slightest reason").

'The psychogenic nature of the last symptom in particular, more especially its ability to derive some secondary profit from illness, was bound to strike everyone: the mere appearance in the ward of the hospital commandant, who came in from time to time to visit the convalescents, a friend's casual remark in the street – "You're looking well, you must be better now" – were all quite enough to set off a prompt attack of vomiting. "Cured . . . that means going back to the front . . . why should I?"'

11) Dr Hanns Sachs gives an account of some other cases of slips in reading induced by wartime experience:

'A close acquaintance had repeatedly told me that when his turn came he would not make any use of his expert training, for which he had gained a diploma, no, he was not going to take advantage of the chance to which it entitled him of employment behind the lines – he would enlist for active service. Shortly before that time actually came he told me one day very briefly, giving no further reason, that he had sent off corroboration of his expert qualifications to the appropriate quarter, and as a result he would soon be working in industry. Next day we met in a local office. I was standing at a desk writing; he came in, looked over my shoulder for a while, and then said, "Oh, I see the word at the top there is really *Druckbogen* [printed sheet]; I'd read it as *Drückeberger* [skiver]" ' (*Internationale Zeitschrift für Psychoanalyse* IV, 1916/17).

12) 'Sitting in the tram, I was thinking that many of the friends of my youth, who had always been considered delicate and frail, now seemed able to stand up to the harshest of conditions which would certainly have a shattering effect on me. In the middle of this unwelcome train of thought, as we were passing a firm's signboard, I was only half aware of registering, as we passed, a word in big black letters saying *Eisenkonstitution* [iron constitution]. A moment later it struck me that this was not really right for a business sign, and turning back quickly I caught another glimpse of the inscription, and saw that it really read *Eisenkonstruktion* [Iron Construction]' (op. cit.).

13) 'The evening papers printed a dispatch from Reuter's, which later proved unfounded, reporting that Hughes had been elected President of the United States. This announcement was followed by a brief biography of the alleged President elect, informing me that Hughes had studied at Bonn University. I thought it odd that this circumstance had never been mentioned in the weeks of press debate leading up to election day. A second glance showed that in fact the report said *Brown* University. This striking case, where considerable violence had to be done to the real words for me to make my slip, is explained not just by the cursory nature of my glance at the newspaper report, but chiefly by the fact that I thought it would be excellent if, as the basis for future good relations, the new President's sympathy for the central European powers derived from personal as well as political causes' (loc. cit.).

B) Slips of the pen

1) I was surprised to find a slip of the pen on a sheet of paper containing brief day-to-day notes, most of them relating to business: among several entries correctly dated to the month of September, I

had written 'Thursday, 20 October'. It was not difficult to account for this anticipation as expressing a wish. A few days earlier I had come back from a holiday, feeling refreshed and ready to tackle a considerable medical caseload, but I still did not have very many prospective patients. On arriving home, I found a letter from a woman patient proposing to visit me on 20 October. When I wrote down the same date of the month, but for September instead, I was probably thinking: I wish X. were here now; what a pity she can't come for another month! And in so thinking, I anticipated the date. The disruptive idea can hardly be called an unwelcome one in this case, and indeed that was why I understood the reason for my slip of the pen as soon as I noticed it. I perpetrated an analogous and similarly motivated slip of the pen in the autumn of the following year. E. Jones has studied similar slips of the pen in recording dates and in most cases has easily recognized them as well motivated.

2) I received the uncorrected proofs of my contribution to the *Jahresbericht für Neurologie und Psychiatrie*, and of course I had to check the names of the authors I had mentioned with particular care, since names of various nationalities commonly cause the typesetter a good deal of difficulty. Sure enough, I did find several foreign-sounding names in need of correction, but there was one that, remarkably enough, the typesetter had changed from the version in my manuscript, and moreover he was perfectly right to do so. I had written *Buckrhard*, which the typesetter had guessed should be *Burckhard*. In this passage I myself had described an obstetrician's account of the influence of childbirth on cases of infantile paralysis as very good, and I had nothing to say against the Burckhard who was its author, but he bore the same name as a Viennese writer who had upset me by writing an ill-informed review of my *Interpretation of Dreams*. It was as if in writing the name of *Burckhard* to refer to the obstetrician I had been thinking something unpleasant about the other man, the author of the review, since spelling a name incorrectly is very often insulting, as I mentioned above in the section on slips of the tongue.[3]

3) There is good support for this statement in a self-observation of A. J. Storfer's where the author, with laudable frankness, sets out

the reasons that made him remember the name of a supposed rival incorrectly and then misspell it when he wrote it down:

'In December 1910 I saw the new book (as it then was) by Dr Eduard *Hitschmann* on the Freudian theory of neurosis in a bookseller's window in Zurich. At the time I happened to be working on the manuscript of a lecture I was soon to deliver to an academic society on the fundamental principles of Freudian psychology. In the introduction to the lecture, which I had already written, I had mentioned the historical development of Freudian psychology from studies in an applied field of medicine, and the resulting difficulty of giving a comprehensive account of those fundamental principles, adding that so far there was no general account. When I saw the book (by an author previously unknown to me) in the shop window I did not at first intend to buy it. However, a few days later I decided that I would, but by then the book was not in the window. I told the bookseller the title of this recently published work, giving the author's name as "Dr Eduard *Hartmann*". The bookseller corrected me – "I expect you mean *Hitschmann*" – and brought me the book.

'The unconscious motive for my slip was obvious. I had been congratulating myself, so to speak, on writing a survey of the fundamental principles of psychoanalytical theory, and my attitude to Hitschmann's book was obviously one of envy and annoyance because it might detract from my own merits. I told myself that, according to the *Psychopathology of Everyday Life* [in an earlier edition], my alteration to the name was an act of unconscious hostility, and for the time being I was satisfied with that explanation.

'A few weeks later I noted down this slip of mine. On that occasion I wondered exactly why I had changed Eduard Hitschmann to Eduard *Hartmann*. Was it just because of the similarity of Hitschmann's name to that of the well-known philosopher Hartmann? My first association was with the memory of something I once heard said by Professor Hugo von Metzl, the authority on Schopenhauer, more or less to the effect that: "Eduard von Hartmann is a failed Schopenhauer – a Schopenhauer turned inside out." The emotional tendency leading to the substituted structure of the forgotten name was thus: "Well, there won't be much in this Hitschmann and his survey of the subject; he probably bears the same relation to Freud as Hartmann does to Schopenhauer."

'I had now recorded this case of predetermined forgetfulness accompanied by a substitute idea. Six months later I came upon the piece of paper on which I had written this note, and I saw that instead of Hitschmann I had twice written *Hintschmann*' (*Internationale Zeitschrift für Psychoanalyse* II, 1914).

4) Next is an apparently more serious case of a slip of the pen, which I might perhaps equally well place under the heading of 'inadvertent actions': I wanted to draw the sum of 300 crowns out of the post office savings bank, and was going to send the money to an absent relative to be used for medical treatment. As I did so I noticed that my account contained 4,380 crowns, and decided to bring it down to the round figure of 4,000 crowns, leaving that sum untouched for the time being. When I had made out my cheque in the usual way, which involved cutting the relevant figures from the sheet with my statement of account, I suddenly noticed that I had withdrawn not the 380 crowns I intended to take out but 438, and was quite alarmed by my own unreliability. I soon realized that there was no call for my alarm; after all, I was no poorer than before. None the less, it took me quite a long time to work out exactly what, without giving any notice to my conscious mind, had made me depart from my original intention. I set out along the wrong lines at first, and tried subtracting 380 from 438, but I could make nothing of the result. Finally, a sudden idea showed me the real connection. 438 was *10 per cent* of the entire account, which contained 4,380 crowns! You get a 10 per cent discount from a *bookseller*. I remembered that a few days earlier I had sorted out a number of medical works that were of no further interest to me, and offered them to a bookseller for exactly 300 crowns. He thought the price too high, and said he would let me know his final answer within the next few days. If he accepted my offer, then he would be replacing the exact sum that I was going to give my sick relative. It cannot be denied that I regretted handing over that sum. My emotion in perceiving my mistake can be better understood as anxiety that I might impoverish myself by making such payments. But both my

regret at parting with the money and the fear of indigence linked to it were entirely outside my conscious mind; I felt no regret when I agreed to pay my relative that sum, and I would have regarded such a motivation as ridiculous. It is likely that I would not have thought myself capable of an emotion of that nature had I not become reasonably familiar with repression in the life of the mind through my practical experience of psychoanalysis with my patients, and had I not had a dream some days earlier which required a similar explanation.[4]

5) I quote the following case from W. Stekel, and can vouch for its authenticity myself: 'An extraordinary instance of the misreading of a slip of the pen happened when a widely distributed weekly journal was being edited. The management of the journal had been publicly accused of venality, so an article of refutation had to be written in defence. And written it was – with much warmth and strong emotion. The editor-in-chief of the journal read the article, the author of course read it several times in manuscript and then in galley proof, and everyone was well satisfied. Suddenly the proofreader spoke up, pointing out a small mistake that had escaped everyone's attention. The wording said, clearly: "Our readers will be well aware that we have always promoted the common good in the most self-interested [*eigennützig*] manner." Of course it should have read *uneigennützig* [disinterested]. But the real thinking behind the emotional article broke through with elemental force.'

6) A reader of the daily *Pester Lloyd* newspaper, Frau Kata Levy of Budapest, recently noticed a similarly unintentional instance of honesty in a report that the journal received from Vienna by telegraph on 11 October 1918:

'On the grounds of the relationship of absolute trust that prevailed throughout the war between us and our German allies, it may be assumed, beyond all doubt, that the two powers will reach unanimous agreement in all cases. There is no need for any explicit mention of the fact that there is still lively and incomplete [*lückenhaft*] co-operation between the allied diplomats.'

Just a few weeks later people could express themselves more freely about this 'relationship of trust', without needing to resort to slips of the pen or misprints.

7) An American staying in Europe, who had parted with his wife on bad terms, thought perhaps they could now make the quarrel up and asked her to cross the Atlantic and meet him on a certain date. 'It would be a good idea if you sailed on the *Mauretania*,' he wrote. However, he did not venture to send the sheet of paper on which he had written this sentence, preferring to rewrite the whole letter in case she noticed the correction he had been obliged to make to the name of the ship. He had originally written *Lusitania*.

This slip of the pen needs no elucidation and can be easily interpreted. By a lucky coincidence, however, more can be added to this instance: his wife had visited Europe for the first time before the war, after her only sister's death, and, if I am not mistaken, the *Mauretania* is the surviving sister ship of the *Lusitania*, which was sunk during the war.

8) A doctor examined a child, and was writing out a prescription containing *alcohol*. While he did so, the child's mother kept bothering him with silly and unnecessary questions. He told himself he was not going to lose his temper, and stuck to this resolution, but his irritation caused a slip of the pen. His prescription contained the word not *alcohol* but *achol*.[5]

9) Since the subjects are related, I will add here a story that E. Jones tells of A. A. Brill. Although Brill never drank at all in the usual way, a friend persuaded him to take a little wine. Next morning a violent headache made him regret agreeing. When he had to write down the name of a woman patient called Ethel, he wrote *Ethyl* instead.[6] Another factor in this case may have been that the lady herself drank rather more than was good for her. Since a doctor's slip of the pen in writing out a prescription can have far greater practical consequences than ordinary slips, I will take this opportunity of giving a full account of the only analysis of such a medical slip yet published:

10) Dr E. Hitschmann, writing on a repeated case of slips of the pen in a prescription: 'A colleague told me that over the years he had several times made mistakes in prescribing a certain medication for women patients of advanced years. He twice prescribed ten times the correct dose, and when he suddenly realized what he had

done, he had to make haste to cancel the prescription, in great alarm lest he had harmed the patient, which would put him in a very unpleasant situation himself. This curious symptomatic action deserves further elucidation by a more detailed account of the individual cases and by analysis.

'In the first case, the doctor prescribed a poor woman on the verge of great old age some belladonna suppositories ten times too strong for her spastic constipation. He then left the outpatients' department of the hospital, and about an hour later, as he was reading the newspaper over lunch, his mistake suddenly struck him. In great alarm, he first hurried back to the outpatients' department to ask for the patient's address and then went straight to her home, which was some way off. He found that the old lady had not yet had her prescription made up, and left feeling greatly relieved, his mind at rest. By way of excuse, and not without some justification, he told himself that the loquacious head of the outpatients' department had been looking over his shoulder as he wrote the prescription and had disturbed his concentration.

'In the second case the doctor had to tear himself away from a flirtatious and good-looking woman patient and leave his consulting rooms in order to examine an elderly spinster lady. He went by car, since he did not have much time for this visit, and he was to have a secret meeting with a young girl of whom he was enamoured near her home at a certain hour. The same medical trouble as in the first case suggested that belladonna was indicated, and yet again he prescribed a dose ten times too high by mistake. The patient said something that, although interesting, was not relevant to her case at present, and although he overtly denied it the doctor showed his impatience and left her in good time to keep his appointment. Some twelve hours later, around seven in the morning, the doctor woke up; the realization that he had committed a slip of the pen came into his conscious mind, almost immediately accompanied by great alarm, and he made haste to send his patient a message, hoping the prescription had not been fetched from the pharmacy yet and asking her to return it so that he could alter it. However, he found that the prescription had already been made up, and went off with a certain stoical resignation – but also with the optimism of experience – to the pharmacy, where the pharmacist calmed his fears by saying that of course (unless it was a mistake of his own?) he had made up a weaker dose than the prescription specified.

'In the third case, the doctor was going to write his old aunt, his mother's sister, a prescription for a harmless dose of a mixture of *Tinct. belladonnae* and *Tinct. opii*. The maidservant took the prescription straight to the pharmacy. Quite soon afterwards it struck the doctor that he had written *extractum* instead of *tinctura*, and the next moment the pharmacist telephoned to query his mistake. The doctor untruthfully excused himself by saying that he was not to blame: he had not finished writing out the prescription before it was snatched up from the desk where he was sitting with unexpected speed.

'The salient points in common between these three cases of slips of the pen are that so far the doctor had perpetrated them only in relation to this one drug, that in all three the patient was female and advanced in age, and that the dose was always too strong. A brief analysis showed that the doctor's relationship to his mother must be of crucial importance here. It struck him that he had once – and very probably before his symptomatic action – written his also elderly mother the same prescription in a dose of 0.03, hoping to bring her radical relief, although he would normally have prescribed the usual dose of 0.02. His mother, whose constitution was delicate, reacted to the drug with congestion in the head and an unpleasantly dry mouth. She complained half jokingly of the dangers of consulting a son on medical matters. And there had been other occasions when his mother, herself a doctor's daughter, had shown a disinclination to take the medicaments recommended by her doctor son, referring in jest to being poisoned.

'So far as the writer can judge the relationship of this son to his mother, he had a natural love for her, but no personal respect or any great opinion of her intellectual qualities. Sharing a household with her and his brother, who was a year younger, he had felt for years that his erotic liberty was inhibited, although as psychoanalytical experience tells us, such reasons are often misused to cover up family ties of too intimate a nature. The doctor accepted this analysis, reasonably satisfied with the explanation, and said, smiling, that the word *belladonna*, "beautiful woman", could also indicate an erotic connection. Earlier, he had sometimes taken the same medication himself' (*Internationale Zeitschrift für Psychoanalyse* I, 1913).

In my view such serious slips occur in exactly the same way as the harmless variety that we usually investigate.

11) The following case of a slip of the pen described by S. Ferenczi will seem particularly innocuous. It may be regarded as a case of compression resulting from impatience (cf. my slip of the tongue in saying *der Apfe*, p. 60), and such a view could have been defended had not close analysis of the incident shown a stronger disruptive factor at work:

'I once wrote in my notebook: "This may be illustrated by the *Anektode*" – meaning of course *Anekdote* ['anecdote', but echoing *Tod*, 'death'], and referring to the tale of a gypsy condemned to death – *zu Tode* – who asked, as a favour, to make his own choice of tree from which he was to be hung himself. (Of course, despite zealous searching, he failed to find any suitable tree.)'

12) On other occasions, in contrast, the most insignificant slip of the pen can express a dangerous secret meaning. An anonymous correspondent writes:

'I concluded a letter by sending "Very best wishes to your wife and *ihren* [her] son." Just before putting the letter in the envelope I noticed the mistake in the initial [which should have been a capital I: *Ihren* – "your" – son], and corrected it. On the way home from my last visit to this married couple, my woman companion had commented that the son looked strikingly like a family friend of theirs and must surely be his child.'

13) A lady sent her sister a few lines of good wishes when she moved into a spacious new apartment. A woman friend present noticed that the writer had put the wrong address on the letter: not the sister's last address, but that of her first home after she was just married, a place from which she had moved long ago. She pointed the mistake out to the letter-writer. 'You're right,' the lady had to admit. 'How on earth did I come to do that, and why?' Her friend said: 'I expect you don't like to think of the beautiful big apartment

she will have while you feel you're short of space yourself, so you wish her back in her first home where she would be no better off than you.' 'Well, of course I'm not really glad she has her nice new apartment,' the other woman honestly admitted, adding: 'What a pity one always has such horrid feelings over these things!'

14) E. Jones reports the following example of a slip of the pen [in English], given him by A. A. Brill: 'A patient wrote to Dr Brill suggesting that his nervous state should be ascribed to his business anxieties during a crisis in the cotton trade. He claimed, in this letter: "My trouble is all due to that damned frigid wave; there isn't even any seed." Of course he meant to write "wave", meaning a current on the money market, but in fact he wrote *wife*. Fundamentally, he was accusing his wife of frigidity and childlessness, and he was not very far from recognizing that his lack of sexual relations were to a considerable extent the cause of his trouble.'

15) Dr R. Wagner writes of himself, in the *Zentralblatt für Psychoanalyse* I, 12:

'On reading through an old college notebook I found that I had made a small slip because of the speed with which I wrote. Instead of *Epithel* [epithelium] I had written down *Edithel*, a word which, if the first syllable bears the stress, becomes the diminutive of a girl's name [Edith, with the Austrian diminutive *l*]. In retrospect, analysis is simple enough. At the time I made this slip of the pen my acquaintance with the girl who bore that name was still entirely superficial, and our friendship did not become intimate until much later. My slip of the pen is thus a neat proof of the emergence of an unconscious fondness for her at a time when I myself really had no notion of it yet, and at the same time my choice of the diminutive illustrates the feelings connected with my slip.'

16) Frau D. von Hug-Hellmuth writes: 'A doctor prescribed *Leviticowasser* [Levitical water] instead of *Levicowasser* [mineral water from Levico] for his woman patient. This mistake, which gave the pharmacist a welcome opportunity to make sarcastic remarks, can easily be given a milder interpretation if we look for possible motives in the unconscious mind and do not deny them some degree of probability out of hand, even if these are only subjective

assumptions on the part of someone who is not close to the doctor concerned. Although he used to accuse his patients, in no uncertain terms, of preferring a poor diet, and it could be said that he read them *die Leviten* ['read them a stern lecture', a colloquial German idiom], he was very popular, and his waiting room was full both before and during surgery hours, a good enough reason for him to wish that once he had finished a consultation his patients would get dressed as quickly as possible – *vite, vite*. As I thought I remembered, and I was correct, his wife was a Frenchwoman by birth, which to some extent supports what may seem my rather bold supposition that he spoke French in urging them to make haste. In fact many people are in the habit of expressing such wishes in a foreign language; my own father used to encourage us children to go faster when we were out on a walk by crying *Avanti gioventù* or *Marchez au pas*, and I remember that a doctor getting on in years, who treated me for a disorder of the throat when I was a young girl, tried to control my movements when they were too quick for his liking with a soothing *Piano, piano*. So it seems to me perfectly possible that this doctor was in the same habit, and thus, in error [thinking of the word *vite*], wrote Levitico Water instead of Levico Water' (*Zentralblatt für Psychoanalyse* II, 5).

The writer mentions other examples from her own youthful memories (*frazösisch* instead of *französisch* [French], and a slip in writing the name Karl).

17) I owe this account of a slip of the pen, which coincides with a familiar bad joke although there was certainly no intention of joking, to Herr J. G., a contribution from whom I have already mentioned.

'As a patient in a tuberculosis sanatorium I found, to my great grief, that a close relation had been diagnosed with the same illness as the one that had sent me to hospital. I wrote to my relative urging him to see a specialist, a well-known professor who was treating me and of whose medical competence I was confident, although on the other hand I had every reason to complain of his incivility: only a little while earlier the professor in question had refused to write me a reference that meant a great deal to me. In replying to my letter, my relation pointed out a slip of the pen, which amused me a great deal, since I could see the reason for it at once. When I wrote to him, I had said: ". . . and anyway I advise you to *in*sult [German: *insultieren*] Professor X. without delay." Of course I had meant to write *con*sult [*konsultieren*]. Perhaps I should point out that my knowledge of Latin and French excludes any possibility of my having made such a mistake out of ignorance.'

18) Omissions in writing can of course be assessed in the same way as slips of the pen. In the *Zentralblatt für Psychoanalyse* I, 12, Dr B. Dattner, a doctor of law, reports a curious example of a 'historical slip'. In one of the legal articles agreed in the settlement between Austria and Hungary in 1867 on the financial obligations of the two states, the word *effective* has been left out in the Hungarian translation, and Dattner considers it probable that the unconscious wish of the Hungarians who drew up the agreement to allow Austria as few advantages as possible had something to do with this omission.

There is also every reason to suppose that frequent repetitions of the same word in writing and copying – perseverations – are not without their significance either. If the writer repeats a word he has already written a second time, he is probably showing that he cannot shake it off so easily, that he could have said more on this point but has refrained, or something of that nature. Perseveration in copying seems to be a substitute for saying: 'Hear, hear!' I have seen long forensic reports with perseverations added by the copyist in particularly outstanding passages, and I could well have imagined, in interpreting them, that he was tiring of his impersonal role and adding a gloss: 'My own case entirely', or: 'Yes, I feel just the same'.

19) Furthermore, there is nothing to prevent us from treating a misprint as a 'slip of the pen' on the part of the typesetter, and regarding it as having some considerable motivation. I have not made a systematic collection of misprints, although something along those lines could be very amusing and informative. Jones has devoted a special paragraph to the misprint in his work (mentioned here several times). The distorted words in telegrams can also sometimes be taken as 'slips of the pen' on the part of the telegraphist. In the summer holidays I received a telegram from my publisher, and could make nothing of it. The text ran:

'*Vorräte* [provisions] received, *Einladung* [invitation] to X. urgent.' The solution to the puzzle comes from the name of the X. mentioned in the telegram. X. is an author for whose book I was to write an introduction [*Einleitung*]. The *Einleitung* had become an *Einladung*. Next I had to remind myself that a few days earlier I had sent the publisher a foreword [*Vorrede*] to another book, and the telegram was confirming its safe arrival. The correct text very probably read: *Vorrede erhalten, Einleitung X. dringend* [Foreword arrived, introduction to X. urgent]. We may assume that it fell victim to reworking by a hunger complex on the telegraphist's part, making a closer connection between the two halves of the message than the sender of the telegram intended. This, incidentally, is a fine example of 'secondary reworking' of the kind evident in most dreams.[7]

H. Silberer, in the *Internationale Zeitschrift für Psychoanalyse* VIII, 1922, mentions the possibility of 'tendentious misprints'. And some misprints that it can hardly be denied are tendentious have been pointed out by other people, for instance by Storfer in the *Zentralblatt für Psychoanalyse* II, 1914: 'The Political Misprinter's Devil', also in ibid. III, 1915, a brief note which I reproduce here:

20) 'There is a political misprint in the number of *März* for 25 April this year. A letter from Argyrokastron reported the remarks of Zographos, leader of the Epirote rebels in Albania, or if you prefer it President of the Independent Government of the Epirus. Among other things he is reported as saying: "Believe me, an autonomous Epirus would be very much in Prince Wied's interests. He could *stürzen* [fall] on it . . ." Very likely the Prince of Albania was well aware that accepting the *Stütze* [support] offered by the Epirotes would mean his *Stürz* [fall], even without that ominous misprint.'

21) I myself recently read in one of our Viennese daily papers an article on 'The Bukovina Region under Romanian Rule', a headline that must be regarded as premature at the very least, since at the time the Romanians had not yet acknowledged their hostility to us. The content showed that the headline should have read not Romanian but *Russian*, but even the censor seems to have found the general idea so likely that he himself overlooked this misprint.

It is difficult not to think of a 'political' misprint in reading the following spelling mistake in the circular issued by the famous printing works of Karl Prochaska in Teschen (formerly the Imperial and Royal Austro-Hungarian printers):

'By order of the Entente, *pleno titulo*, it is declared that the River Olsa is the frontier, dividing not only Silesia but also Teschen into two, one half of which [*zuviel*, 'too much', in error for *zufiel*, 'fell to'] went to Poland, the other to Czechoslovakia.'

Theodor Fontane once, and amusingly, had to defend himself against an only too meaningful misprint. On 29 March 1860 he wrote to the publisher Julius Springer:[8]

Dear Sir

It seems that my modest wishes are not to be granted. A glance at the proofs I enclose will show you what I mean. Moreover, I was sent only *one* set of proofs, although for the reasons I have given you I need two. And you have not yet sent back the first set for me to look through it again – *for the sake of the English words and phrases*. I am extremely anxious to do so. On page 27, for instance, in a scene between John Knox and the Queen of Scots, the present proof has the phrase '*worauf Maria aasrief* ['whereupon Mary cried 'Carrion!', in error for *ausrief* 'cried out']. In view of such brilliant notions one would like to be sure that the error really has been corrected. The unfortunate *aas* for *aus* is all the worse in that there is no doubt she (the Queen) really must have called him names of that nature in her mind. With kind regards.

> Yours sincerely,
> Theodor Fontane.

Wundt gives an interesting reason for the readily confirmed fact that we find it easier to commit slips of the pen than slips of the tongue (op. cit., p. 374). 'In normal speech the inhibitory function of the will is constantly operating to reconcile the workings of the imagination with the process of articulation. If the movement of expression following on from ideas is slowed by mechanical causes, as in writing [. . .] such anticipations will be especially likely to occur.'

Observation of the conditions in which mistakes in reading are made suggests a doubt which I would not like to leave unmentioned, since I believe that it can be the point of departure for a fruitful investigation. Everyone knows how often, when someone is reading aloud, the reader's attention wanders away from the text and turns to his own thoughts. Quite often, and because of this inattention, he cannot say anything about the content of the text if he is interrupted and asked what it was. He has been reading almost automatically, but nearly always correctly. I do not believe that mistakes in reading are noticeably greater in such conditions. We are used to assuming that a whole series of other functions is meticulously but automatically performed, and little conscious attention is paid to them. It would seem to follow that whether or not one's attention is alerted must, in the case of slips of the tongue, reading and writing, be determined in some way other than Wundt's idea of the cessation or neglect of attention. The examples subjected to analysis have not really allowed the assumption of a quantitative decrease in attention; what we found, and it may not be quite the same thing, was the disruption of attention by another thought that emerged and claimed it.

Neglecting to add a signature should come somewhere between slips of the pen and ordinary forgetfulness. An unsigned cheque means a forgotten cheque. To illustrate the significance of such an omission I will cite a passage in a novel, which caught the attention of Dr H. Sachs:

'There is a very clear and informative example of the creative writer's sure touch in dealing with the psychoanalytic handling of slips and symptomatic actions in a novel by John Galsworthy, *The Island Pharisees*. The plot turns on the hesitation of a young man, a member of the rich bourgeoisie, between deep social sympathy and the conventions of his own class of society. Chapter XXVI describes his reaction to a letter from a young vagabond to whom he had given aid several times in the past, feeling drawn to his unconventional way of life. The young man's letter does not contain any direct request for money, but describes a situation of great need which allows no other interpretation. At first its recipient rejects the idea of throwing money away on someone so incorrigible, rather than supporting charitable institutions.

'To give a helping hand, a bit of himself, a nod of fellowship to any fellow being irrespective of a claim, merely because he happened to be down, was sentimental nonsense! The line must be drawn! But in the muttering of this conclusion he experienced a twinge of honesty. "Humbug! You don't want to part with your money, that's all!"

'Thereupon he wrote a friendly letter, ending with the words: "I enclose a cheque. Yours sincerely, Richard Shelton."

'Before he had written out the cheque, a moth fluttering round the candle distracted his attention, and by the time he had caught and put it out he had forgotten that the cheque was not enclosed.'

And the letter is sent off just as it stands. Its writer's forgetfulness, however, is more subtly motivated even than in the way in which his selfish wish to spare himself expense, although apparently overcome, finally wins the day.

Staying at the country house of his future parents-in-law, with his fiancée, her family and their guests, Shelton feels lonely; his slip tells us that he misses his protégé, whose past history and attitude to life make him a complete contrast to Shelton's present blameless company, all of them the products of one and the same convention. As it turns out, his correspondent, who cannot remain in his post any longer without support, arrives a few days later to find out why the cheque promised in the letter never arrived.'

Notes

1. Darmstadt 1898, H. L. Schlapp.
2. W. Heymann: *Kriegsgedichte und Feldpostbriefe* [*War Poems and Letters from the Front*], p. 11: 'Den Ausziehenden' ['To Those Going to War'].
3. Cf., for instance, the passage in *Julius Caesar*, Act III, Scene 3:

CINNA: Truly, my name is Cinna.

A CITIZEN: Tear him to pieces; he's a conspirator.

CINNA: I am Cinna the poet! I am not Cinna the conspirator.

A CITIZEN: It is no matter, his name's Cinna; pluck but his name out of his heart, and turn him going.

4. This was the dream I used as the paradigm in a short paper 'Über den Traum' ['On Dreaming'] (no. VIII of *Grenzfragen des Nerven- und Seelenlebens* [*Borderline Problems of Nervous and Mental Life*], ed. Löwenfeld and Kurella, 1901; vol. III, *Gesammelte Werke*.

5. Meaning something like 'Without anger' (from *choler*).

6. Ethyl alcohol.

7. Cf. *Interpretation of Dreams* [VI.I], *Gesammelte Werke* vols. II/III, section on dream work.

8. The subject was the printing of Fontane's book, published in 1860 by Julius Springer, *Jenseits des Tweed. Bilder und Briefe aus Schottland* [*Beyond the Tweed, Pictures and Letters from Scotland*].

VII

Forgetting Impressions and Intentions

Should anyone feel inclined to overestimate the present state of our knowledge of the life of the mind, one need only mention the function of memory to induce a sense of humility. No psychological theory has yet succeeded in giving a full account of the basic phenomena of remembering and forgetting. Indeed, overall analysis of what can in fact be observed has hardly begun. Perhaps we find forgetfulness more of a riddle than memory today, now that the study of dreams and of pathological cases has shown that something we thought long forgotten can suddenly surface in the memory again.

However, we are now in possession of a few insights which may be expected to be generally acknowledged. We assume that forgetting is a spontaneous process involving a certain lapse of time. We emphasize the fact that when something is forgotten, a kind of selection is made from among the available impressions, and that the same thing happens with the details of any impression or experience. We know some of the conditions for the tenacity of certain memories and for the possibility of retrieving a memory that would otherwise be forgotten. However, countless occasions in everyday life show how incomplete and unsatisfactory our knowledge of the subject is. One has only to listen to two people who have received external impressions together, for instance on a journey in each other's company, and who are exchanging memories some time later. An incident that has lodged firmly in the mind of one of them has often been forgotten by the other as completely as if it had never been, even when there is no reason to claim that the impression was any more psychically significant for one than the other. A considerable number of the factors determining what the memory selects obviously still elude our understanding.

With the intention of making a small contribution to our knowledge of the causes of forgetfulness, I am in the habit of subjecting my own instances of forgetting to psychological analysis. As a rule I study only a certain group of these cases, those in which I am surprised to find I have forgotten something because I would have expected to know it. I will just add that I am not inclined to forgetfulness in general (I mean to forgetting experiences, not to forgetting something I have learnt!), and I was capable of unusual feats of memory for a short time in my youth. When I was a schoolboy I thought it quite natural that when I had read a page of a book I could recite its contents by heart, and shortly before going to university I was able to write down popular lectures on scientific subjects almost word for word directly after hearing them. I must still have been using what remained of that ability during the stressful period before my last oral examination for my doctorate of medicine, since I almost automatically gave the examiners answers in some subjects faithfully echoing the text of a book that I had once leafed through in great haste.

Since then my ability to gain access to what is stored in my memory has deteriorated, but until quite recently I have been able to convince myself that with the aid of a certain trick I can remember far more than I would otherwise have thought I could. For instance, if a patient in my consulting rooms mentions that I have seen him before, and I cannot remember when, or indeed recollect meeting him at all, I try guessing, that is to say, thinking quickly of a number of years running from the present backwards. Where written notes or the patient's own certainty make it possible for me to check my ideas, it turns out that I am seldom wrong by more than six months within a period of over ten years.[1] It is much the same when I meet someone I do not know particularly well, and for the sake of politeness I ask how his small children are. If he tells me about their progress then I try to work out how old the child is now, check that age against what the father says, and I am wrong by a month at the most, or three months with older children, although I cannot say what points of reference I used for making my estimate. Recently I have felt bold enough to bring out my guess spontaneously, so as to run no risk of hurting the father's feelings by revealing my ignorance of his offspring. In this way I extend my conscious recollections by calling on my unconscious memory, which in any case contains far more material.

I will therefore give an account of *striking* examples of forgetfulness, most of them observed in myself. I distinguish the forgetting of impressions and experiences, that is to say things I have seen or done, from the forgetting of intentions, that is to say, omitting to do something. I will begin by stating the uniform result of a whole series of observations: *in all cases the motive for forgetting something proved to be based on aversion.*

A) *Forgetting impressions and knowledge*

1) One summer my wife made me very cross, although the reason was harmless in itself. We were sitting at the *table d'hôte* opposite a gentleman from Vienna whom I knew, and who obviously remembered me too. However, I had my own reasons for not reviving our acquaintance. My wife, who had heard only the well-known name of the man opposite, made it too obvious that she was listening to what he said to his neighbours at table, for she turned to me from time to time with questions referring to the theme of their conversation. I grew impatient and finally short-tempered. A few weeks later, I was complaining to a woman relative about my wife's conduct, but I could not remember a single word the man had said. As I am usually rather inclined to bear a grudge, and do not forget any of the details of an incident that has annoyed me, my amnesia in this case was probably motivated by consideration for my wife. A similar thing happened to me only recently. I was going to invite a close friend to laugh at something my wife had said just a few hours earlier, but found that I could not put this intention into practice because, remarkably, I had completely forgotten what it was. I had to ask my wife herself to remind me. It is easy to see that this

forgetfulness of mine should be regarded as analogous to the typical disruption of the powers of judgement we encounter in dealing with members of our immediate family.

2) A lady who had just arrived in Vienna and did not know the city wanted a small iron safe in which she could keep documents and money, and I had said I would get her one. When I made this offer the unusually vivid image of a shop window in the inner city where I must have seen such safes came before my mind's eye. I could not remember the name of the street, but I felt sure I would find the shop on a walk through Vienna, since my memory told me I had passed it countless times. To my annoyance, however, and although I combed the inner city, I could not find the shop with safes on display. There was nothing for it, I thought, but to get the names of manufacturers of safes from the addresses in a trade directory, and then go round the area again to identify the shop window I was looking for. However, there was no need for all that; among the addresses listed was one that I could instantly identify as the shop I had forgotten. It was true that I had passed the display window countless times – every time I visited the M. family, who had lived in the same building for years. But now that we were no longer close friends, and indeed were not on good terms at all, I was in the habit of avoiding both the area and the building without stopping to wonder why. On that walk of mine through the city in search of the display of safes I had gone down every other street in the area, avoiding only this single one as if it were forbidden. The aversion motivating my poor sense of direction in this case was palpably obvious. The mechanism whereby I forgot, however, was less simple than in the first example. My dislike was not, of course, for the safes manufacturer, but for someone else whom I did not want to think about, and it transferred itself from that other person to the present occasion, causing me to forget. In exactly the same way, as in the *Burckhard* case, my resentment of one person had caused a slip of the pen in the name of another. The effect of their identical names in that case, linking two essentially different trains of thought, had its parallel in spatial contiguity and indissoluble proximity in the example of the display window. In fact this latter

case had a firmer factual basis; there was a second link, one of content, since money had played some part in the reasons for my estrangement from the family living in that building.

3) I was called in by the firm of B. & R. to give medical advice to one of its employees. On the way to his home I was preoccupied by the idea that I must have been in the building where the firm had its offices many times before. I felt that I had noticed the nameplate on a lower floor while I was visiting a patient on a floor higher in the same building, but I could remember neither what the building was nor whom I had been visiting there. Although the whole thing was trivial and unimportant, I could not get it out of my mind, and finally, trying to take my usual long and circuitous route around the subject by assembling my ideas on it, I worked out that the Pension Fischer, where I have frequently visited patients, is one floor above the offices of the firm of B. & R. I now knew which building accommodated both the firm's offices and the boarding house, but I still could not think why I had forgotten. I could discover nothing repellent in my memory about the firm itself, or the Pension Fischer, or my patients who lodged there. I suspected that it could not be anything very unpleasant, or I would have been unable to recollect what I had forgotten simply by thinking round the subject without, as in the previous case, calling on other aids. It finally occurred to me that only just now, on my way to visit my new patient, a man had spoken to me in the street, and I had found it quite difficult to recognize him. Months before I had seen this man in what looked like a very serious condition, and had diagnosed progressive paralysis, but then I heard that he had recovered, so my diagnosis was wrong. Or perhaps he was in one of those remissions that do occur in *dementia paralytica*, in which case I would have been right after all! It was this encounter that had affected my memory of the neighbourhood of the offices of B. & R., and my interest in finding out what I had forgotten had been transferred from that case of a doubtful diagnosis. The link associating the two, although slight in terms of content – the man who had recovered contrary to my expectations was also an employee of a large firm which used to send me patients – was another instance of an identical name. The doctor who had

been with me when I saw the possibly paralytic patient was called Fischer, like the forgotten name of the boarding house in the same building as the B. & R. offices.

4) *Mislaying* something means simply forgetting where you have put it down, and like most people who have a great deal to do with written papers and books, I know what is where on my desk, and can lay my hands on anything I want. What looks like disorder to other people is, to me, order of what is eventually a historical nature. But why did I recently mislay so completely a catalogue of books which had been sent to me that it simply could not be found? I had intended to order a book advertised in it, *Über die Sprache* [*On Language*], because it was by an author whose lively, amusing style I like and whose knowledge of cultural history and psychological insights I admire. I believe that was the very reason why I mislaid the catalogue. In the usual way, I lend this author's books to my acquaintances for their information, and a few days ago someone returning me a book said: 'His style reminds me very much of yours, and he thinks in the same way too.' The speaker did not know what an effect this remark would have on me. Years ago, when I was younger and needed to establish good contacts, an older colleague to whom I had praised the writings of a well-known medical author said much the same to me. 'Yes, just your style, very much in your own line.' I was encouraged by this to write to the medical author suggesting we might become acquainted, but was put in my place by a cool reply. And perhaps there were also other and even earlier deterrent experiences behind this one, for I never did find the mislaid catalogue, and was probably prevented by this ominous sign from ordering the advertised book, although the disappearance of the catalogue did not really put any difficulty in my way, since the name of the book and its author were lodged in my memory.[2]

5) Another case of mislaying something deserves our attention because of the circumstances in which the mislaid item was found again. A young man told me: 'A few years ago there were some misunderstandings in my marriage. I felt my wife was too cool, and although I was very ready to acknowledge her excellent qualities we lived together without any tenderness between us. One day she

came home from a walk bringing me a book that she had bought, thinking it might interest me. I thanked her for this kind attention, promised to read the book, put it somewhere and couldn't find it again. Months passed by, and now and then I thought of the missing book and tried in vain to find it. About six months later my beloved mother, who did not live with us, fell ill. My wife left our home to care for her mother-in-law. The invalid's condition became serious, and gave my wife an opportunity of showing herself in her best light. One evening I came home, feeling great admiration and gratitude for what my wife had done. I went to my desk, opened a certain drawer in it without any particular intention, but with a sleep-walker's unerring sense of direction, and at the top of the drawer I found the book that had been missing so long.'

J. Stärcke (op. cit.) gives an account of a case of a mislaid item that greatly resembles this one in its concluding feature: the curious certainty with which the lost item was found.

6) 'A young girl was going to make a collar, but she had spoiled the fabric in cutting the collar out. A dressmaker had to be called in to put her mistake right. When she had arrived, and the girl went to fetch the collar from the drawer where she thought she had put it away, she couldn't find it. She turned the drawer right out, but it was nowhere to be found. Feeling annoyed with herself, and wondering why it had suddenly disappeared and whether perhaps the fact was that she didn't *want* to find it, she realized that of course she was ashamed to let the dressmaker see that she had spoiled something as simple as a collar. Once that had occurred to her she stood up, went to another cupboard, and produced the cut-out collar at once.'

7) The next example of 'mislaying' conforms to a type that is familiar to every psychoanalyst. I should say that the patient who mislaid something in this instance found the key to the puzzle himself:

'A patient in psychoanalysis whose treatment was to be interrupted by a summer holiday during a period of resistance, when he was not feeling well, put his key-ring down in the usual place, as he thought, on getting undressed in the evening. Then he remembered that he wanted to fetch a few items from his desk in readiness for his departure next day, which was also the last day of his course of treatment, when the fee for it would be due. He had put the money in the desk as well. But he found that his keys had disappeared. He began searching his small apartment systematically and with increasing agitation, but in vain. Since he recognized that "mislaying" the keys was a symptomatic action, and therefore something he had really done with intent, he woke his manservant so that he would have an impartial person's help as he went on with his search. After another hour he gave up, fearing he really had lost the keys. Next morning he ordered new keys from the maker of the cashbox on his desk, and they were provided in great haste. Two acquaintances who went home in the cab with him thought they had heard something clink on the ground as he got out, and he felt sure that the keys had fallen out of his pocket. That evening his manservant triumphantly presented him with the original keys. They were tucked between a thick book and a thin pamphlet (a paper by one of my pupils), which he meant to take away to read on holiday, and were so skilfully concealed that no one would have suspected they were there. He found it impossible to replicate the concealment of the keys to make them equally invisible. The unconscious skill with which an item is mislaid as a result of secret but strong motivation is very reminiscent of the sleep-walker's "unerring sense of direction". Of course his motives were dislike of the idea of interrupting his treatment, and his secret annoyance at having to pay a high fee when he still felt so unwell.'

8) A man, writes A. A. Brill, was urged by his wife to attend a social occasion in which he took no interest. He finally gave way to her pleas and began taking his evening dress out of the chest where it was kept, but then interrupted himself and decided to shave first. When he had finished shaving he came back to the chest, but it was closed and locked, and the key could not be found. It was impossible to get hold of a locksmith, since it was a Sunday evening, so the couple had to excuse themselves from the party. When the chest was opened next morning, the key was found inside. Absent-mindedly, the man had dropped it into the chest and then closed the lid. He did assure me, says Brill, that he had done so unintention-

ally and entirely without his own knowledge, but I knew that he did not want to go to the party, so there were reasons for him to mislay the key.

E. Jones noticed that he always used to mislay his pipe when he had been smoking too much and consequently felt unwell. The pipe would then turn up in all kinds of places where it had no business and where it was never usually kept.

9) An innocuous case in which the motivation was admitted has been recorded by Dora Müller:

Fräulein Erna A. said, two days before Christmas: 'Guess what – yesterday evening I took out my packet of spiced biscuits and ate some. I thought that when Fräulein S. (her mother's companion) came in to say good night to me I ought to offer her some, not that I really wanted to, but all the same I decided I would. Later, when she did come in and I put my hand out to my little table to pick up the packet, it wasn't there. When I looked for it afterwards I found it in my wardrobe. I'd put the packet in there without knowing it.' There was no need for any analysis; the narrator was clear about the connection herself. She had just repressed a wish to keep all the biscuits for herself, but it made itself felt all the same, automatically, although in this case the phenomenon was reversed by her subsequent conscious action.

10) H. Sachs describes the way he once mislaid something to avoid having to work. 'Last Sunday afternoon I was hesitating: should I work, or should I go out for a walk and pay a call? I struggled with myself for a while, but decided to work. After about an hour I noticed that I had run out of paper. I knew I had been keeping a stack of paper somewhere in a drawer for years, but I searched my desk and other places where I thought I might find it in vain, although I went to a great deal of trouble, rummaging everywhere and looking in between old books and pamphlets and so forth. So I felt I had no alternative but to stop work and go out after all. When I came home in the evening I sat down on the sofa, and half in thought, half absent-mindedly, looked at the bookcase opposite. A drawer in it caught my eye, and I remembered that it was a long time since I had examined its contents. I went over and opened it.

On top was a leather folder full of blank paper, and only when I had taken it out and was just putting it in the drawer of my desk did I realize that this was the same paper I had been looking for in vain that afternoon. I should add that although I am not thrifty by nature I am very careful about paper, and keep every scrap that can still be used. It was obviously this habit, nurtured by an instinctive drive, that made me remedy my forgetfulness as soon as the present motive for it had gone.'

11) In the summer of 1901 I once told a friend with whom I used to have lively exchanges of scientific ideas at the time that neurotic problems can be solved only if we take it as read that individuals are originally bisexual. He replied: 'But I told you that myself two and a half years ago in Br., when we were out for an evening walk, and you wouldn't hear of it at the time.' It is painful to be required to surrender one's claim to originality in that way. I could remember no such conversation, nor what my friend had said. One of the two of us was obviously mistaken, and on the principle of who benefits – *cui prodest?* – it must be me. Over the next week I did in fact remember everything just as my friend had tried to remind me of it. I even remembered what I had replied at the time: 'No, I can't agree with you, and I don't want to get drawn into that line of argument.' But since then I have become more tolerant if I come upon one of the few ideas with which my name can be linked elsewhere in medical literature, and find that I have been given no credit for it.

Criticisms of one's wife – friendship that has turned to its opposite – a mistake in medical diagnosis – rejection by people working along the same lines – borrowed ideas: it can hardly be coincidence that a number of examples collected at random like this require me to face such painful subjects in order to explain them. I suspect that anyone else trying to examine his own forgetfulness for its motives could draw up a similar sample card of unpleasant ideas. The tendency to forget unpleasantness seems to me general; the ability to do so is probably developed to a different degree in different people. Much of the *refusal* to acknowledge something that we encounter in the field of medicine may probably be put down to *forgetfulness*.[3] Our view of such forgetfulness, however, restricts the difference between these behavioural phenomena to purely psychological conditions, allowing us to see the same motive expressed in both ways of reacting. Of all the many examples of the refusal to entertain unpleasant memories that I have seen in relatives of the sick, one remains in my mind as particularly strange. A mother was telling me about the childhood of her nervous son, who was now going through puberty, and said that like his siblings he had wet the bed until quite a late age, something not without significance in a case history of neurosis. A few weeks later, when she wanted to know what stage his treatment had reached, I had occasion to mention the young man's signs of a constitutional disposition to illness, and referred to the bed-wetting she had mentioned in her account of his medical history. To my surprise she denied that either he or her other children ever used to wet the bed, asked me what made me think I knew that, and I finally said that she herself had told me so quite recently, although now she had forgotten it.[4]

Healthy people who are not neurotic also display many signs of resisting the memory of painful impressions and the recollection of unwelcome ideas.[5] The full significance of this phenomenon, however, can be assessed only with reference to the psychology of neurotics, when it becomes obvious that such an *elementary resistance* to ideas that can arouse unpleasant ideas – a resistance comparable only to the flight reflex in reaction to painful stimuli – is to a great degree responsible for the mechanism producing hysterical symptoms. One cannot protest against the acceptance of such a tendency of resistance by claiming that on the contrary, we often enough find it impossible to shake off the painful memories that pursue us and rid ourselves of such unpleasant emotions as remorse and the pangs of conscience. I am not saying that this tendency to resistance will come into effect everywhere, or that in the interplay of psychic forces it may not encounter factors which are working in the opposite direction for purposes of their own, and can defy it. *A structure of multiple stratified agencies can be seen as the architectonic principle of the mental apparatus*, and it is perfectly likely that the tendency to resistance belongs to a lower psychic agency which can be inhibited by a higher authority. However, it says much for the existence and forcefulness of that tendency when we can derive from it processes such as those in the above examples of forgetfulness. We can then see that a good deal is forgotten for its own sake, and where that is not possible the tendency to resistance shifts its aim and at least causes us to forget something else, something less important but associated with whatever it is that really upsets us.

The view proposed here, that painful memories are particularly apt to be forgotten for good motives, deserves to be related to several areas in which it has so far received insufficient or no attention. For instance, it seems to me that we still do not look at the idea keenly enough in considering the credibility of evidence in a law-court,[6] where the oath a witness has taken is obviously far too easily credited with exerting a purifying influence on the interplay of psychic forces in his mind. It is generally accepted that one must consider such motives as they affect the rise of racial traditions and legends, eliminating incidents painful to national feeling from the memory. On closer examination the way in which national traditions and the individual's childhood memories are formed might turn out to be entirely analogous. The great Darwin's insight into the motive of aversion in causing forgetfulness has become a 'golden rule' for scientists.[7]

False memories can occur when impressions are forgotten, just as they occur in the forgetting of names, and, in this case, when the person affected believes them, they are described as paramnesia. The phenomenon of false memory in pathological cases – and in paranoia, when it acts as a constituent factor in the patient's illusions – has given rise to an extensive body of literature, but nowhere do I find any account of its motivation. Since this phenomenon is also part of the psychology of neuroses it is outside the scope of my subject here. Instead, let me describe a curious example of a false memory of my own, obviously motivated by unconsciously repressed material; the way in which the two were linked is also clear enough.

When I was writing the final sections of my book on the *Interpretation of Dreams* I was on my summer holiday and had no access to libraries and reference books. I was obliged to insert all references and quotations in my manuscript from memory, intending to check them later. In the section on daydreams I thought of the well-drawn character of the poor bookkeeper in Alphonse Daudet's *Le Nabab*, through whom the author was probably describing his own day-dreaming. I thought I clearly remembered one of the fantasies entertained by this man – I called him Monsieur Jocelyn – on his walks through the streets of Paris, and began describing it from memory. When M. Jocelyn boldly stands in the way of a bolting horse in the street and brings it to a halt, the door of the carriage opens, a distinguished personage gets out, presses M. Jocelyn's hand, and says: 'My saviour! I owe you my life. What can I do for you?'

I told myself that I could easily correct any inaccuracies in my account of this fantasy at home, when I had the book to hand. But when I did leaf through *Le Nabab* to compare the passage in print with my manuscript, I was dismayed and abashed to find nothing about any such daydream by a M. Jocelyn, which was not even the poor bookkeeper's name; he was called M. Joyeuse. This second mistake soon provided the key to the first, my false memory. *Joyeux* (the man's surname being the feminine form of the adjective) is the way my own name *Freud* would translate into French. So where did the incorrectly remembered fantasy that I had attributed to Daudet come from? It could be only a product of my own mind, a daydream I had invented myself without being conscious of it, or perhaps I had once been conscious of it and had then entirely forgotten it. It was possible that I had it in Paris, where until Charcot took me into his circle I often enough walked the streets alone and full of longing, in great need of some friend and patron to help me. Subsequently I met the author of *Le Nabab* several times at Charcot's home.[8]

Another case of false memory that proved capable of satisfactory explanation is reminiscent of the phenomenon of *fausse reconnaissance*, which will be discussed later: I had told one of my patients, an ambitious and capable man, that a young student had recently introduced himself into my circle with an interesting paper on 'The Artist: An Attempt at a Sexual Psychology'. When this paper was printed a year and a quarter later, my patient said he could remember it perfectly well, since he had read the announcement of its forthcoming publication somewhere before I had first mentioned it (a month or half a year before), perhaps in a bookseller's advertisement. This notice had come straight to his mind at the time, and he said, moreover, that the author had changed the title, since it was now called not an 'essay' or 'attempt' [*Versuch*] but 'approaches' [*Ansätze*] to a sexual psychology. However, careful questioning of the author and comparison of all the dates involved showed that my patient was claiming to remember something impossible. No advertisement for the work had appeared anywhere before its publication, certainly not a whole year and a quarter in advance. When I refrained from analysing this false memory, the same man came up with a similar but new variation. He thought that recently he had seen a work on *Agoraphobia* in the display window of a bookshop, and tried to get hold of it by consulting all the publishers' catalogues. I was then able to explain why his efforts were bound to be unsuccessful: the work on agoraphobia existed only in his imagination as an unconscious intention, because he was planning to write such a book himself. His ambition to emulate the other man and become a member of my circle through producing a scientific work of that kind had led him to both the first and the second false memory. He then remembered that the bookseller's advertisement which he had used as the basis for his first false memory referred to a work entitled *Genesis, das Gesetz der Zeugung* [*Genesis, the Law of Procreation*]. I was responsible, however, for the change of title that he mentioned, since it was I who had misquoted it myself as *Versuch* instead of *Ansätze*.

B) *Forgetting intentions*

No other group of phenomena is more suitable than the forgetting of intentions to prove the hypothesis that inattention is not enough to explain a slip in itself. An intention is an impulse to perform an action upon which one has already decided, while postponing its execution to some appropriate time. Now, in the interval of time thus created a change in motivation can occur, a change of such a nature that the intention is not carried out, but it has not been actually forgotten, merely revised and rejected. Forgetting intentions, as we are apt to do every day and in all kinds of situations, is not something we usually explain to ourselves by reassessing our motives. We generally leave it unexplained, or look for some psychological elucidation by assuming that around the time it was to have been carried out, the requisite attention to the subject was no longer present, although it would have been an essential condition for the forming of the original intention and must thus have been available at that time for putting it into practice. But observation of our normal attitude to intentions allows us to dismiss this attempt at explanation as arbitrary. If I form an intention in the morning, meaning to carry it out in the evening, I may be reminded of it several times before then, but it does not have to be consciously present in my mind during the day at all. When the time to carry it out approaches, I shall suddenly remember it, and it will impel me to make the preparations necessary for the intended action. If I go out for a walk taking a letter to the post, as a normal rather than a nervous individual I am not in the habit of clutching it in my hand the whole time, constantly looking out for a letterbox in which to post it; instead, I put it in my pocket, go for my walk, allowing my thoughts to wander as they will, and expect that one of the next letterboxes I see will remind me to put my hand in my pocket and take the letter out. Normal behaviour once an intention has been formed coincides exactly with the experimentally induced behaviour of people to whom 'long-term post-hypnotic suggestion' has been given under hypnosis.[9] This phenomenon is usually described as follows: the suggested intention lies dormant in the person concerned until the time to carry it out approaches. It is then aroused and impels the person into action.

In two situations in life, even lay people realize that forgetting an intention cannot by any means be regarded as an elementary phenomenon incapable of being traced further back, and will conclude that tacit motives exist. The two situations I mean are love and military matters. A lover who misses his rendezvous will not find that an excuse to the effect that, unfortunately, he forgot goes down well with his inamorata. She will not hesitate to retort: 'You wouldn't have forgotten a year ago. You don't love me any more.' Even if he were to resort to the psychological explanation mentioned above and try excusing himself by pleading pressure of business, he would only make the lady – as perceptive by now as any psychoanalyst – reply: 'How odd that business worries never used to trouble you!' The lady will not, of course, deny that he may have forgotten; she will merely think, with some justification, that much the same conclusion – a certain cooling of his ardour – can be drawn from unintentional forgetting as from a conscious excuse.

In the same way, any distinction between unintentional and intentional forgetting is ignored in the army on principle, and rightly so. The soldier *must* not forget what his military service requires of him. If he does forget, even though he knew what he had to do, the motives urging him to do his military duty are opposed by other motives running counter to them. For instance, the man doing a year's military service who tries excusing himself on parade by saying he *forgot* to polish his buttons until they shone can be sure of punishment. But that punishment is as nothing compared to what he would risk if he told his superior officers the real reason for his omission: 'I hate army service and all this wretched drill.' It makes economic sense, so to speak, to use forgetting as an excuse or as a compromise solution to spare himself the punishment he would then incur.

Courtship and army service demand that everything to do with them must be impossible to forget, thus suggesting that it is permissible to forget unimportant things; to forget something important, however, shows that it is being treated as unimportant and is tantamount to denying that it matters at all.[10] The standpoint of psychic evaluation cannot be dismissed here. No one forgets to do something that seems to him important without being suspected of mental disturbance. Our study can therefore cover only the forgetting of more or less trivial intentions; but no intention can be considered entirely unimportant, for in that case it would certainly never be formed at all.

As with the functional disturbances described above, I have collected cases observed in myself of neglecting to do something because I forgot, and have tried to cast light on them. I have found in general that they could be traced back to the intervention of unknown and unadmitted motives – or, one might say, to a *counter-will* implying negativity. In some of these cases I found myself in a situation similar to that of military service, under a compulsion which I had not entirely given up resisting, so that I was making my protest by forgetfulness. For instance, I am particularly apt to forget to send good wishes on birthdays, anniversaries, weddings and professional promotions. I always intend to send congratulations, and am increasingly convinced that I shall not succeed. I am now about to give up that intention and consciously allow the motives resisting it to have the upper hand. While I was in the transitional stage I told a friend in advance, when he had asked me to send a telegram of congratulations on his behalf as well as my own on a certain date, that I would forget both, and not surprisingly my prophecy came true. The reason why I feel unable to offer expressions of goodwill that are bound to sound excessive, since the appropriate phrases do not match the very minor amount of emotion I really feel, is to do with painful experiences in my own life. Ever since realizing that I have often taken other people's words of goodwill at face value, I have felt a dislike for conventional expressions of sympathy, although I can see that they are socially useful. Condolences on someone's death are an exception to my ambivalent attitude; when I have made up my mind to send them I do so at once. Nor is the expression of my feelings inhibited by forgetfulness when it has nothing to do with social duty.

First Lieutenant T. gives an account, from his experience as a prisoner of war, of a case of forgetfulness in which an intention initially suppressed made itself felt as an act of 'counter-will' and led to an unfortunate situation: 'The highest-ranking officer in a prisoner-of-war camp was insulted by one of his companions. To avoid further problems, he intended to make use of the one form of authority still available to him and have the other man moved to a different camp. Only on the advice of several friends did he decide, against his secret wishes, to refrain and take the conventionally honourable line of a challenge, which was bound to have a number of undesirable consequences. The same morning this commanding officer, under the supervision of the camp guard, had to take the roll-call of the officers. He had known his companions for a long time, and had never before made any mistake in reading out the list. Today, however, he omitted the name of the man who had insulted him, who therefore had to stay behind in the parade square after all his companions had left, until the mistake was cleared up. The forgotten name was in a perfectly obvious position in the middle of a sheet of paper. This incident was regarded by one of the parties concerned as an intentional insult, and by the other as an unfortunate and awkward accident which might well be misinterpreted. However, the protagonist in this drama later read Freud's *Psychopathology* and drew the correct conclusions about what exactly had been going on.'

There is a similar explanation for cases where people forget to carry out actions that they have promised to perform as a favour to someone else, because this conventional duty conflicts with their unadmitted personal opinion of it. In such cases it is usual for only the person who was supposed to do the favour to think that forgetting it is any excuse, while the person who asked him to do it undoubtedly gives himself the correct answer: he isn't interested or he wouldn't have forgotten. Some people are commonly described as forgetful, and are forgiven for it in much the same way as a short-sighted person is forgiven for failing to greet an acquaintance in the street.[11] These people forget all the minor promises they have made, and neglect all the tasks they are asked to perform, thus showing themselves unreliable in small things and suggesting that such minor offences in them should not be taken ill – that is to say, should not be explained by their characters but ascribed to something organic in them.[12] I am not one of them myself, and have had no opportunity of analysing the actions of such people in order to discover the motivation for their omissions by looking at what they choose to forget. However, I cannot help suspecting, by analogy, that unusually great if unadmitted contempt for another person is a motive employing that constitutional factor for its own ends.[13]

In other cases the motives for forgetfulness are not so easy to find, and once discovered arouse more of a sense of surprised dissatisfaction. I noticed in the past that when I was paying a great many visits to sick patients, the only ones I ever forgot were those made to people I was treating free of charge or to colleagues. Feeling ashamed of this, I made it my habit to note down in the morning the visits I was going to make that day. I do not know if any other doctors have adopted this habit in the same way, but it does give some idea of what causes a so-called neurasthenic to write down the information he wants to give the doctor in his notorious 'notes'. He seems to lack confidence in the ability of his memory to reproduce his symptoms. And he may well be right, but what happens is usually this: the patient has described his various complaints and put his questions in a very long-winded way. When he has finished, he pauses for a moment, then brings out his notes and says apologetically: 'I wrote a few things down because I have such a bad memory.' As a rule the notes contain nothing new. He goes over each point again, answering it himself: 'Oh yes, I've already asked you that.' His notes are probably just the demonstration of one of his symptoms: the frequency with which his intentions are disrupted by the intervention of unclear motives.

I shall be mentioning something which afflicts the majority of healthy people I know when I admit that, especially in the past, I have found that I easily forget to return books I have borrowed, keeping them for a long time, and I was particularly inclined to put off paying bills by forgetting them. Not long ago I left the tobacco-nists where I had made my daily purchase of cigars one morning without paying. It was a perfectly innocent omission, since I am a regular customer there, and could therefore expect to be reminded of what I owed next day. But the small forgetfulness, the attempt to run up a debt, must certainly have been connected with the thoughts about my finances that had been occupying me all the previous day. It is easy to find traces of an ambivalent attitude even in most so-called well-conducted people when it comes to money and property. The baby's primitive greed in trying to grab everything it can (and stuff it into its mouth) may prove to have been only incompletely overcome in general by culture and education.[14]

I am afraid that all the examples above have been rather banal. However, I do not mind referring to matters known to everyone and, by the same token, understood by everyone, since my intention is solely to collect everyday examples and subject them to scientific study. I do not see why the insights that reflect our common experience of life should be denied admission to the category of scientific findings. The essential character of scientific study lies not in the disparity of its subjects, but in its strict approach to the establishment of its findings and in trying to make far-reaching connections.

Intentions of moderate importance are found, in general, to be forgotten when opposed by unclear motives. In even less important intentions, the transference to the intention of a negative counter-will from some other source, once an external association has been established between that other source and the content of the intention, constitutes a second mechanism for forgetting. The following example belongs in that category: I like to use good blotting paper, and on my afternoon walk into the inner city I meant to buy some. But on four successive days I forgot to do so, until I stopped to ask myself why. I found my forgetfulness easy to explain when I had recollected that I am in the habit of writing *Löschpapier* [blotting paper], but in speech I use the alternative term *Fliesspapier*. 'Fliess' is the name of a friend in Berlin who had caused me much anxious and painful reflection on the days concerned. I could not shake off such thoughts, but my tendency to resistance (cf. above, p. 139) was expressed by transference, through the similarity of the word, to my not very important and therefore not very resistant intention.

Direct counter-will and more distant motivation coincide in the following case: in the collection *Grenzfragen des Nerven- und See- lenlebens* [*Borderline Problems of Nervous and Mental Life*], I had written a short essay on dreaming, which summed up the content of my *Interpretation of Dreams*. The publisher, Bergmann of Wies- baden, sent me a set of proofs and asked to have them back by return, because he wanted to bring the collection out before Christmas. I corrected the proofs that night and put them on my desk, ready to take them out with me next morning. In the morning I forgot, and remembered the proofs only that afternoon when I saw their wrapper on my desk. I continued forgetting to send off the proofs that afternoon, that evening and the next morning, until I pulled myself together and took them to a letterbox on the afternoon of the second day, wondering what the reason for my delay might be. Obviously there was some reason why I did not want to send them, but I could not think what it was. However, on the same walk I looked in on my Viennese publisher, the publisher of the book on dreams itself, ordered something from him, and then said, as if struck by a sudden idea: 'I suppose you know I've rewritten my *Dreams*?' 'Oh, no!' he exclaimed. 'No, don't worry,' I said, 'it's only a brief essay for the Löwenfeld-Kurella collection.' But he was still upset; he feared that my contribution to the collection would harm sales of my own book. I assured him it wouldn't, and finally said: 'If I'd asked you in the first place, would you have forbidden me to publish the article?' 'No, of course not.' I myself think I acted entirely within my rights, and did only what everyone usually does, but it seems to me certain now that I had some reservations about writing the article, along the same lines as the doubts expressed by my publisher, and those reservations had motivated my unwilling-ness to send off the proofs. They derived from an earlier occasion on which another publisher made a fuss when, unavoidably, I took several pages of text from an earlier work of mine on cerebral infantile paralysis published by another firm, and included them unaltered in my discussion of the same subject in Nothnagel's *Handbuch* [*Manual*]. Once again, there was no good reason for anyone to blame me; on that occasion too I had duly told my first publisher (in fact the publisher of the *Interpretation of Dreams*) what I intended to do. But if I look back yet further in this series of memories, it brings me to an even earlier occasion and a translation from the French, when I really did infringe the rights of intellectual property in a publication. I had added notes of my own to the translated text without asking the author's permission, and a few years later I had reason to think that he was not happy with this unauthorized action of mine.

A proverb revealing the popular knowledge that intentions are not forgotten by chance runs: 'What you forget to do once you will forget to do again.'

Sometimes, in fact, it is difficult to avoid the impression that everything which can be said about forgetting and other slips is already known to humanity and accepted as perfectly natural. How odd, then, that one still has to point out such well-known facts to the conscious mind! Time and again I have heard someone say: Oh, don't ask me to do that, I'm sure to forget! There can then surely be nothing mysterious about the accuracy of the prophecy. The person who made it was aware of intending not to carry out the task, and was merely unwilling to admit to it.

Light is also cast on the way in which we forget intentions by what could be called the forming of false intentions. I once promised a young author to write a review of his brief work, but I put it off because of some internal resistance, of which I was not unaware, until one day his urging induced me to promise that I would do it that very evening. And I seriously intended to do so, but I had forgotten that the same evening I was to write a report which could not be postponed. Once I had recognized my intention as a false one, I gave up the battle against my resistance and told the author that I would not write the review.

Notes

1. During the consultation the details of the patient's first visit on the earlier occasion then usually emerge into my conscious mind.
2. I would suggest similar explanations for many of the coincidental occurrences that have been ascribed, since T. Vischer wrote about them, to 'the malice of objects'.
3. If you ask someone whether he suffered from a syphilitic infection ten or fifteen years ago, it is easy to forget that psychically he will think of this disease in quite different terms from, say, acute arthritis. In the accounts given by parents of their neurotic daughters' medical history it is difficult to distinguish for certain between what they have forgotten and what they are concealing, since everything that might stand in the way of the girl's subsequent marriage is automatically eliminated, that is to say, repressed by both parents. A man whose much-loved wife recently died of a lung infection told me the following case of misleading medical information,

which can be ascribed only to such forgetfulness. 'When my poor wife's pleurisy was still no better after many weeks, Dr P. was called in as consultant. In taking down the history of her case, he asked the usual questions, among them whether anyone else in my wife's family had suffered from pulmonary disorders. My wife said no, and I could not remember any either. When Dr P. left, the conversation turned by chance to excursions out of town, and my wife said, "Yes, and it's a long way to Langersdorf *where my poor brother is buried.*" This brother had died some fifteen years earlier after suffering from tuberculosis for several years. My wife had loved him dearly, and often talked to me about him. Indeed, it occurred to me that she herself, when her pleurisy had been diagnosed, had been very anxious and had thought, sadly: *My brother died of lung trouble too.* But now she had repressed the memory to such an extent that even after what she had just said about expeditions to L., she could see no reason to correct what she had told the doctor about her family's medical history. I myself had noticed her failure to remember at the very moment when she mentioned Langersdorf.' E. Jones describes an analogous experience in his work, mentioned already several times above. A doctor whose wife was suffering from a disorder of the lower abdomen, which resisted diagnosis, said as if to comfort her: 'It's a good thing there are no cases of tuberculosis in your family.' The wife, much surprised, replied: 'Have you forgotten that my mother died of tuberculosis, and my sister did not recover from the disease until the doctors had given her up?'

4. At the time when I was writing these pages I suffered the following almost incredible instance of forgetfulness: on 1 January I was looking through my medical records so that I could send out the invoices for my fees, and in doing so came upon the name of M . . . for the month of June. I could not remember anyone with that name. My surprise grew as I noticed, looking forward through my records, that I had treated this case in a sanatorium, visiting daily for weeks. A doctor does not, a mere six months later, forget a patient whom he has treated in such circumstances. Had the patient been an uninteresting person, I wondered, a paralytic? At last, a note about having received my fee restored all the facts that were trying to elude my memory to my mind. M . . . had been a girl of fourteen, the most remarkable case I had treated the previous year and one that taught me something I am unlikely ever to forget. Its outcome was very painful to me. The child fell sick, unmistakably with hysteria, and swiftly and fundamentally improved under my treatment. But after this improvement the child's parents withdrew her from my care. She was still complaining of abdominal pains, which had featured prominently as a symptom of her hysteria, and

two months later she died of cancer of the abdominal glands. The hysteria to which the child was also predisposed had used the formation of the tumour as a cause provoking it, and I, with my mind on the obvious but harmless hysterical symptoms, had perhaps overlooked the first signs of her progressive and incurable illness.

5. A. Pick has recently gathered together papers by a series of authors ('Zur Psychologie des Vergessens bei Geistes- und Nervenkranken', *Archiv für Kriminal-Anthropologie und Kriminalistik* by H. Gross) on the influence on the memory of emotional factors, more or less clearly recognizing the contribution that resistance to unpleasant ideas makes to the memory. None of us, however, has described the phenomenon and its psychological basis as exhaustively and impressively as Nietzsche in one of his aphorisms (*Jenseits von Gut und Böse* [*Beyond Good and Evil*], part II, 68): 'I have done this, says my memory. I cannot have done that, says my pride, and insists upon it. At last it is the memory that gives way.'

6. Cf. Hans Gross, *Kriminalpsychologie*, 1898.

7. Ernest Jones points to the following passage in Darwin's autobiography, which tellingly reflects his scientific honesty and psychological acuteness: 'I had, during many years, followed a golden rule, namely, that whenever a published fact, a new observation or thought came across me, which was opposed to my general results, to make a memorandum of it without fail and at once; for I had found by experience that such facts and thoughts were far more apt to escape from the memory than favourable ones.'

8. Some time ago, one of my readers sent me a little volume from F. Hoffmann's series of books for young people, containing an extensive account of a scene involving a rescue, much like the one I had imagined in Paris. The coincidence even went so far as certain rather unusual expressions that appeared in both sources. The possibility of my having in fact read this book as a boy cannot be rejected. The library of my high school contained Hoffmann's collection and was always ready to lend volumes to the school-boys instead of other intellectual nourishment. The fantasy that I thought I remembered at the age of 45 as someone else's, and then had to recognize as my own and dating from my 29th year, may therefore easily have been the faithful reproduction of an impression absorbed between the ages of 11 and 13. The rescue fantasy I ascribed to the unemployed bookkeeper in *Le Nabab* was only to pave the way for a fantasy of my own rescue, making my wish for a patron and protector tolerable to my pride. No student of the mind will be surprised to hear that even in my conscious life I have felt great resistance to the idea of being dependent on any protector, and have not borne the few real situations in which something similar has occurred

with a very good grace. The deeper significance of fantasies involving such subjects, with an almost exhaustive explanation of their characteristics, has been shown by Abraham in a work entitled 'Vaterrettung und Vatermord in den neurotischen Phantasiengebilden' ['Saving and Murdering the Father in Neurotic Fantasies'], 1922 (*Internationale Zeitschrift für Psychoanalyse* VIII).

9. Cf. Bernheim, *Neue Studien über Hypnotismus, Suggestion und Psychotherapie* [*New Studies of Hypnotism, Suggestion and Psychology*], 1892.

10. In Bernard Shaw's play *Caesar and Cleopatra*, Caesar, about to leave Egypt, torments himself for some time with the idea that he intended to do something and has now forgotten what it was. At last it turns out that what Caesar had forgotten was to say goodbye to Cleopatra! This small incident is meant to illustrate – in complete contrast to the historical facts – how little Caesar thought of the Egyptian princess. (From E. Jones, op. cit, p. 488.)

11. Women, with their subtler understanding of the unconscious workings of the mind, are usually more inclined to be offended if someone fails to recognize and greet them in the street than to think of the obvious explanation: that their acquaintance is short-sighted, or so deep in thought that he or she has not seen them. They conclude that they would have been noticed if they were truly valued.

12. S. Ferenczi says that he himself was 'absent-minded' and notorious among his acquaintances for the frequency and peculiarity of the slips he made. However, the signs of this 'absence of mind' have almost entirely disappeared since he began psychoanalytical treatment of his patients, and found himself obliged to turn his attention to his own ego as well. He thinks that slips are abandoned if one learns to extend one's own responsibility, and therefore he contends, in my view correctly, that absence of mind is a condition which depends on unconscious complexes, and can be cured by psychoanalysis. One day, however, he was blaming himself for making a professional mistake in the psychoanalysis of a patient, and all his earlier symptoms of 'absent-mindedness' returned. He stumbled several times walking down the street (reflecting the *faux pas* he had made in treating his patient), left his wallet at home, offered a kreuzer too little for his tram fare, did not button up his clothing neatly, and so forth.

13. On this subject, E. Jones points out: 'Often the resistance is of a general order. Thus a busy man forgets to post letters entrusted to him – to his slight annoyance – by his wife, just as he may "forget" to carry out her shopping orders.'

14. For the sake of thematic unity I will break into my scheme in this book here, and add to what I have said above by pointing out that human memory is especially selective in financial matters. False memories of having paid something already, as I myself know, are often very persistent. When the intention to make a profit is allowed free rein, over and beyond the major interests of life and thus, so to speak, for fun, for instance in a game of cards, the most honest of men are inclined to make mistakes, fail to remember or calculate properly, and find themselves involved in minor frauds without really knowing how. The psychically enjoyable nature of the game is based in part on such liberties. The proverb saying that a person's real character is revealed in gaming may be admitted, so long as his manifest character is not meant. When head waiters make unintentional mistakes of calculation they are often to be regarded in the same way. Businessmen frequently show a certain hesitation to provide sums of money, pay bills, and so on, in a way that will bring them no profit but can be understood only psychologically, as an expression of the counter-will to get rid of money. Brill points out, with epigrammatic cogency: 'We are more apt to mislay letters containing bills than checks.' It is in connection with their most intimate and least clearly understood emotions that women in particular show especial aversion to paying a doctor. They have usually left their purses at home, and cannot pay in the consulting rooms; they then regularly forget to send the fee from home, and thus achieve the effect of having been treated free – for the sake of their charms. They pay, as it were, with their glance.

VIII

Inadvertent Actions

I take the following passage from the work by Meringer and Mayer, mentioned above (p. 98):

'Slips of the tongue do not stand in isolation, but correspond to those slips that often occur during other kinds of human activities, and are ascribed, in a rather simple way, to forgetfulness.'

I am therefore by no means the first to have suspected that there is significance and intention behind the small functional disturbances in the daily life of healthy people.[1]

If slips of the tongue – and speaking is a motor function – allow of such an interpretation, it seems obvious that we may expect mistakes in our other motor functions to operate in the same way. I have drawn up two groups of cases here: those in which the essential factor seems to be the effect of failure itself – the departure from an intention – I have described as 'inadvertent actions', and those in which, by contrast, the entire action appears inappropriate I call 'symptomatic and fortuitous actions'. However, no clear-cut distinction can be drawn; one has to acknowledge that all the categories mentioned in this work have only a descriptive significance, running counter to the general consistency we find in such phenomena as a whole.

The psychological understanding of 'inadvertent actions' obviously gets no notable encouragement if such actions are classified as instances of ataxia, more particularly cortical ataxia. Let me try instead to trace some individual examples back to the conditions in which they occurred. Again, I shall use self-observations, although instances of the phenomenon are not particularly frequent in me.

a) In the past, when I used to visit patients at home more frequently than I do now, I would often happen to reach the door
where I was to knock or ring the bell, and then take my own
front-door key out of my pocket – and put it back again, feeling
rather abashed. When I work out which patients this happened with,
I can only suppose that the inadvertent action – getting out my own
key instead of ringing the bell – was a compliment to the place
where I perpetrated this slip. It amounted to thinking: 'I feel at
home here,' since it occurred only when I had come to like the
patient. (And of course I never ring my own front-door bell.)

The inadvertent action was therefore the symbolic representation
of an idea determined by something which was not really a serious
conscious assumption, for in reality, as a neurologist, I know perfectly
well that patients will remain close to me only as long as they expect
to benefit from the relationship, and the neurologist himself takes
an unusually warm interest in his patients merely so that he can
offer psychic help.

It is clear from many self-observations by others that this significant manoeuvre with the key was not by any means peculiar to
myself.

A. Maeder ('Contrib. à la psychopathologie de la vie quotidienne',
Archives de Psychologie VI, 1906) describes a case almost identical
with my own experiences: 'Il est arrivé à chacun de sortir son
trousseau, en arrivant à la porte d'un ami particulièrement cher, de
se surprendre pour ainsi dire, en train d'ouvrir avec sa clé comme
chez soi. C'est un retard, puisqu'il faut sonner malgré tout, mais
c'est une preuve qu'on se sent – ou qu'on voudrait se sentir – comme
chez soi, auprès de cet ami [Almost everyone has found himself
getting out his keys on arriving at the door of a particularly close
friend, has surprised himself, so to speak, in the act of opening the
door as if it were his own. He is delaying himself, since he will have
to ring the bell after all, but it is evidence that he feels – or would
like to feel – very much at home with that friend].'

E. Jones (op. cit., p. 509): 'The use of keys is a fertile source of
occurrences of this kind, of which two examples may be given. If I
am disturbed in the midst of some engrossing work at home by

having to go to the hospital to carry out routine work, I am very apt to find myself trying to open the door of my laboratory there with the key of my desk at home, although the two keys are quite unlike each other. The mistake unconsciously demonstrates where I would rather be at the moment.

'Some years ago I was acting in a subordinate position at a certain institution, the front door of which was kept locked, so that it was necessary to ring for admission. On several occasions I found myself making serious attempts to open the door with my house key. Each of the permanent visiting staff, of which I aspired to be a member, was provided with a key to avoid the trouble of having to wait at the door. My mistakes thus expressed my desire to be on a similar footing, and to be quite "at home" there.'

Dr Hanns Sachs gives an account of a similar incident: 'I always carry two keys with me, one of which opens the door of my office and the other my front door at home. They are not at all easy to mix up, since the key to the office is at least three times the size of my front-door key, and furthermore I carry the former in my trouser pocket and the latter in my waistcoat pocket. All the same, as I stood outside one of the doors I quite often noticed that I had taken out the wrong key as I climbed the stairs. I decided to make a statistical experiment: as I approached the two doors in more or less the same state of mind every day, my mixing up the two keys ought to show some regular tendency if there were some psychic determination of a different kind for it. My subsequent observations showed that I regularly produced my front-door key outside the door of my office, but I did the reverse only once, when I came home feeling tired but knew there was a guest waiting for me. I then tried to open the front door with the office key, which of course was much too large.'

b) In a certain building I used to come to a door on the second floor twice a day at fixed times over a six-year period. On two occasions during this long period of time (with a short interval between them) I happened to climb a floor too high. I had thus climbed the wrong way [*verstiegen*, past participle of *versteigen*, 'to become lost when mountaineering']. On the first occasion I was absorbed in a daydream of an ambitious nature in which I was 'climbing onward and upward'. I even failed to hear the door in question opening as I started up the first of the steps leading to the third floor. The second time I once again climbed too far while lost in thought; when I noticed I turned back, and tried to pin down the fantasy occupying my mind. I found that I was feeling angry with imaginary criticism of my writings which accused me of always 'going too far', and in which I now had to insert the not very respectful expression of being *verstiegen* [literally, see above, 'having climbed the wrong way', but colloquially, 'high-flown, eccentric' in literary style].

c) For many years a reflex hammer and a tuning fork lay side by side on my desk. One day I was hurrying off at the end of my consulting hours because I wanted to catch a certain local city train, and in full daylight I put the tuning fork instead of the hammer in my coat pocket. The weight of the object dragging down my pocket alerted me to my mistake. Someone unused to thinking much about such small incidents would undoubtedly explain and excuse it by the haste I was in. Instead, I asked myself just why I had picked up the tuning fork instead of the hammer, for my haste might equally well have been a good reason for me to perform the correct action, so that I need not lose any time putting things right.

The question that now came into my mind was: who last touched the tuning fork? The answer was that it had been an *idiot child* a few days ago, when I was checking his sensory impressions. He had been so fascinated by the tuning fork that I had difficulty getting him to let go of it. Did that mean I was an idiot too? It certainly seems so, because the next idea I associated with 'hammer' [German: *Hammer*] was *chamer* (Hebrew: 'donkey').

But why call myself an idiot? I now had to look at the situation itself. I was hurrying off to a consultation in a place on the Western Railway line, to visit a woman patient who, in her medical history as described to me in a letter, had fallen from her balcony months ago and had been unable to walk ever since. The doctor who had turned to me as a consultant wrote that he still was not sure whether this was a case of injury to the spinal cord or traumatic neurosis –

hysteria. I had been called in to decide. Here I had to remind myself to be particularly careful in the delicate matter of differential diagnosis. My colleagues are very ready in any event to believe that diagnoses of hysteria are much too glibly made when in fact the trouble is more serious. That, however, did not account for my calling myself an idiot! But now I recollected that years ago I had seen a young man who could not walk properly, as the result of an emotional disturbance, in the same place for which I was about to catch a train to take me to its little railway station. I had diagnosed hysteria at the time and subsequently took the patient into psychiatric treatment, but it turned out that while my diagnosis was not actually incorrect, it did not cover everything. A considerable number of my patient's symptoms had been hysterical, and sure enough they promptly disappeared in the course of treatment, but it was then possible to see remaining symptoms that were inaccessible to therapy, and could only indicate multiple sclerosis. Doctors who saw the patient after me easily enough identified his organic ailment. I could hardly have done other than I did, nor could I have reached a different conclusion, but an impression was left that I had made a serious mistake, and of course I could not, as I had promised, cure him. My mistake in picking up the tuning fork instead of the hammer could thus be put into words as follows: you fool, you donkey, come on, pull yourself together and make sure you don't diagnose hysteria again where there is really an incurable illness present, as you did with that poor man at the same place years ago! And luckily for the sake of my little analysis, although it did nothing for my state of mind, that same man, my patient with severe spastic paralysis, had been in my consulting rooms only a few days before, the day after I had seen the idiot child.

It will be noted that on this occasion the voice of self-criticism made itself heard through the inadvertent action, and such occurrences are particularly apt to be a means of self-reproach. The inadvertent action here represents a similar action perpetrated elsewhere.

d) An inadvertent action can also, of course, be serving a whole series of other obscure intentions. Here is one example: I do not often break things. I am not particularly good with my hands, but there is nothing the matter with the anatomical integrity of my nervous and muscular systems that would account for my making clumsy movements with unfortunate consequences, so I cannot remember ever breaking any household item. There is not much space in my study, where I have a small collection of antique pottery and stone objects, and when handling them I therefore often have to do so in very awkward positions. People watching me used to express a fear that I would knock something over and break it, but I never did. So why did I once drop the marble top of my plain inkwell to the floor and break it?

My inkstand was a slab of Untersberg marble hollowed out to take the glass inkwell, which had a lid made of the same stone and with a knob. There was a row of bronze statuettes and terracotta figurines arranged in a circle behind this inkstand. I sat down at my desk to write, made a curiously clumsy, sweeping movement with the hand holding my pen and knocked the lid of the inkwell, which was already lying on my desk, to the floor. It is not difficult to find the explanation. A few hours earlier my sister had been in the room to see some of my new acquisitions. She admired them, and then said: 'Your desk looks really nice now, except for the inkstand, which doesn't suit the rest. You ought to have a prettier one.' I left the room with my sister and did not come back for some hours. But then, or that is how it seems, I carried out the sentence she had pronounced and executed the condemned inkstand. Did I perhaps conclude from my sister's words that next time she had occasion to make me a present she was going to give me a better inkstand, and had I broken the plain, old one to make sure that she put the plan she had indicated into practice? If so, then my sweeping movement was only apparently clumsy, and in reality was both dextrous and purposeful, since I contrived to avoid all the more valuable objects standing close to the inkstand.

I really do think we must assume that a great number of clumsy movements which appear to be accidents can be explained in this way. It is true that there is something violent and jerky about them, as if they were spastic or ataxic movements, but they betray their intentional nature and fulfil their purpose with a certainty that cannot always be attributed to conscious and voluntary movements. They have two characteristics, violence and a sure aim, in common with the motor expressions of hysterical neurosis and to some extent with the motor phenomena of somnambulism, and in both cases these features indicate the same unconscious modification of the process of innervation.

A self-observation recounted to me by Frau Lou Andreas-Salomé convincingly shows how persistent 'clumsiness' can be very skilfully put to the service of unacknowledged intentions.

'Just when milk was in short supply and had become very expensive I found, to my frequent alarm and annoyance, that I kept letting it boil over. I tried in vain to get the better of this tendency, although I cannot accuse myself of being absent-minded or careless in other ways, and I would have been more and not less likely to have a reason for that after my much-loved white terrier died; he was called "Friend" (Russian: Drujok), a name he deserved as much as any human being. But as it happened, I never let so much as a drop of milk boil over again after his death. My first thought was: "What a good thing, because milk boiling over on the stove and dripping to the floor would be no use to anyone now!" And at the same time I saw my "Friend" in front of me, sitting watching me as I was cooking, with his head slightly to one side, already wagging the end of his tail hopefully – waiting confidently for my enjoyable accident to happen. That explained it all, and showed that I had been even fonder of him than I knew.'

In the last few years, since I began collecting such observations, I have happened to damage or break objects of some value on several occasions, and study of these incidents has convinced me that they were never the result of chance or my unintentional clumsiness. For instance, one morning as I was walking through a room in my dressing gown, wearing straw slippers, I obeyed a sudden impulse and kicked one slipper off my foot and against the wall, where it brought down a pretty little marble Venus from her bracket. As she smashed into pieces, I cheerfully quoted Wilhelm Busch's verse:

Ach! Die Venus ist perdü –
Klickeradoms! – von Medici.

[Dear me – crash! The Medici Venus is broken!]

This wanton violence and my lack of concern at the damage can be explained by my situation at the time. A member of the family was seriously ill, and I already had private doubts of her recovery. But that morning I was told of a great improvement, and I know that I said to myself: She will live after all. My destructive outbreak served to express gratitude to fate and enabled me to make a 'sacrifice', as though I had vowed that if she recovered I would indeed sacrifice something! My choice of the Medici Venus as victim can only have been a gallant tribute to the convalescent. But I still find it extraordinary that yet again I could make up my mind so quickly, aim so well, and ensure that I did not hit any of the other items so close to the statuette.

Another breakage, also with the significance of a sacrifice, this time to avert evil, was made with a pen that slipped out of my hand. I had allowed myself to blame a good and loyal friend for something that depended on no more than my interpretation of certain signals made by his unconscious mind. He took it ill, and wrote me a letter asking me please not to subject my friends to psychoanalysis. I had to agree that he was right, and was writing him a conciliatory answer. As I wrote this letter my latest acquisition, a fine glazed Egyptian figurine, was standing in front of me. I broke it as I have just described, and knew at once that I had done the damage to avert a greater one. Luckily it proved possible to mend both the friendship and the figurine so well that no one would ever have noticed the cracks.

A third breakage happened in a less serious context: it was simply, to borrow a phrase used by T. Vischer in his *Auch Einer* [*Another One*], a camouflaged 'execution' of an object I no longer liked. For some time past I had been carrying a walking stick with a silver handle; when the thin silver plate of the handle was damaged, not by my own fault, it was poorly repaired. Soon after the stick came back from being mended, and when I was in a cheerful mood one day, I used the crook of the handle to angle for one of my children's legs, and during this game of course it broke and I was rid of it.

The indifference with which I regarded the damage in all these cases may be taken as proof that I had some unconscious intention to inflict it.

There are times when, in looking for the reasons behind so small a slip as breaking an object, one uncovers connections going deep into someone's past history and still affecting his present situation. The following analysis by L. Jekels may serve as an example.

'A doctor owned a very pretty although not expensive earthenware flower vase. It had once been given to him by a patient, a married woman, along with a number of other objects, some of them valuable. When the woman's psychosis became obvious he returned all the presents she had made him to her family – except for the comparatively cheap vase from which he felt unable to part, allegedly because it was so attractive. But withholding this item cost the doctor, who was usually very scrupulous, a certain internal struggle, for he was well aware of the impropriety of his conduct and could calm his guilty conscience only by making excuses: the vase was really of no material value, it would have been difficult to pack up, and so forth. A few months later, when he was about to instruct a solicitor to claim and recover the outstanding fees for this patient's treatment, which were the subject of dispute, his self-reproach returned; fleetingly, he felt alarm in case the woman's relatives discovered what might be termed his misappropriation of the vase and brought it up against him during legal proceedings. The first factor in particular, his self-reproach, was so strong for a time that he actually entertained the idea of giving up his demand for the fees owed – worth about a hundred times more than the vase – as a kind of compensation for the item he had failed to return. However, he immediately saw that this idea was absurd and rejected it.

'While he was in this frame of mind, it happened that although in the normal way he very seldom broke anything, and had excellent control of his muscular system, he swept the vase off the table while he was refilling it with water, making a curiously clumsy movement which had no organic connection with what he was doing, so that it broke into five or six large pieces. This happened when the previous evening, and only after much hesitation, he had decided to fill this very vase with flowers and put it on the dining-room table in front of some guests he had invited. Just before he broke it he had thought of it, was taken aback to find that it was not in his living room as usual, and then fetched it back from the dining room himself! When, after his initial shock, he had picked up the pieces of the vase and found, by fitting them together, that it could still be mended to look almost as good as new, two or three of the larger fragments slipped out of his hands, smashed into a thousand pieces, and with them went all hope of a successful repair.

'Undoubtedly this slip had the effect of allowing the doctor to take his case to court by destroying the vase he had withheld, which to some extent was inhibiting him from demanding what, in turn, had been withheld from himself. But as well as this direct determination, any psychoanalyst can see a further, much deeper, more important and symbolic meaning behind his slip: a vase, after all, clearly symbolizes a woman.

'The protagonist of this anecdote had suffered the tragic loss of his young, beautiful and dearly loved wife; he fell into a state of neurosis dominated by the idea that he himself was responsible for his misfortune ("he had broken his beautiful vase"). He could no longer relate to women, and felt a distaste for marriage or any long-term loving relationship, which his unconscious regarded as inconstancy to his dead wife, but which he rationalized in his conscious mind as meaning that he brought women bad luck, a woman might kill herself for his sake, and so forth. (Then, of course, he need not keep the vase permanently!)

'As he had a strong libido, it is not at all surprising that he saw relationships with married women, fleeting of their very nature, as the most suitable kind for him (hence the significance of his withholding someone else's vase).

'There is good confirmation of this symbolism in the following two factors: first, he underwent psychoanalytical treatment for his neurosis. Later in the session when he described breaking the earthenware vase, he reverted to the subject of his relationships with women, and said he was ridiculously demanding: he insisted, for instance, that women must be of "unearthly beauty". This clearly emphasized the fact that he still loved his wife (who was dead, and therefore unearthly) and wanted no ordinary "earthly beauty"; hence the breaking of the earthenware (earthly) vase. And at the very time when, in the course of transference, he was constructing a fantasy of marrying his doctor's daughter, he gave the doctor a present – of a vase, as if indicating the kind of present he would like to be given in return.

'It is likely that the symbolic meaning of his slip could be susceptible to many other variations, for instance not wishing to fill the vase, and so on. However, it strikes me as more interesting to surmise that the presence of several motives – two at least, probably operating separately in the preconscious and unconscious minds – is reflected in the duplication of the slip: knocking it over and then dropping the pieces a second time.'[2]

e) Dropping objects, knocking them over and breaking them often seems to be a way of expressing unconscious trains of thought, and while this can sometimes be proved by analysis it is more often evident from the superstitious or jocular ideas contained in popular sayings. Everyone knows what spilling salt is supposed to indicate, or knocking over a wine glass, dropping a knife so that it sticks in the floor point down, and so on. I shall return later to the claims such superstitions have on our attention; here I will merely point out that a clumsy action in isolation by no means has a fixed meaning, but offers itself as a method of representing some intention or another, depending on the circumstances.

Recently there was a time when unusual quantities of glass and china were broken in my household; I myself contributed by damaging several items. This violent little psychic epidemic could easily be explained; it happened in the days leading up to my eldest daughter's wedding. On festive occasions such as a wedding it is common to break something on purpose, accompanying the breakage by wishes of good luck. This custom may both suggest a sacrifice and have the significance of yet another symbolic meaning.

When servants drop and break something fragile our minds do not immediately fly to some psychological explanation, but once again it is not unlikely that hidden motives are involved. Nothing is further from an uneducated person's mind than an appreciation of art and works of art. Unspoken hostility towards artistic items prevails among the servant classes, particularly when the objects, whose value they do not understand, give them extra work to do. People of the same origin and educational attainments, on the other hand, often prove very skilful and reliable in handling delicate objects in scientific institutes once they have begun to identify with their employers and regard themselves as important members of staff.

I will add here some remarks from a young technician which give us an insight into the mechanism whereby property can be wilfully damaged. 'Some time ago I was working with several colleagues in the university laboratory on a set of complicated experiments on elasticity, a task for which we had volunteered, although it was beginning to take up more time than we had expected. One day, when I went into the laboratory with my colleague F., he said that today in particular he disliked losing so much time, for he had a great many other things to do at home; I could only agree with him, and said half jokingly, referring to something that had happened the week before: "Well, let's hope the machinery goes wrong again so that we can stop work and go home early!" When our duties were allotted to us, it so happened that my colleague F. had to control the valve of the hydraulic press, which meant letting the liquid under pressure flow slowly out of the accumulator and into the cylinder by carefully opening the valve. The man in charge of the experiment was standing by the manometer and called out a loud "Stop!" when the right pressure was reached. At this command F. took the valve and turned it as hard as he could – to the left (all valves without exception are turned to the right to close them!). This made the full pressure of the accumulator suddenly felt in the press. The tubing was not adjusted to take it, and a connection burst – a perfectly harmless accident to the machinery, but enough to mean that we had to stop work for the day and go home. Characteristically, some time later, when we were talking about the incident, my friend F.

said he could remember absolutely nothing about it, although I recalled it perfectly.'

Nor need falling over, stumbling and slipping always be interpreted as a purely accidental disturbance to one's motor action. The double meaning of such an expression as *faux pas* in itself indicates the kind of concealed fantasies that can be betrayed when our physical equilibrium is lost in this way. I remember a number of mild nervous disorders in women and girls which manifested themselves after a harmless fall, and were regarded as traumatic hysteria resulting from the alarm they had felt at falling. Even then, I had the impression that this was not the real explanation, that the fall itself had been a result of neurosis, expressing those unconscious sexual fantasies which one might suspect to be the motive forces behind the symptoms. After all, there is a proverb that runs: 'When a young lady falls, she falls on her back', and which could be regarded in the same way.

Cases in which we give a beggar a gold coin by mistake for a copper or small silver coin can also be described as inadvertent actions. It is easy enough to resolve the meaning of such slips; they are sacrifices intended to placate destiny, avert misfortune, and so forth. If a loving mother or aunt is heard expressing anxiety about a child's health just before going for a walk, and on that walk she inadvertently gives generous alms in this way, there can be no doubt of the meaning of her apparent mistake. Such slips allow us to observe all those pious and superstitious customs that the conscious mind cannot now acknowledge, because our rational thinking rejects them with incredulity.

f) The fact that fortuitous actions are really intentional will be especially readily accepted in the field of sexual activity, where the borderline between chance and intention really does seem blurred. A few years ago I observed in myself a good example of the way in which an apparently clumsy movement can be subtly exploited for sexual ends. I was in a friend's house, where I met a young girl who was also a guest and who aroused feelings in me that I had thought were long gone, thus putting me in a cheerful, talkative and forthcoming frame of mind. Even then I wondered why; a year before the same girl had left me cold. When her uncle, a very elderly gentleman, came into the room, we both jumped up to bring him a chair standing in a corner. She was nimbler than I, and probably closer to the armchair, so she got hold of it first and carried it over in front of her with the back towards her, both her hands on the sides of the chair. As I joined her, still claiming my own right to carry the chair, I was suddenly standing right behind her. I put both arms around her, so that my hands momentarily met in front of her lower belly. Of course I brought the situation to an end as quickly as it had arisen, and no one seemed to notice how skilfully I had exploited my unskilful movement.

I have also sometimes told myself that the annoying and clumsy attempt to avoid someone else in the street, when you step to one side or another for several seconds but always end up on the same side, until you are both left facing each other and 'barring the way', duplicates some earlier improper form of provocative conduct, pursuing sexual intentions in the guise of clumsiness. From my psychoanalysis of neurotics I know that what is regarded as *naïveté* in children and young people is often only a disguise of this kind, enabling them to express indecency directly and unimpeded by embarrassment.

W. Stekel has made similar self-observations: 'I entered someone's home, and gave the lady of the house my right hand. Oddly enough, in the process I untied the bow holding her loose morning dress together. I was not aware of any dishonourable intentions, yet I had performed this unskilful movement with a conjuror's sleight of hand.'

I have repeatedly provided evidence that literary writers see various slips as being meaningful and motivated in the way I suggest here. It is not surprising, then, to find another example of a writer's seeing significance in a clumsy movement and using it as an omen prefiguring later events.

In Theodor Fontane's novel *L'Adultera* (vol. II, p. 64 of the *Collected Works* published by S. Fischer) we read: '[...] and Melanie jumped up and threw her husband one of the large balls, as if in greeting. But she had not aimed accurately, the ball flew to one side, and Rubehn caught it.' On returning from the expedition that led up to this little incident, Melanie and Rubehn have a conversation which betrays the first signs of attraction between them. This attraction turns to passion, and Melanie finally leaves her husband to give herself entirely to the man she loves. (Contributed by H. Sachs.)

g) The effects of inadvertent actions when perpetrated by normal people are usually of an extremely innocuous nature. For that very reason it is particularly interesting to see whether actions of this kind, which actually can have weighty and far-reaching consequences, for instance if perpetrated by a doctor or a pharmacist, come into these categories of ours in any way.

Since I very seldom practise as a physician, I can describe only one example of an inadvertent action in a medical context from personal experience. I had been visiting a very old lady twice a day for years, and my medical activity on my morning visit was confined to two procedures: I put a few eye-drops in one of her eyes and gave her a morphine injection. I had two little bottles regularly prepared and ready, a blue one for the collyrium and a white one for the morphine solution. During both procedures, my thoughts were usually elsewhere; I had carried them out so often that I did not need to give them my full attention. But one morning I noticed that in working automatically I had made a mistake: I had dipped the eye-dropper into the white bottle instead of the blue one and put morphine instead of collyrium in my patient's eye. I was much alarmed, but then calmed myself by reflecting that a few drops of a 2 per cent morphine solution could do no harm even in the conjunctival sac. The reason for my sense of alarm was obviously to be sought elsewhere.

In trying to analyse this little slip I thought first of the phrase *sich an der Alten vergreifen* ['to assault the old woman'; *vergreifen* is also the verb for 'performing inadvertent actions', used here in German], which seemed the shortest way to the answer. I was still thinking of a dream told to me the previous evening by a young man, the content of which could only be interpreted as sexual intercourse with his own mother.[3] The curious fact that the classical legend does not seem to balk at Queen Jocasta's age seems to me to bear out the idea that a sense of being in love with one's own mother never relates to her person as she is now, but to her youthful image remembered from childhood. Such incongruities always appear when a fantasy oscillating between two periods comes into the conscious mind and becomes fixed on one of them. Deep in thoughts of this nature, I went to visit my patient, who was over ninety years old, and I must have been on my way to seeing the generally human character of the fable of Oedipus as corresponding to the destiny foretold by the oracles, for I did then 'make the mistake' of 'committing an assault on' the old lady [German: *sich vergreifen*, see above]. However, this slip was innocuous in itself: of the two possible mistakes, using the morphine solution as eye-drops or injecting the eye-drops into my patient, I had chosen by far the least harmful. But we still cannot say whether inadvertent actions that could in fact do severe damage can be traced back to an unconscious intention in a similar way to the one described above.

For here, as might be expected, my own material lets me down, and I have to fall back on assumptions and conclusions. It is well known that self-injury is sometimes a symptom in severe cases of psychoneurosis, and that the ending of psychic conflict by suicide can never be excluded in such cases. I have known instances, well vouched for, of many apparently accidental injuries that are really self-inflicted, when a latent tendency to self-mortification, which is usually expressed in self-reproaches or contributes to the formation of symptoms, skilfully exploits an external situation that happens to offer itself, or gives it a little extra help to achieve the desired effect of injury. Such incidents are by no means rare even in cases of only moderate severity, and betray the part played by unconscious intentions through a series of particular features, for instance the notable composure with which the patients contemplate what they claim to have been accidents.[4]

I will give a detailed account of a single example from my medical experience, rather than citing several: a young woman broke one of her shinbones in a carriage accident, and was confined to her bed for weeks. A striking feature of her misfortune was the fact that she did not complain of the pain and bore it with equanimity. This accident led to her developing a severe neurotic disorder which lasted a long time, and of which she was finally cured by psychoanalysis. In treatment, I discovered the attendant circumstances of the accident, and certain incidents that had preceded it. The young woman and her husband, a very jealous man, were staying on her married sister's estate in the company of her many other siblings and their spouses. One evening, in this close-knit family circle, she performed one of her party pieces, dancing a very good cancan to the plaudits of her relations but much to the displeasure of her husband, who whispered to her afterwards: 'There you go again, behaving like a tart as usual!' His accusations hit home; we will leave aside the question of whether he was referring only to her dancing. She slept poorly that night, and next morning said she would like to go for a drive. She chose the carriage-horses herself, rejecting one pair and demanding another. Her youngest sister wanted her baby and his nurse to go on the drive too, but she energetically opposed that idea. During the drive she acted nervously, warned the coachman that the horses were getting restive, and when the nervous animals really did create momentary trouble she jumped out of the carriage in alarm and broke her leg, while the others, who had stayed inside, got away unscathed. Once we know these details, can anyone doubt that this accident was really staged in advance? One has to admire the skill that caused the accident to make the punishment fit the crime so well, since the lady would not be able to dance a cancan for quite a long time to come.

I cannot say that I have inflicted any injuries on myself at times when my mind is calm, but I find that they can happen under stress. If one of my family complains of having bitten his or her tongue, pinched a finger, or so on, I am inclined to ask: 'What did you do that for?' instead of offering the sympathy expected of me. I myself pinched my thumb very painfully after a young patient told me during his hour of treatment that he planned to marry my eldest daughter (of course I did not take him seriously), while I knew that at that very moment she was lying in a sanatorium, in mortal danger of her life.

One of my sons, whose lively temperament made it difficult for anyone to nurse him when he was unwell, fell into a temper one morning because he had been told to spend the morning in bed, and threatened to kill himself, an idea he had picked up from the newspaper. That evening he showed me a bump on his ribcage, caused when he ran into the door-handle. When I asked why he had done that, and what the idea of it was, my son, then aged eleven, said as if suddenly enlightened: 'Oh, it was my suicide attempt, the one I threatened this morning.' I do not think, incidentally, that my children knew anything about my views on self-inflicted injuries at the time.

Anyone who believes that semi-intentional self-inflicted injuries do happen – if I may be allowed that rather clumsy way of putting it – will be prepared to accept that besides conscious and intentional suicides there are also cases of semi-intentional suicide attempts, made for reasons unconsciously nurtured, ingeniously exploiting life-threatening situations and dismissing them as chance accidents. Such a thing is by no means uncommon. A suicide wish is present to some extent in many people who never actually try to kill themselves; self-inflicted injuries are generally a compromise between this drive and the forces countering it, and even when the suicide wish does prevail, a tendency in that direction has been present for a long time already, either to a lesser degree or as an unconscious, suppressed tendency.

A conscious intention to commit suicide also picks its time, method and opportunity; it is entirely consistent with this for the unconscious intention to wait for an occasion that can act as the partial cause, freeing the intention from suppression by the subject's powers of rejection by making other demands on them.[5] These ideas of mine are by no means put forward at random; I have heard of more than one case of what looked like a riding or carriage accident which, when more closely investigated, gave grounds for the suspicion that it was an unconscious suicide attempt. For instance, during a horse-race between some army officers, one officer fell and injured himself so badly that he died some days later. His behaviour when he returned to consciousness is striking in many respects, but even more remarkable was his conduct before the race. He was deeply depressed by the death of his mother, whom he had loved dearly, was overcome by fits of weeping in the company of his comrades, and told his close friends that he was tired of life, saying he planned to leave the army and go to fight in a war in Africa which had nothing to do with him.[6] Once a daring horseman, he now avoided riding whenever possible. Finally, he expressed gloomy forebodings before the race, although he could not back out, and, as I see it, it was not surprising that his presentiments came true. It may be objected that it was understandable for a man in a state of such nervous depression to be unable to control his mount as well as he would in full health. I agree entirely, but I would locate the mechanism of his motor inhibition by 'nervousness' in the intention of suicide which I have been describing here.

S. Ferenczi of Budapest has let me see his analysis of a case of an apparently accidental shooting injury, which he interprets as an unconscious suicide attempt. I can only say that I agree with his interpretation:

'J. Ad., a journeyman cabinetmaker aged 22, came to see me on 18 January. He wanted me to tell him whether the bullet that had entered his left temple on 20 March 1907 could or should be removed by an operation. He felt perfectly well apart from occasional headaches, which were not too bad, and examination showed only the characteristic powder-blackened scar on his left temple caused by the entry of the bullet, so I advised against the operation. When I inquired into the circumstances of the case, he said he had shot himself by accident. He was playing with his brother's revolver, *thinking that it was not loaded*, held it against his left temple with his left hand (he is not left-handed), put his finger on the hammer, and the gun went off. *There were three cartridges in the revolver, which had six chambers*. I asked him what induced him to pick up the revolver. He replied that he was about to be examined to see if he was physically fit to do his military service, and he had taken the gun to the tavern with him the evening before because he was afraid of a brawl. When the medical examination took place he was declared unfit for the army because of varicose veins, and felt deeply ashamed.

He went home and fiddled about with the revolver, but without any intention of harming himself. Then the accident happened. When I made further inquiries, asking whether he was happy with his life in other respects, he sighed and told me that he was in love with a girl who returned his affection but had none the less left him; she had emigrated to America, just because she wanted to make some money. He would have liked to follow her, but his parents prevented him. His inamorata had left on 20 January 1907, two months before the incident, but despite all these suspect factors the patient insisted that the shot really had been an "accident". I, however, am firmly convinced that his failure to look at the weapon to see if it was loaded before playing with it was psychically determined, and so was his self-inflicted injury. He was still under the depressing influence of his unhappy love affair, and obviously wanted to join the army in order to "forget". It was when he was deprived of even this hope that the game with the gun occurred – or, rather, that he made his unconscious suicide attempt. The fact that he held the revolver in his left and not his right hand strongly supports the idea that he really was just "playing", that is to say, he did not consciously mean to commit suicide.'

Another analysis of an injury apparently self-inflicted by chance was given to me by an observer, and reminds one of the saying: 'He who digs a pit for others may fall into it himself.'

'Frau X., of a good middle-class background, was married with three children. She was slightly neurotic but had never needed intensive treatment, since she was able to cope with life well enough. One day she disfigured her face temporarily, but for the time being rather obviously, as follows. She tripped over a pile of stones in a street where the road was being mended, and struck her face against the wall of a building. It was badly scratched, her eyelids were blue and bruised, and feeling afraid that her eyes themselves might be damaged she called me in as a physician. When I had set her mind at rest on that point I asked: "But what made you fall like that?" She said that just before she went out she had warned her husband, who for some months had suffered from a disorder of the joints which made him unsteady on his feet, to take good care if he was walking along that street, and she had often noticed that when she warned someone else against an accident, she suffered the very same accident herself.

'I was not satisfied with this explanation of her accident, and asked whether she could tell me anything else. Well, yes: just before the accident she had seen a pretty picture in a shop on the opposite side of the street, and all of a sudden she thought it would look nice hanging in her children's room. She decided to buy it at once, went straight towards the shop, forgetting to look down at the road surface, stumbled over the pile of stones and fell against the wall of the building, without making the slightest attempt to protect herself with her hands. She immediately forgot about wanting to buy the picture, and went straight home. "But why didn't you take more notice of the road surface?" I asked. "Well," she said, "perhaps it was a *punishment*! Because of that incident – the one I told you about in confidence." "Does it still haunt your mind, then?" "Oh yes – afterwards I regretted it very much, I felt I was wicked, criminal and immoral, but I was quite beside myself with my poor nerves at the time."

'The incident of which we were speaking was an abortion that she had undergone with her husband's consent, since their financial situation meant they did not want to be blessed with any more offspring. It had been induced by a back-street abortionist, but had to be concluded by a qualified specialist.

'"I often tell myself reproachfully: you had your baby killed, didn't you? I was afraid something like that couldn't go unpunished. Now that you've told me I shan't have any trouble with my eyes, I feel much better: I've been *punished enough* as it is."

'In one way, therefore, this accident was a punishment in penance for her sin, but in another it was self-inflicted to escape punishment of an unknown nature and perhaps much worse, something she had been constantly fearing for months. Just as she hurried towards the shop to buy the picture her memory of the whole incident, with all her fears, which had been working quite strongly in her unconscious as she warned her husband about the street, got the upper hand. Her thinking might perhaps be put into words along these lines:

why would you need something pretty for your children's room? You had your own child killed! You're a murderess! Punishment is surely on its way!

'This thought did not reach her conscious mind, but instead she took the occasion at what might be called this psychological moment of punishing herself, making surreptitious use of the pile of stones, which seemed just the right means to her end; as a result she did not even put out her hands to save herself as she fell, nor did she feel too badly frightened. The second and probably less important factor in causing her accident was self-punishment for her *unconscious* wish to see her husband removed from the scene – for he, after all, had been a guilty party too. She had given away that wish in her warning to him to take great care in the street where the stones were lying about, which was quite unnecessary, since for the very reason that he was not good on his feet her husband took great care in walking.'[7]

If we look at all the circumstances of the next case, we shall be inclined to agree with J. Stärcke (op. cit.) when he describes a burn apparently self-inflicted by chance as a 'sacrificial action':

'A lady whose son-in-law had to go to do his military service in Germany scalded her foot in the following way. Her daughter was soon to have a baby, and the thought of the dangers of war naturally did nothing to cheer the family as a whole. The day before her son-in-law left she had asked him and her daughter to dinner. She cooked the meal herself in her own kitchen, but first, oddly enough, changed out of her high laced boots with their instep raisers, in which she could walk comfortably and which she usually wore at home, and put on a pair of her husband's slippers. The slippers were too large for her and were open on top. As she was taking a large pan of boiling soup off the heat she dropped it, scalding one foot quite badly, including the back of it, which was not protected by the open slipper. Naturally everyone put this accident down to her understandably "nervous" state. For the first few days after making this "burnt offering" she was very careful with anything hot, which did not prevent her from scalding her wrist with hot broth a few days later.'[8]

When anger like this directed against one's own integrity and even one's own life can be concealed by apparently chance clumsiness and motor inadequacy, it is not such a very great step further to believing it possible that the same concept is at work in slips which seriously endanger the life and health of others. The evidence I can produce for the validity of this idea comes from my experience with neurotics, and therefore does not entirely comply with my present require-ments. I will describe a case of what was not exactly an inadvertent action, but rather what may be called a symptomatic or fortuitous action, and which put me on the right lines to enable me to resolve my patient's conflict. I was once trying to improve the marriage of a very intelligent man who certainly had some genuine reasons for his quarrels with his young wife, who loved him dearly, but as he admitted himself those reasons did not fully explain the situation. He was constantly dwelling on ideas of divorce, which he then ruled out again because he loved his two small children so much. None the less, he kept coming back to the idea, and would try no means of making the marriage tolerable for himself. I saw this inability to deal with a conflict as evidence that unconscious and repressed motives had already reinforced the opposing conscious motives, and in such cases I try to resolve the conflict by psychic analysis. The man told me one day about a small incident that had alarmed him very much. He was romping about with his elder child, who was easily his favourite, swinging him up and down in the air, and once, from a certain place in the room, he swung the child up so high that the top of his head almost hit the heavy gas chandelier hanging from the ceiling. Almost, but not quite – or had it? No harm had come to the child, but he was quite dizzy with alarm. The father stood there, horrified, with the child in his arms, the mother became hysterical. The particular dexterity of this incautious movement and the parents' extreme reactions suggested that the accident should be seen as a symptomatic action expressing ill-will towards a much-loved child. I could remove any contradiction between that action and the father's present real love for his child if I transferred the impulse to harm him back to the period when this son was the only child, and still too small for his father to need to take an affectionate interest in him. Then I could easily suppose that at the time the husband, left unsatisfied by his wife, thought or projected something along these lines: I'm not at all fond of this little creature; if he died I should be free and could get a divorce from my wife. Unconsciously, therefore, he must still wish for the death of the child he now loved so much. It was easy to find my way from here to the manner in which the wish became an unconscious fixation. A powerful motive existed in my patient's childhood memory of his own little brother's death; their mother had blamed their father's negligence for it, and as a result there were violent arguments between his parents, accompanied by threats of divorce. The successful effect of my therapy on the subsequent course of my patient's marriage confirmed my deductions.

J. Stärcke (op. cit.) gave an example of the way in which writers may have no scruples in substituting an inadvertent action for an intentional action, in such a way as to cause the most serious consequences:

'A sketch by Heyermans[9] contains an example of an inadvertent action, or more precisely a blunder, which the author takes as a dramatic subject.

'The sketch is called "Tom and Teddie", and the characters are a couple of divers performing in a variety theatre, with an act in which they stay under water for a long time and do tricks in an iron tank with glass sides. One of the couple, the wife, has been having an affair with another man, an animal trainer. The husband has just caught them together in the dressing room before the performance. They freeze, threatening glances are exchanged, and the male diver says: "Just wait till later!" The performance begins. The husband is about to do his most difficult trick, staying, as the sketch announces, "two and a half minutes under water in a hermetically sealed container". It is a trick they have often done before, the container is closed, and "Teddie" – the wife – "shows the audience the key as they began checking the time on their watches." She also drops the key into the tank a couple of times on purpose, and then dives quickly in after it so as to be on the spot when the tank is ready to be opened.

'On the evening of 31 January, Tom had been locked in, as usual, by his merry little wife's nimble fingers. He was smiling behind the peep-hole – she was playing with the key, waiting for him to give the signal. Backstage stood the third party in the eternal triangle, the animal trainer in his immaculate frock-coat with his white tie and riding whip. He gave a brief whistle to attract her attention. She looked at him, smiled, and with the clumsiness of someone whose attention is distracted threw the key into the air so wildly that it fell beside the tank, after exactly two minutes twenty seconds of the show by a careful count, and landed on the bunting covering the trestles. No one had seen it. Indeed, no one could see it. The view from the auditorium produced an optical illusion: the audience all thought they had seen the key fall into the water – and none of the scene shifters noticed, because the bunting deadened the sound.

'Smiling, without hesitation, Teddie climbed over the rim of the tank. Smiling – Tom was doing well – she climbed down the ladder. Smiling, she disappeared to look under the trestles, and on failing to find the key at once, she bowed, standing at the front of the bunting-covered trestles with a scene-stealing expression on her face as if saying, "Oh, what a bore this is!"

'Meanwhile, Tom was making funny faces behind the peep-hole, as if he too were becoming uneasy. The spectators could see the white gleam of his false teeth, his lips working beneath his blond moustache, the comic bubble-blowing act he had done before when eating an apple. They could see his white knuckles as his hands clutched and contorted, and they roared with laughter as they had done before that evening.

'Two minutes fifty-eight seconds . . .

'Three minutes seven seconds . . . twelve seconds . . .

'Bravo! Bravo! Bravo!

'But then there was dismay in the theatre, and feet began scraping on the floor as the scene shifters and the animal trainer began looking for the key too. The curtain fell before the tank was opened.

'Next on stage were six English dancing girls – then the man with the ponies, the dogs and the monkeys, and so on.

'Only next morning did the public learn that there had been an accident, and Teddie was now a widow . . .

'The sketch described above clearly shows how well its author must have understood the nature of a symptomatic action, enabling him to present so cogent an account of the underlying cause of the fatal act of clumsiness.'

Notes

1. A second publication by Meringer later showed me that I had misjudged this author in assuming that he had such an understanding of the subject.

2. *Internationale Zeitschrift für Psychoanalyse* I, 1913.

3. I call it 'the Oedipal dream' because it provides the key to understanding the legend of King Oedipus. In the play by Sophocles, the connection with such a dream is put into Jocasta's own mouth. (Cf. *The Interpretation of Dreams* [V.D], p. 182. (*Gesammelte Werke*, 8th edition.)

4. Self-injury falling short of suicide has no choice in our present civilized state but to conceal itself behind an appearance of accident, or make itself felt by simulating some ailment that has arisen spontaneously. In the past it was a customary sign of mourning, or could sometimes express piety and renunciation of the world.

5. In essence, this case is like that of a sexual attack on a woman in which all the woman's muscular strength cannot prevail against the man's violence because some part of the victim's unconscious emotions is encouraging him. It is sometimes said that in such a situation the woman's strength is *paralysed*; we need only add the reasons for this paralysis. Here the amusing judgement passed by Sancho Panza in his capacity as governor of his island is psychologically inaccurate (*Don Quijote*, part II, chapter XLV). A woman drags a man before the judge, claiming that he has robbed her of her honour by violence. Sancho provides her with compensation in the form of the full purse he takes from the accused man, and once she has left gives the man permission to run after her and snatch the purse away again. They both come back struggling, and the woman boasts that the wicked fellow had not been able to get hold of her purse. To which Sancho replies: 'If you had defended your honour half as hard as that purse, the man could not have robbed you of it.'

6. It is a plausible idea that the battlefield is a situation conducive to a conscious intention of committing suicide, which none the less shrinks from taking the direct way. Cf., in *Wallenstein*, the Swedish captain's words on the death of Max Piccolomini: 'They say he wished to die.'

7. Van Emden, 'Selbstbestrafung für Abortus' ['Self-punishment for Abortion'], *Zentralblatt für Psychoanalyse* II/12. A correspondent writes, on the subject of 'self-punishment by slips': 'Watching the way people behave in the street, one can see how often men who – as they commonly do – glance at women walking by suffer some small accident. A man may sprain his ankle, even on level ground, or bump into a lamp-post, or hurt himself in some other way.'

8. In a very great number of such cases of accidental injury or death the interpretation is doubtful. Those at a distance from the accident will see no reason to regard it as anything but chance, while someone close to and with intimate knowledge of the victim will have grounds to suspect the unconscious intention behind it. The following account by a young man whose fiancée was run down in the street is a good example of the kind of knowledge I mean, and the other circumstances involved:

'In September last year I met a Fräulein Z., aged 34. She lived in comfortable circumstances, and had been engaged before the war, but her fiancé, an officer on active service, fell in 1916. We came to know and love each other, at first without any idea of marriage, since the circumstances did not seem to either of us to admit it on account of the age difference – I myself was 27. Since we lived opposite each other in the same street, and saw one another every day, our friendship eventually became intimate. At this point the idea of getting married became more likely, and I finally thought it would be a good idea myself. We were going to get engaged at Easter of that year, but first Fräulein Z. intended to visit her relations in M. However, a railway workers' strike resulting from the Kapp putsch prevented her from going. The dismal long-term prospects that the workers' victory and its consequences held out were soon reflected in our own minds, more particularly by Fräulein Z., since she thought she saw new obstacles in our way. On Saturday 20 March, however, she was in an exceptionally cheerful frame of mind, a circumstance which quite surprised me, so that I too was swept away by it, and we thought we saw everything in the rosiest of hues. A few days earlier we had spoken of going to church together some time, without fixing on a definite date. Next morning, Sunday 21 March, around 9.15 a.m., she called me by telephone asking me to call for her and we would go to church at once, but I objected, since I could not have been ready in time, and anyway I had work to do. Fräulein Z. was very disappointed, set off by herself, met an acquaintance on the steps outside her house and went with him the short way through Tauentzienstrasse to Rankestrasse in a cheerful enough mood, without saying anything about our conversation. The gentleman said goodbye, making a joke as he did so.

Fräulein Z. now had only to cross the Kurfürstendamm, which had been broadened just there, giving a good view – when she was run over close to the pavement by a horse-drawn cab (her liver suffered contusions and she died a few hours later). We had crossed the road here hundreds of times before; Fräulein Z. was very careful and had often kept me back when I made an incautious move, that morning there were almost no vehicles about, since the trams, omnibuses, etc., were on strike – there was almost *absolute* calm at the time, and the cab-driver must have heard her even if he couldn't see her. Everyone thought it was an accident. My own first reaction was: impossible – how could anyone say she did it on purpose? But I looked for a psychological explanation, and after a while I thought I had found it in your *Psychopathology of Everyday Life*. In addition, Fräulein Z. had sometimes expressed certain suicidal tendencies, and had also tried to infect me with them. I had often enough talked her out of such thoughts. Two days earlier, for instance, on coming back from a walk, she had begun to speak for no reason at all of her death and of making a will, although she had not in fact done so – a sign that she was certainly not serious about what she said. If I may express my own humble opinion, I should say that I see this accident not as chance, and not as the effect of a clouding of the conscious mind, but as an intentional suicide carried out with unconscious intention, masquerading as an accident. I was supported in this opinion by what Fräulein Z. had said about her relations, both earlier, when she did not know me, and later, as also expressed to me up to those last days – all to be understood as arising from the loss of her first fiancé, whom nothing could replace in her eyes.'

9. Hermann Heyermans, *Schetsen van Samuel Falkland*, 18th bundle, Amsterdam, H. J. W. Becht, 1914.

IX

Symptomatic and Fortuitous Actions

The actions described up to this point, in which we found an unconscious intention carried out, manifested themselves as disturbances to other, intentional actions, and took cover behind the excuse of clumsiness. The fortuitous actions to be discussed now are distinguished from inadvertent actions only in not requiring any conscious intention to support them, and thus needing no excuse. They stand alone, and are tolerated because we do not assume that there is any purpose or intention behind them. They are performed 'unthinkingly', 'purely by chance', 'for something to do with one's hands', and we count on such remarks to nip any inquiry into the significance of these actions in the bud. Since they no longer claim the excuse of clumsiness, they must fulfil certain conditions in order to enjoy their exceptional position: they must be *unobtrusive*, and their effects must be minor.

I have collected a large number of such fortuitous actions from my own studies and those of others, and after thorough study of the various examples I think they ought rather to be termed *symptomatic actions*. They express something that passes unsuspected even by the person executing them, and which he does not as a rule intend to impart, but to keep to himself. They therefore act as symptoms, just like all the other phenomena considered in this work so far.

The richest yield of such fortuitous or symptomatic actions, however, is to be found in the psychoanalytic treatment of neurotics, and I cannot resist taking two illustrations from that field to illustrate how wide and subtle is the determination of these little incidents, arising from unconscious ideas. In fact the borderline between symptomatic and inadvertent actions is so blurred that I could quite well have placed these examples in the previous section.

1) A young woman told me during our session about something that had occurred to her: as she was cutting her nails the day before, she had 'cut into the flesh while trying to remove the soft cuticle at the base of the nail'. This seemed so trivial that I wondered, in surprise, why she had remembered and mentioned it at all, and I began to suspect that we were dealing with a symptomatic action. Sure enough, it was her ring finger that suffered this little accident: the finger on which a wedding ring is worn. Furthermore, it had happened on her wedding anniversary, which gave the injury to the cuticle a very distinct and easily divined meaning. She told me at the same time about a dream referring to her husband's clumsiness and her own lack of sexual feeling in her marriage. But why did she hurt herself on the ring finger of her left hand, since she would usually have worn a wedding ring on the right hand? Her husband is a lawyer, a doctor of law [German: *Doktor der Rechte, Recht* meaning both 'law' and 'right'] and as a girl she had been secretly attracted to a doctor of medicine (described jocularly as a *Doktor der Linke* [doctor on the left-hand side]). And marriage on the left hand [a partnership without legal basis] has its own specific meaning.

2) An unmarried young lady told me: 'Yesterday, quite unintentionally, I tore a hundred-gulden note in half and gave one of the halves to a lady who was visiting me. Would you call that a symptomatic action too?' Closer inquiry revealed the following details. Let us take the hundred-gulden note first: the young woman devoted some of her time and her means to charitable works. She and another lady were financing the upbringing of an orphan child. The hundred gulden had been this other lady's contribution, which she put into an envelope when it arrived and placed temporarily on her desk.

The visitor she had mentioned was a distinguished lady whom she assisted in another charitable project, and who wanted to make a note of the names of people to whom they might apply for support. There was no piece of paper ready to hand, so my patient picked up the envelope on her desk and tore it in half without stopping to think what was in it, keeping one half herself so as to have a copy of the list of names and giving the other to her visitor. Notice the harmless nature of this action, inexpedient as it was, since as everyone knows a hundred-gulden note does not lose its value if it is torn, so long as the torn pieces can be reassembled complete. The importance of the names on the piece of paper guaranteed that my patient's visitor would not throw it away, and similarly there was no doubt that she would return its valuable contents as soon as she realized what they were.

But what unconscious idea did this chance action, resulting from forgetfulness, actually express? My patient's visitor approved of the treatment I was giving her, in fact it was she who had recommended me to her in the past, and I believe that my patient felt she owed her gratitude for her advice. Was the half of the hundred-gulden note meant to represent a kind of fee for her good offices? No, that would still be odd.

But there was more to it than that. A day before, a woman intermediary of quite a different kind had asked a relation of my patient whether she, my patient, would like to make the acquaintance of a certain gentleman, and in the morning, a few hours before the other lady visited her, the suitor's letter pleading his cause had arrived and had aroused much mirth. When her visitor opened the conversation by asking after her health, my patient may well have thought: 'Yes, you recommended me the right doctor, but I'd be even more grateful if you could help me to find the right husband' ('and a child', an idea concealed behind that of a husband). This repressed idea made her merge the two intermediaries into one, and she gave her present visitor the fee that, in her imagination, she was prepared to give the other woman. It is an interpretation which carries even more conviction when I add that I had been telling my patient about such fortuitous or symptomatic actions only the evening before – and she took the first opportunity to produce something along the same lines.

One could divide occurrences of fortuitous or symptomatic actions, which are very frequent, into various categories according to whether they are customary, regular in certain circumstances, or occur in isolation. The first kind (like playing with a watch-chain, twirling a moustache, and so on), which may almost look like personal habits, are close to the many kinds of nervous tics and should probably be studied in connection with them. Among the second group I would classify playing with a stick one is holding, doodling with a pencil in one's hand, chinking coins in the pocket, kneading crumbs and other plastic substances, fiddling with one's clothes in a number of ways, and many other such actions. Psychic treatment commonly shows that sense and meaning, which have been denied any other expression, are concealed beneath these playful activities. Usually the person concerned has no idea that he is doing anything of the kind or that he has made certain modifications to his usual idle actions, and he fails to notice the effects. He will not, for instance, hear the sound he makes chinking coins, and he will be surprised and incredulous if it is pointed out to him. Similarly, fiddling with one's clothing, which often passes unnoticed, is significant and worthy of a doctor's attention. Any change of one's usual appearance, any small act of negligence – for instance a button left undone – every exposure means something which the person wearing that clothing does not want to say directly, indeed generally does not intend to say at all. The interpretation of these little fortuitous actions and the evidence for its validity will always emerge clearly enough from circumstances mentioned during the session, from the subject under discussion itself, and from the ideas produced when the patient's attention is directed to something that apparently happened by chance. But the context is such that I shall refrain from supporting my theories here by citing and analysing examples. I mention these things, however, because I believe they do have the same significance in normal people as in my neurotic patients.

And I cannot refrain from giving at least one example that shows how closely a symptomatic action habitually performed may be linked to the most intimate and important factors in a healthy person's life:[1]

'As Professor Freud has taught us, symbolism plays a greater part in the childhood of normal people than was expected from earlier psychoanalytical studies; in this respect the following short analysis may be of some interest, in particular because of its medical insights.

'A doctor on rearranging his furniture in a new house came upon an old-fashioned, straight, wooden stethoscope, and, after pausing to decide where he should put it, was impelled to place it on the side of his writing-desk in such a position that it stood exactly between his chair and the one reserved for his patients. The act in itself was certainly odd, for in the first place the straight stethoscope served no purpose, as he invariably used a binaural one; and in the second place all his medical apparatus and instruments were always kept in drawers, with the sole exception of this one. However, he gave no thought at all to the matter until one day it was brought to his notice by a patient, who had never seen a wooden stethoscope, asking him what it was. On being told, she asked why he kept it just there; he answered in an off-hand way that that place was as good as any other. This started him thinking, however, and he wondered whether there had been any unconscious motive in his action. Being interested in the psycho-analytic method he asked me to investigate the matter.

'The first memory that occurred to him was the fact that when a student of medicine he had been struck by the habit his hospital interne had of always carrying a wooden stethoscope on his ward visits, although he never used it. He greatly admired this interne, and was much attached to him. Later on, when he himself became an interne, he contracted the same habit, and would feel very uncomfortable if by mistake he left his room without having the instrument to swing in his hand. The aimlessness of the habit was shewn, not only in the fact that the only stethoscope he ever used was a binaural one, which he carried in his pocket, but also in that it was continued when he was a surgical interne and never needed a stethoscope at all.

'From this it was evident that the idea of the instrument in question had in some way or other become invested with a greater psychical significance than normally belongs to it [. . .] I will forestall the rest of the analysis by saying what this secondary idea was – namely, a phallic one [. . .]

'Then came a number of childhood memories relating to his family doctor. He had been strongly attached to this doctor as a child, and during the analysis long-buried memories were recovered of a double phantasy he had in his fourth year concerning the birth of a younger sister – namely, that she was the child (1) of himself and his mother, the father being relegated to the background, and (2) of the doctor and himself; in this he thus played both a masculine and feminine part [. . .]

'He had had his chest repeatedly examined by the doctor at the age of six, and distinctly recollected the voluptuous sensation of feeling the latter's head near him pressing the wooden stethoscope into his chest, and of the rhythmic to-and-fro respiratory movement of his breathing. He had been struck by the doctor's habit of carrying his stethoscope inside his hat; he found it interesting that the doctor should carry his chief instrument concealed about his person, always handy when he went to see patients, and that he only had to take off his hat (i.e., part of his clothing), and "pull it out". At the age of eight he was impressed by being told by an older boy that it was the doctor's custom to get into bed with his women patients. It is certain that the doctor, who was young and handsome, was extremely popular among the women of the neighbourhood, including the subject's own mother. The doctor and his "instrument" were therefore the objects of great interest throughout his boyhood.

'It is probable that, as in many other cases, unconscious identification with the family doctor had been a main motive in determining the subject's choice of profession. It was here doubly conditioned, (1) by the superiority of the doctor on certain interesting occasions to the father, of whom the subject was very jealous, and (2) by the doctor's knowledge of forbidden topics and his opportunities for illicit indulgence. The subject admitted that he had on several occasions experienced erotic temptations in regard to his women patients; he had twice fallen in love with one, and finally had married one.

'The next memory was of a dream already mentioned in print elsewhere,[2] plainly of a homosexual-masochistic nature; in it a man, who proved to be a replacement-figure of the family doctor, attacked the subject with a "sword" [. . .] The thought of a sword reminded the subject of the passage in the "Nibelung Saga", where Sigurd sleeps with his naked sword (*Gram*) between himself and Brunhilda, an incident that had always greatly struck his imagination.

'The meaning of the symptomatic act now at last became clear. The subject had placed his wooden stethoscope between himself and his patients, just as Sigurd had placed his sword (an equivalent symbol) between him and the maiden he was not to touch. The act was a compromise-formation; it served both to gratify in his imagination the repressed wish to enter into nearer relations with an attractive patient (interposition of phallus), and at the same time to remind him that this wish was not to become a reality (interposition of sword). It was, so to speak, a charm against yielding to temptation.

'I would add that a passage from Lord Lytton's *Richelieu* had made a great impression on the boy:

> '"Beneath the rule of men entirely great
> The pen is mightier than the sword"[3],

that he had become a prolific writer, and uses an unusually large fountain pen. When I asked him why he needed it, he characteristically replied: "I have so much to say."

'This analysis reminds us once again what far-reaching insights into mental life "innocent" and "pointless" actions afford us, and how early in life a tendency to symbolization is developed.'

I can add, from my own psychotherapeutic experience, an account of a case in which a hand made an eloquent statement simply by playing with some breadcrumbs. My patient was a boy of not quite thirteen, who had been severely hysterical for almost two years and whom I finally took into psychoanalytical treatment. He had spent a good deal of time in a spa resort, but showed no improvement. I set out by assuming that he must have had sexual experiences and was troubled by sexual matters, which is natural for a lad of his age; however, I was careful not to help him out by offering explanations, since I wanted to put my assumptions to the test. Inevitably, I was curious to see just how the facts I was seeking would emerge in him. One day I noticed him rolling something about in the fingers of his right hand, putting his hand in his pocket, where he went on playing with it, bringing it out again, and so on. I did not ask what he had there, but he showed me when he suddenly opened out his hand. It contained some breadcrumbs kneaded together into a lump. At our next session he brought another such lump with him, and while we were talking formed it into little model figures with extraordinary speed, keeping his eyes closed. The figures attracted my interest. They were undoubtedly little men, each with a head, two arms and two legs, like the most primitive of prehistoric idols, and with a protrusion between the two legs, which he pulled out into a long point. No sooner was the little man finished than he kneaded it together again; later he left one alone but pulled the dough out into similar protrusions on the back and in other places, to hide the significance of the first one. I wanted to show him that I understood, but without giving him the excuse of being able to say he had nothing at all in mind while he was making his little men. With this in view, I suddenly asked if he remembered the story of the Roman king who answered his son's envoy in mime in his garden. The boy claimed not to remember it, although he must have heard the tale much more recently than I had. He asked if it was the story of the answer written on a slave's shaven skull. No, I said, that one was out of Greek history, and I told him the Roman story: King Tarquinius Superbus sent his son Sextus to take soundings in secret in an enemy city of Latium. The son, having found adherents there, sent the king a messenger asking what to do next. The king did not answer in words, but went into his garden, got the messenger to repeat the question, and struck off the largest and finest of the poppy heads growing there in silence. The messenger could tell Sextus no more than this. But Sextus understood his father, and realized that he was instructed to have the most prominent citizens assassinated.

As I was talking the boy stopped kneading his figure, and when I was telling him about the king's mimed answer in the garden he tore the head off his little man with a lightning movement as soon as I reached the words 'struck off . . . in silence'. He had understood what I meant, and he knew that I understood him. Now I could ask him direct questions, give him the information he needed, and we very soon put an end to his neurosis.

Those symptomatic actions that can be observed in almost inexhaustible profusion in both the healthy and the sick deserve our interest for several reasons. They often give the doctor valuable help in finding his way in new or unfamiliar circumstances, and they are extremely revealing to the observer of human nature, sometimes uncovering even more than he wanted to know. Anyone with a good understanding of them must sometimes feel like King Solomon, said in oriental legend to know the language of animals. One day I was to give a medical examination to a young man previously unknown to me in his mother's house. When he came to meet me I noticed a large stain of egg white on his trousers, identifiable by its character-istically clear-cut rim. After a moment's embarrassment, the young man apologized by saying he had been eating a raw egg to ease his hoarse voice, and some of the slippery egg white must have been spilt on his clothing. By way of confirmation, he pointed to the eggshell still lying on a little plate in the room. This was an innocuous enough explanation of the suspect stain, but when his mother had left us alone together I thanked him for making my diagnosis so much easier, and I immediately took his admission that he suffered from the ills attendant on masturbation as the starting-point of our conversation. On another occasion I was visiting a lady as rich as she was avaricious and foolish, who used to make her doctor work his way through a host of complaints before he could get to the simple reason for her condition. When I arrived she was sitting at a small table building silver gulden into little piles, and as she rose she knocked some of the coins on the floor. Helping her to pick them up, I soon interrupted her description of her wretched state of health, and asked: 'Dear me, has your distinguished son-in-law wormed so much money out of you?' She denied the very idea bitterly, only to launch soon afterwards into the pathetic tale of the anxiety her son-in-law's extravagance gave her. She did not call me in again; it cannot be said that those who are told the meaning of their symptomatic actions always like one for it.

Another 'confession' conveyed by a slip is reported by Dr J. E. G.

van Emden of The Hague: 'When I was paying the bill in a small Berlin restaurant the waiter claimed that the price of a certain dish had risen by ten pfennigs because of the war; when I wondered why the menu did not show this price rise he said it must have been left off by mistake, but he could assure me that he was right! As he was taking my payment he fumbled with the coins and let a ten-pfennig coin fall on the table, as if for me!

' "Well," I said, "now I know for certain that you've overcharged me. Do you want me to inquire at the cash desk?"

' "If you'd be good enough to wait a moment . . ." and off he went.

'Naturally I allowed him his face-saving retreat, and a couple of minutes later, when he apologized and said that for some mysterious reason he must have mixed up one dish with another, I gave him the ten pfennigs to reward him for his contribution to the psycho-pathology of everyday life.'

Anyone watching his fellow men eating will notice some very interesting and instructive symptomatic actions.

Dr Hanns Sachs gives us the following account:

'I happened to be present when two of my family, an elderly married couple, were eating their evening meal. The lady had a delicate stomach and was obliged to stick to a very strict diet. A helping of roast meat had just been put in front of the husband, and he asked his wife, who was not allowed to share this dish, to pass the mustard. His wife opened the sideboard, reached into it, and put her little bottle of digestive drops on the table in front of her husband. Of course the barrel-shaped mustard jar was not in the least like the bottle of digestive drops, so there was no similarity to explain the mistake, but the wife noticed what she had done only when her husband pointed it out to her with a smile. The meaning of that particular symptomatic action needs no explanation.'

I owe an excellent example of this kind, very ingeniously explained by the observer himself, to Dr Bernhard Dattner of Vienna:

'I was sitting in a restaurant having lunch with my colleague from the department of philosophy, Dr H. He was talking about the trials and tribulations of academics with only probationary status, and mentioned in passing that before the end of his studies he had been secretary to the Chilean ambassador, or rather the Chilean plenipotentiary minister extraordinary. "But then the minister was moved elsewhere, and I did not introduce myself to his successor." As he said this last sentence he carried a piece of tart to his mouth, but let it drop off the fork as if out of clumsiness. I immediately saw the hidden meaning of this symptomatic action, and said as if casually to my colleague, who was not familiar with psychoanalysis: "Well, you let a choice morsel go there." Failing to notice that my remark could equally well apply to his symptomatic action he repeated, in a curiously attractive and surprising lively tone, as if I had literally taken the words out of his mouth, exactly what I had just said: "Yes, that was indeed a choice morsel I allowed to go." He then relieved his feelings by giving me an exhaustive account of the awkwardness that had lost him his well-paid post.

'Further light is cast on his symptomatic action by the fact that my colleague felt some scruples in telling me about his straitened finances, since I am not a close friend, and that the thought coming to the forefront of his mind thus emerged in the form of a symptomatic action symbolically expressing what ought to have been hidden, helping the speaker's unconscious to relieve his feelings.'

Dr B. Dattner tells us that: 'A colleague of mine was visiting a girl he had known and been very fond of in his youth for the first time since her marriage. He told me about this visit, saying that while he had meant to stay with her for only a short time he had not stuck to this intention, which surprised him. Then he told me about a curious slip he had made while he was there. His friend's husband, who took part in the conversation, looked round for a box of matches, which had certainly been on the table when my colleague arrived. He too searched his clothing to see if he might have "picked it up" by mistake, but in vain. [In German the pronoun for 'it' here is *sie*, agreeing with the gender of *die Zündhölzchenschachtel*, 'matchbox', and thus could by inference mean 'her'.] Some time later he actually did find the box in his pocket, and noticed that there was only a single match left in it. A few days later a dream in which the matchbox symbol figured prominently, together with the friend of my colleague's youth, confirmed my explanation that his

193

symptomatic action found him trying to reclaim his right of priority and demonstrate that he had sole possession of the lady (there was only one match in the box).'

Dr Hanns Sachs describes the following incident: 'Our maidservant is particularly fond of eating a certain tart – a fact that admits of no doubt, for it is the only dish which she always, without exception, makes well. One Sunday she was going to serve us this tart, put it on the sideboard, took the used plates and cutlery from the previous course and stacked them on the tray on which she had carried in the tart. She then put the tart back on the tray too on top of the pile of plates, instead of placing it on the table in front of us, and bore it off back into the kitchen. At first we thought she had seen something about the tart that needed to be put right, but when she failed to reappear my wife rang the bell and asked, "Betty, what happened to the tart?" "What do you mean?" asked the maid, at a loss. We had to point out that she had taken the tart away with her; she had loaded it on the tray, taken it out and put it down in the kitchen again "without noticing". Next day, when we were about to eat what remained of the tart, my wife remarked that all we had left of it the day before was still there, so the maid had refrained from eating the slice of her favourite dish which was properly hers. When asked why she said, in some embarrassment, that she didn't feel like it. There are clear signs of an infantile attitude on both occasions; first the child-like greed that does not want to share the object of its desires with anyone else, then the equally childlike and defiant reaction: if you won't let me have it then you can just keep it, I don't want any now.'

Those fortuitous or symptomatic actions that occur in a marriage are often of very considerable significance, and could persuade people who know nothing about the psychology of the unconscious mind to believe in omens. It is not a good start for a young wife to lose her wedding ring on her honeymoon, although in most such cases it has just been mislaid and is soon found again. I know a lady now divorced from her husband who would often sign documents relating to the management of her property with her maiden name, for some years before she did in fact revert to it. I was once visiting a young married couple and heard the young wife, laughing, tell the tale of a recent experience of hers: the day after she came home from a journey, she had visited her unmarried sister, as she habitually did, to go shopping while her husband went out to work. She had suddenly seen a gentleman on the other side of the street, nudged her sister, and said: 'Oh, look, there's Herr L.' She had forgotten that Herr L. had actually been her husband for some weeks. A shiver ran down my spine at this tale, but I did not venture to draw conclusions. I remembered the little incident only years later, when the marriage had come to an unhappy end.

I take the following observation, which could equally well have been included in the chapter on 'Forgetfulness', from the interesting works of A. Maeder,[4] published in French in Zurich.

'Une dame nous racontait récemment qu'elle avait oublié d'essayer sa robe de noce et s'en souvint la veille du mariage à huit heures du soir, la couturière désespérait de voir sa cliente. Ce détail suffit à montrer que la fiancée ne se sentait pas très heureuse de porter une robe d'épouse, elle cherchait à oublier cette représentation pénible. Elle est aujourd'hui . . . divorcée [A lady recently told us that she had forgotten to try on her wedding dress, and remembered only at eight in the evening on the day before her marriage, by which time the dressmaker despaired of seeing her client. This detail was quite enough to show that the fiancée was not very happy about wearing a wedding dress, and was trying to forget this painful idea. Today . . . she is divorced].'

A friend who had learnt to pay attention to meaningful signs told me that the great Eleonora Duse introduced a symptomatic action into one of her roles, clearly illustrating what a consummate actress she was. The play was a drama of adultery; Duse's character had just quarrelled with her husband, and was now standing to one side in thought before her would-be seducer approached. In this brief pause she played with the wedding ring on her finger, taking it off, putting it on again, then taking it off once more. She was now ready for the other man.

Here I will add some remarks by T. Reik about other symptomatic actions involving rings.

'We know about the symptomatic actions performed by married people when they take off a wedding ring and put it on again. My colleague M. described a whole series of similar symptomatic actions. He had been given a ring as a present by a girl whom he loved, and who told him that if he lost it she would know he had stopped loving her. After that he felt increasingly anxious about losing the ring. When he took it off now and then, for instance to wash his hands, he regularly mislaid it and often had to search for a long time before finding it again. When he put an envelope into the letterbox he could not help fearing that his ring might be pulled off by the edges of the slot, and once he did in fact post a letter so clumsily that his ring fell into the box. The letter concerned on this occasion was a farewell to a former lover, he felt guilty about her – and at the same time his desire for her was reawakened, conflicting with his feelings for the present object of his affections' (*Internationale Zeitschrift für Psychologie* III, 1915).

Yet again, the theme of a ring shows how difficult it is for a psychoanalyst to discover any new insight that has not already been clear to a creative writer before him. In Fontane's novel *Vor der Sturm* [*Before the Storm*] there is a game of forfeits in which Councillor of Justice Turgany says: 'Believe it or not, ladies, forfeits are a clue to the deepest secrets of human nature.' One of the examples he gives to prove his claim is of special interest: 'I remember a professor's wife who showed some middle-aged spread, and who kept pulling her wedding ring off her finger. You must allow me to refrain from describing the marital happiness of that household.' He then continues: 'There was a gentleman in the same company who never tired of dropping his English pocket-knife into the ladies' laps – it had ten blades, a corkscrew and a flint and steel. At last, after tearing rents in several silk gowns and in the face of general and horrified outcry, that monstrosity of a knife disappeared.'

It is not surprising that an object of such great symbolic significance as a ring can also feature in slips that mean something but do not denote an erotic link, as with a wedding or engagement ring. Dr M. Kardos has given me the following example of such an incident: 'Several years ago a much younger man attached himself to me;

he shared my intellectual interests, and in some ways he stood in the same relation to me as a pupil to his teacher. On a certain occasion I had given him a ring, which had caused him to make certain slips or perform a symptomatic action several times already, whenever something in our relationship displeased him. He recently told me the following particularly neat case, which is easily interpreted: he had made some excuse for missing a weekly meeting where he regularly used to see and talk to me, because he had an appointment with a young lady which was a more attractive prospect. Next morning he noticed, but only long after leaving home, that the ring was not on his finger. He thought no more of it, assuming that he had left the ring behind on the bedside table where he placed it every evening, and would find it there when he got home again. And as soon as he returned he did look for it, but in vain; so now, equally unsuccessfully, he began searching the whole room. At last it struck him that the ring had been lying on the bedside table, just where he had left it at night for over a year, beside a small knife, which he used to put in his waistcoat pocket, and he began to think that he might "absent-mindedly" have put away the ring with the knife. He felt inside the pocket, and sure enough found the ring he was looking for. Proverbially, a man puts his wedding ring in his waistcoat pocket when he is planning to be unfaithful to the woman who gave it to him. His guilty conscience first made my friend punish himself ("You don't deserve to wear this ring any more"), and second to confess his unfaithfulness, although merely in the form of a slip to which there were no witnesses. Only in the circuitous process of giving an account of the outcome – which could easily be foreseen – did he admit to the little act of "unfaithfulness" that he had committed.'

I also know of a gentleman getting on in years who married a very young girl, and was going to spend the wedding night in a city hotel before going away on honeymoon. No sooner did the couple arrive at the hotel than he realized with alarm that his wallet was missing. It contained the entire sum of money intended for the honeymoon trip, and he had either mislaid or lost it. He managed to get in touch with his manservant by telephone; the manservant found the missing wallet in the coat the bridegroom had been wearing for the wedding and brought it round to the hotel, where the husband who had thus embarked on marriage penniless, with nothing to offer his bride, was waiting. He was therefore able to set out on his honeymoon with his young wife next morning, but on the wedding night itself, just as his fears had predicted, he had 'nothing to offer her'.

It is comforting to think that our human way of 'losing' things is more of a symptomatic action than we divine, and is therefore not unwelcome to the loser's secret intentions. Often it conveys no more than a low opinion or secret dislike of the lost object or the person from whom it came. Alternatively, the inclination to lose something has been transferred to the object concerned from other and more important items, through a symbolic train of thought. Losing something valuable often serves to express all kinds of emotional impulses; the loss may symbolically represent a suppressed idea, and thus repeats a warning that we would rather not hear, but above all it may be a sacrifice to those dark powers of fate which we still feel we should propitiate.

Here are just a few examples to illustrate my remarks above about losing things:

From Dr B. Dattner: 'A colleague told me that he had unexpectedly lost his Penkala pencil, which he had had for over two years. He thought a lot of it because it was such a good one. Analysis showed that the previous day my colleague had received a distinctly unpleasant letter from his brother-in-law, which concluded: "I do not have the time or inclination just now to support your light-minded and idle conduct." The emotion stirred up by this letter was so strong that next day my colleague promptly sacrificed his Penkala pencil, *a present from his brother-in-law*, to avoid having to feel too grateful to him.'

A lady I knew refrained, for understandable reasons, from going to the theatre while she was in mourning for her old mother. There were only a few days left before the formal year's mourning came to an end, and she let some friends persuade her to accept a ticket for a particularly interesting theatrical performance. When she reached the theatre she discovered that she had lost the ticket, and thought later that she must have thrown it away with her tram ticket as she got out of the vehicle. But this same lady boasts of never carelessly losing anything.

One must assume, therefore, that another occasion on which she lost something was also well motivated.

On arriving at a spa resort, she decided to visit a boarding house where she had stayed on an earlier occasion. She was welcomed as an old friend, well entertained, and when she wanted to pay for her meal she was told that she must consider herself a guest, although she did not feel very happy about that. She was allowed, however, to leave a tip for the waitress, so she opened her purse to put a one-mark note on the table. That evening the manservant from the boarding house came round with a five-mark note that had been found under the table, and that the owner of the boarding house thought must belong to her. It had fallen out of her purse when she took out the waitress's tip – she was probably trying to pay her bill after all.

Otto Rank has written a paper of some length[5] casting light on the sacrificial attitude behind such actions, and their more profound motivation, with the aid of the analysis of dreams.[6] Interestingly, he adds that on occasion not only losing but also *finding* something seems to be predetermined. His own observations, which I quote here, show how we are to understand this. Obviously, when something is lost its nature is already known, whereas when something is found, its nature has to be identified first.

'A young girl who was financially dependent on her parents saw and wanted to buy an inexpensive piece of jewellery. She asked the price of the item in the shop, and was sorry to learn that it cost more than her savings. Yet the sum of only two crowns prevented her from enjoying this small pleasure. She was walking home in downcast mood through the hurry and bustle of the city streets during the evening. In one of the busiest squares, and although according to her own account of it she was deep in thought, she suddenly realized there was a little piece of paper lying on the ground; she had just passed it by without noticing it. She turned back, picked it up, and saw to her surprise that it was a folded two-crown note. Fate has put this in my way so that I can buy the piece of jewellery I saw, she told herself, happily turning back to put the idea into practice. At the same moment, however, she told herself not to, since the money she had found was "lucky money", which one is not supposed to spend.

'The small amount of analysis required to understand this "fortuitous action" could probably be gleaned from the situation, even without information provided by the girl herself. Among the thoughts occupying her on her way home, her poverty and her material restrictions were probably to the forefront of her mind, and we may suspect that they took the form of wish-fulfilment as she imagined being liberated from her difficult circumstances. How she could most easily come by the sum of money she needed is an idea that will not have been very far from her mind, interested as it was in satisfying her modest wish, and that idea will have suggested the simple solution of finding it. In this way her unconscious (or pre-conscious) mind was already open to the idea of "finding" the money, even if she was not to become fully conscious of it because of other claims on her attention (she was "deep in thought"). On the basis of the analysis of similar cases, we may even say that an *unconscious* "readiness to search" can more easily lead to success than a conscious and attentive decision to do so. It would be difficult to find any other explanation of the way in which this one person, out of all the many hundreds of people in the street, could make the find that surprised her so much, particularly as the dim street-lighting in the evening and the dense crowds did not favour her chances. The strong extent to which this unconscious or pre-conscious readiness actually existed is evident from the curious fact that even after making her find, that is, after her readiness to find something had already become superfluous, and was certainly no longer in her conscious mind, the girl also found a handkerchief in a dark and isolated place in a suburban street as she continued on her way home.'[7]

It must be said that it is such symptomatic actions that often provide the best access to an understanding of the intimate mental life of human beings.

Of the kinds of fortuitous actions that occur in isolation, I will choose an example which allowed deeper interpretation even without analysis, is a cogent illustration of the conditions in which such symptoms can be very inconspicuously produced, and to which I may add a note of practical significance. While I was away on a summer holiday I happened to have to wait some days in a certain place for my travelling companion to arrive. During this time I made the acquaintance of a young man who also seemed to be feeling lonely and was very ready to keep me company. As we were staying in the same hotel, we easily fell into the habit of eating all our meals together and going for walks with each other. On the afternoon of the third day, my new friend suddenly told me that he was expecting his wife to arrive by express train that evening. This aroused my psychological interest, for that morning I had already noticed that my companion had declined my suggestion of a longer walk, and while we were out on our little stroll he had been disinclined to take a certain path, saying that it was too steep and dangerous. On our walk that afternoon he suddenly told me I must be hungry, and said I wasn't to postpone my evening meal on his account; he would take his own with his wife after her arrival. I understood the hint and sat down at the supper table while he went to the station. Next morning we met in the hotel lobby. He introduced his wife to me, and added: 'I hope you'll join us for breakfast?' I had a small purchase to make in the next street, and told them I would be back soon. When I entered the breakfast room I saw the couple both sitting on the same side of a little table in the window. There was only one chair on the opposite side of the table, but the man's large, heavy loden coat was draped over the back of it, covering the seat. I had a very good idea of the reason for this arrangement of his coat, which was certainly not intentional but was all the more eloquent for that; it said: there's no room here, you're superfluous to requirements now. The man did not notice me standing by the table, unable to sit down, but the lady did, and she immediately nudged her husband and whispered: 'Look, you've taken the gentleman's seat.'

In this and similar incidents, I have concluded that actions unintentionally performed are bound to be a source of misunderstanding in human intercourse. The perpetrator, who has no idea that there is any intention linked to them, does not credit himself with one, nor does he consider himself responsible for them. The second person concerned, however, since he regularly draws conclusions about the intentions and attitudes of the first from such actions, knows more about that first person's psychic processes than he is ready to admit himself or thinks he has imparted. He will be indignant if faced with any such conclusions made on the basis of his symptomatic actions, declaring them groundless, since he was unaware of having any intention to carry them out, and he will complain that the second person misunderstands him. Such misunderstandings, strictly speaking, actually arise from too great and too subtle a process of understanding. The more 'edgy' two people are, the more likely they are to give each other occasion for disagreements, each denying his own responsibility for them while taking it as proven for the other party. This may well be the penalty we pay for our inner dishonesty in allowing ourselves to express certain ideas only through the devices of forgetfulness, inadvertent and unintentional actions, ideas that, even if we cannot control them, we would do better to admit to ourselves and to others. In general, it may be said that everyone is always psychoanalysing his fellow men, and as a consequence learns to know them better than they know themselves. The way to carrying out the famous injunction to *know thyself* is through studying our own apparently fortuitous actions and omissions.

Of all the creative writers who have sometimes expressed their opinions of such small symptomatic actions and slips, or have used them in some way in their work, none has recognized their secret nature so clearly or described them with such uncanny faithfulness as Strindberg – whose brilliant perception, however, rested on his own profound psychic abnormality. Dr Karl Weiss of Vienna has drawn our attention to the following passage in one of his works (*Internationale Zeitschrift für Psychoanalyse* I, 1913, p. 268):

'After a while the count did arrive, and went calmly up to Esther as if he had arranged a rendezvous with her.

' "Have you been waiting long?" he asked, in a quiet voice.

' "Six months, as you know," replied Esther. "But didn't you see me yesterday?"

' "Why, yes, in the tram, and I looked into your eyes and felt as if I were speaking to you."

' "A great deal has 'happened' since last time."

' "Yes, I thought it was all over between us."

' "Why?"

' "All the little presents you had given me broke in a most mysterious way. But noticing such things is nothing new."

' "Why, goodness me! Now that you say so, I remember a whole series of incidents which I took for chance. While we were on good terms my grandmother once gave me a pair of pince-nez. They were made of polished rock crystal and very useful when I was carrying out post-mortems – in fact they were wonderful, and I looked after them carefully. One day I quarrelled with the old lady, and she was cross with me. Next time I was performing a post-mortem the lenses fell right out. I thought the pince-nez were simply broken and sent them off to be repaired, but it was no use, they would not work for me, so I put them away in a drawer and lost track of them."

' "Well, think of that! How strange that anything to do with the eyes is so particularly sensitive! I had been given a pair of opera glasses by a friend; they suited my eyes so well that it was a pleasure to use them. Then my friend and I fell out. You know how these things happen, for no obvious reason; it seems as if one just can't agree. Next time I was going to use the opera glasses I couldn't see clearly through them: the shank was too short and I saw two images instead of one. I hardly need to tell you that the shaft was no shorter than before, nor had the distance of the lenses from my eyes increased! Peculiar things like this happen all the time, although the unobservant don't notice them. So what is the explanation? Why, *the psychic force of hatred must be greater than we think*. Oh, and that ring you gave me lost its stone and absolutely refuses to be repaired. So – do you want to break with me now?" ' (*The Gothic Rooms*).

Psychoanalysts must also give precedence to literary writers in the field of symptomatic actions. We can only repeat what they said long ago. Herr Wilhelm Stross has pointed out to me the following passage in the famous humorous novel *Tristram Shandy* (part VI, chapter V):

'. . . and I am not at all surprised that Gregory of Nazianzum, upon observing the hasty and untoward gestures of Julian, should foretell he would one day become an apostate; or that St Ambrose should turn his amnuensis out of doors, because of an indecent motion of his head, which went backwards and forwards like a flail; – or that Democritus should conceive Protagoras to be a scholar, from seeing him bind up a faggot, and thrusting, as he did it, the small twigs inwards. – There are a thousand unnoticed openings, continued my father, which let a penetrating eye at once into a man's soul; and I maintain it, added he, that a man of sense does not lay down his hat in coming into a room, – or take it up in going out of it, but something escapes, which discovers him.'

Here is a small collection from the many kinds of symptomatic actions observed in both healthy people and neurotics:

An older colleague, who does not like losing at cards, one evening lost quite a large sum of money, and paid it without a murmur but in a noticeably muted frame of mind. When he had gone home he turned out to have left behind almost everything he had with him: his glasses, his cigar case and his handkerchief. Translated into words, his action meant: well, you thieves, you've well and truly fleeced me.

A man who suffered from occasional sexual impotence because his childhood relationship with his mother had been so close said he used to mark his writings and drawings with an S, the initial of her name. He could not bear letters from home to be in contact with other and less sacrosanct correspondence on his desk, and was obliged to keep them somewhere else.

A young lady suddenly opened the door of the consulting room where the previous patient was still sitting. She apologized, excusing herself on the grounds of 'thoughtlessness', but it soon turned out that she was showing the same kind of curiosity which had led her to burst into her parents' bedroom in the past.

Girls who are proud of their beautiful hair arrange their combs and hairpins so skilfully that their hair is bound to come down in the middle of a conversation.

Many men will scatter small change out of their trouser pockets while they are lying down during their treatment, thus symbolically paying the fee for the session according to their own estimate of its value.

Patients who forget something they have brought with them when visiting a doctor – pince-nez, gloves, a wallet – are suggesting that it is hard to tear themselves away and that they want to come back soon. E. Jones has said: 'One can almost measure the success with which a physician is practising psychotherapy, for instance by the size of the collection of umbrellas, handkerchiefs, purses, and so on, that he could make in a month.'

The smallest actions habitually and inconspicuously performed, for instance winding up one's watch before going to sleep, putting out the light before leaving the room, and so forth, are sometimes prone to disruptions that unmistakably illustrate the influence of unconscious complexes on what appear to be the most firmly established of habits. Maeder writes in the journal *Coenobium* of a hospital doctor who had important business one evening in town, and decided to go out although he was on call and ought not really to have left the hospital. On coming back he was surprised to see his room lit up. He had forgotten to put the light out when he left, something that had never happened before. But he soon pinpointed the motive for his forgetfulness: the director of the hospital, who lived in the same building, would conclude from seeing his houseman's light on that he too was in the building.

A man with many anxieties who was sometimes subject to fits of depression told me that he regularly found his watch had run down in the morning if life had seemed to him too harsh and forbidding the evening before. Failing to wind his watch was a symbolic expression of his disinclination to face the coming day. Another man, not personally known to me, writes: 'When a hard blow of fate fell on me, life seemed so hostile that I felt I could not summon up the strength to live another day, and then I noticed that almost daily I forgot to wind my watch, something I had never been in the habit of forgetting before, when I regularly and unconsciously or almost mechanically did so before going to bed. Now I very seldom remembered to wind it, in fact only when I had some important project next day, or something was to happen in which I took a particular interest. Could that be a symptomatic action as well? I couldn't explain it to myself at all.'

Anyone who, like Jung (*Über die Psychologie der Dementia praecox*, 1907, p. 62) and Maeder ('Une voie nouvelle en psychologie – Freud et son école', *Coenobium*, Lugano 1909), takes the trouble to listen to the tunes people involuntarily hum to themselves, often without noticing, will regularly find some connection between the words to the tune being hummed and a subject preoccupying the person who hums it.

Subtler determination of the way in which we express our ideas in speaking or writing deserves close study. We generally believe that we can choose the words in which we clothe our ideas, or the image in which we cloak them. But closer observation shows that this choice is made for other reasons, and that a deeper and often unintentional sense shows faintly through in the form taken by the idea. The images and style that people use for preference seldom prove irrelevant to assessment of their characters, while other phrases often turn out to refer to a background subject which has taken strong hold on the speaker. There was a time when I often heard a man using the expression, in theoretical discussion: 'When something suddenly shoots through your mind [German: *Kopf*, 'head'],' when in fact I knew he had recently heard that a Russian bullet had passed right through the army cap his son was wearing on his head.

Notes

1. E. Jones, 'Beitrag zur Symbolik im Alltag' ['Symptomatic Acts'] (*Zentralblatt für Psychoanalyse* 1, 3, 1911).
2. 'Freud's Theory of Dreams', *American Journal of Psychology*, April 1910, p. 301, no. 7.

3. Cf. Oldham's 'I wear my pen as others do their sword.'

4. Alphonse Maeder, 'Contributions à la psychopathologie de la vie quotidienne', *Archives de Psychologie*, vol. VI, 1906.

5. 'Das Verlieren als Symptomhandlung' ['Losing Something as a Symptomatic Action'], *Zentralblatt für Psychoanalyse* I, 10/11.

6. Other accounts on this subject are to be found in the *Zentralblatt für Psychoanalyse* II, and the *Internationale Zeitschrift für Psychoanalyse* I, 1913.

7. *Internationale Zeitschrift für Psychoanalyse* III, 1915.

X

Making Mistakes

Making mistakes in remembering facts is to be distinguished from forgetfulness attended by a faulty memory in only one feature: we do not realize that we have made a mistake, but think we are right. The use of the term 'mistake', however, seems to depend on a different aspect of the phenomenon. We speak of 'making mistakes' instead of faulty memory when we want to emphasize the objective reality of the mental material we are reproducing, that is, when we want to remember something outside our own psychic lives, something which is capable of confirmation or refutation by other people's memories. In this sense, ignorance is the opposite of a mistaken memory.

In my book *The Interpretation of Dreams* (1900),[1] I was guilty of a series of falsifications of historical facts and indeed factual material in general, and became aware of them, to my own surprise, only after the publication of the book. On closer examination I found that they did not derive from my ignorance, but could be traced back to mistakes of memory which I could clear up by analysis.

1) On p. 266 [VI.G] of the first edition, I had said that Schiller's birthplace was the Hessian city of *Marburg*, a place name also found in Styria. This mistake comes in the analysis of a dream I had while travelling by night, from which I was woken when the guard called out the name of Marburg station. The content of the dream refers to a book by Schiller. In fact Schiller was born not in the university town of Marburg, but in *Marbach* in Swabia, as I am sure I have always known.

2) On p. 135 [V.B] I gave the name of *Hannibal's* father as *Hasdrubal*. I found this a particularly annoying mistake to have

made, but it did much to confirm my ideas of the way in which such mistakes occur. Few of the readers of the book will have known more about the history of the Barca family than the author himself, yet I put the wrong name down and let it pass through three sets of proofs. Hannibal's father was *Hamilcar Barca – Hasdrubal* was the name of Hannibal's brother, and also of his brother-in-law who preceded him as commander of the Carthaginian army.

3) On pp. 177 [V.D] and 370 [VII.F] I said that *Zeus* castrated his father Kronos and usurped his throne. By mistake I had shifted this grisly act one generation forward; in Greek mythology, it was *Kronos* who castrated his father *Uranus*.[2]

How can I explain the way in which my memory provided false information on these points, while as readers of the book can see for themselves it placed other material of a most obscure and unusual nature at my disposal? What is more, how could I have missed seeing the mistakes, as if afflicted by sudden blindness while I was carefully correcting three sets of proofs?

Goethe said of Lichtenberg: 'When he makes a joke, there is a problem behind it.' Something similar could be said of the passages from my book cited here: where I had made a mistake, some repression lay behind it. Or, more accurately, some insincerity or distortion, ultimately based on a repression. In the analysis of the dreams that I gave there, the nature of the subjects to which the dream ideas related meant that at some times I had to break off the analysis before it was complete, and at others I was forced to distort an indiscreet detail slightly in order to blur its point. I had no other choice, and indeed there was no alternative if I were to cite any examples and produce any evidence at all; the situation in which I found myself derived inevitably from the very nature of dreams, their ability to bring out what has been repressed and is incapable of conscious expression. Even so, there seems to have been enough left to give offence to certain more sensitive souls. The modification or elimination of ideas when I myself knew how they would continue could not, however, be carried out without leaving any trace. What I wanted to suppress often made its way, against my will, into what I did say, emerging as a mistake that passed unnoticed. In addition, the same subject lies at the heart of all three of the examples I mentioned above; my mistakes arose from repressed ideas connected with my late father.

1) It will be partially obvious to readers of the dream analysed on p. 266 [VI.G], and they will be able to draw further conclusions from some hints, that I stopped short there of expressing adverse criticism of my father. Part of the train of thoughts and memories as it would have continued depends on a painful story involving books and a business friend of my father's, a man whose name was Marburg, the same name that woke me from sleep when I heard it called out at Marburg station on the Southern Railway. In the course of analysing the dream I wanted to leave this Herr Marburg out, concealing his existence from both myself and my readers, but he avenged himself by intruding where he did not belong and changing the name of Schiller's birthplace from *Marbach* to *Marburg*.

2) The mistake *Hasdrubal* instead of *Hamilcar*, where I gave the name of Hannibal's brother instead of his father, was made in a context concerning my Hannibal fantasies when I was at secondary school and my dislike of my father's attitude to the 'enemies of our people'. I could have gone on to mention that my relationship with my father was altered after a visit to England, where I met my half-brother from my father's first marriage, who lived in that country. His eldest son is my own age, so there was no age difference in the way of my fantasies when I thought how different it would have been if I had come into the world as my brother's son and not my father's. These suppressed fantasies falsified the text of my book just where I interrupted the analysis by making me put the name of Hannibal's brother instead of his father.

3) I ascribe my shifting the mythological horrors enacted by the gods of ancient Greece one generation forward to the influence of the same brother's memory. One of the pieces of advice he gave me remained in my mind for a long time: 'As your life goes on,' he told me, 'don't forget that you are really in the third rather than the second generation of our father's family.' In fact he – our father – was getting on in years by the time he remarried, so that he was a great deal older than the children of that second marriage. I made

the mistake mentioned above in the book at the very place where I was discussing the dutiful relationship between parents and children.

Friends and patients whose dreams I have described or referred to in dream analysis have sometimes told me that my account of the details we shared with each other was inaccurate. Again, these mistakes could be called historical in nature, for I checked the various passages concerned after being set right, and realized that my memory of facts was at fault only where I had intentionally distorted or concealed some part of the analysis. Once again, *a mistake passed unnoticed as the substitute for an intentional omission or repression*.

Mistakes deriving from repression can be clearly distinguished from mistakes that are the result of real ignorance. It was plain ignorance, for instance, when I thought that I had seen Emmersdorf, where the revolutionary Fischhof lived, while I was on an expedition to the Wachau area. In fact there are two places of that name, and the Emmersdorf where Fischhof lived is in Carinthia, but I knew no better.

4) Another humiliating but instructive mistake was what I might describe as a case of temporary ignorance. A patient reminded me one day that I had promised to lend him two books on Venice to read in preparation for his Easter holiday. I told him that I had got them out ready for him, and went to my library to fetch them. In fact I had forgotten to look them out, for I was not too pleased about my patient's journey; I regarded it as an unnecessary interruption to his treatment, and also financially disadvantageous to me as his doctor. I quickly glanced around the library looking for the two books I had thought of. One was a book on *The Art of Venice*, and I was sure I also had another historical work in a similar series. Sure enough, there it was: *The Medici*. I took it off the shelf and gave it to my waiting patient, only to confess my mistake with some embarrassment, since I really knew quite well that the Medici have nothing to do with Venice. For a brief moment, however, it had seemed to me not at all unlikely. Now in all fairness – since I had so often pointed out the patient's own symptomatic actions to him – I could retrieve my authority in his eyes only by being honest and

telling him the reasons, which I had not mentioned to him, for my reservations about his journey.

In general, it is surprising to find that our compulsion to tell the truth is so much stronger than is usually thought. It may be a result of my study of psychoanalysis, but I now find it very difficult to lie. Whenever I try to be evasive, I make a mistake or some other slip that gives away my devious intentions, as in this and the previous examples.

The mechanism whereby mistakes are made seems to be more flexible than in other kinds of slips; that is to say, making a mistake in general shows that the mental activity involved was in conflict with some disruptive influence, but the nature of the mistake is not determined by the quality of the disruptive idea, which remains obscure. I should add at this point, however, that the same may be assumed in many simple cases of slips of the tongue or pen. Whenever we make such a slip we must suppose that mental processes outside our intention have disrupted it, but one has to admit that slips of the tongue and pen often operate through similarity of sound, laziness or a tendency to be hasty, and the disruptive factor does not succeed in making its own character felt in the resultant mistake. Co-operation on the part of the verbal material alone both facilitates and limits determination of the mistake.

To avoid citing nothing but mistakes of my own, I will add a few examples which could, however, equally well have been classified as slips of the tongue or actions that missed their mark, but that makes little difference in view of the similarity between all these kinds of slips.

5) I had a patient who wanted to end a relationship, and I strongly advised him not to talk to his lover on the telephone, since every conversation made it harder for him to break with her. I said he should write instead, although there was some difficulty in getting letters delivered to her. He visited me at one o'clock to tell me he had found a way round that problem, and asked, among other things, whether he could cite my medical authority. At two o'clock, when he was busy writing the farewell letter, he suddenly interrupted himself and said to his mother, who was in the room: 'Oh, I forgot

to ask the professor if I could mention him by name in the letter.' He hurried to the telephone, was connected, and put his question: 'Could I speak to the professor if he's finished lunch, please?' His answer was a startled: 'Are you out of your mind, Adolf?' in the very voice that, had he followed my advice, he would not have heard again. He had simply 'made a mistake', and called his lover's number instead of his doctor's, mine.

6) A young lady was going to call on a recently married friend in Habsburgergasse. She was talking about her visit around the family table, but said by mistake that she had to go to Babenbergergasse. Laughing, her companions at table pointed out the mistake – or slip of the tongue, if you prefer. Two days previously, the Austrian republic had been declared in Vienna, the black and yellow colours of the former empire had gone, to be superseded by the red, white and red of the old Ostmark, home of the House of Babenberg, and the Habsburgs were stripped of power; the speaker had made the same substitution in her friend's address. There is, as it happens, a very well-known street in Vienna called Babenberger*strasse*, but no Viennese would speak of it as a *Gasse* or alley-way.

7) The local schoolteacher at a holiday resort, a poor but handsome young man, had been courting the daughter of a man from the city who owned a villa there until the girl fell passionately in love with him. In spite of the differences of race and social standing between them, she persuaded her family to agree to the marriage. One day the schoolmaster wrote his brother a letter, commenting: 'The girl is not beautiful, but very sweet-natured, so everything would be all right there. But I can't say whether I shall be able to bring myself to marry a Jewess in the end.' When he sent this letter to his fiancée the engagement was broken off, while his brother was surprised to receive a missive full of loving vows. The source of this story assured me that it really was a mistake, not a clever ruse. However, I have heard of another case in which a lady was dissatisfied with her doctor, but did not want to say so and leave him openly, instead achieving her end by mixing up two letters, and there at least I can guarantee that this familiar comic device was a real mistake and not a device consciously employed.

8) Brill gives an account of a lady who asked after another woman whom they both knew, and erroneously called her by her maiden name. When he drew her attention to the mistake, she admitted that she did not like their friend's husband and was not at all happy about her marriage.

9) This is a mistake that could also be called a slip of the tongue: a young father went to the registrar's office to report his second daughter's birth. When asked the child's name he replied: 'Hanna.' 'But you already have a child called Hanna,' the registrar told him. We may infer that this second daughter was not quite such a welcome addition to the family as the first.

10) Here are some further observations of names being confused. Again, they could just as well have been included in other sections of this book.

A lady had three daughters, two of whom had been married for some time, while the youngest had not yet become engaged. Another lady, who was a friend of the family, had given the identical present of a valuable silver tea set at the two weddings. Whenever anyone mentioned this tea set, the mother made the mistake of naming her third daughter as its owner. Obviously the mother's mistake expressed her wish to see her third and last daughter married too; she was assuming that she would get the same wedding present.

It is equally easy to interpret the frequent cases in which a mother mixes up the names of her daughters, sons or sons-in-law.

11) A good and easily explained example of the persistent confusion of names is provided by the self-observation of one Herr J. G. while he was in a sanatorium: 'At dinner in the sanatorium one day I used a particularly attentive phrase to my neighbour at table during a conversation which did not much interest me, and was very conventional in tenor. This neighbour of mine, a spinster getting on in years, could not help observing that I was not usually so attentive and gallant to her – an observation that conveyed a certain regret, but even more clearly was a derogatory reference to a lady we both knew and to whom I was accustomed to pay more attention. Of course I knew what she meant at once. During the rest of our conversation – and I found this very embarrassing – my neighbour

pointed out several times that I had just addressed her by the name of the lady whom she saw, not without justification, as her more successful rival for my affections.'

12) An instance with a serious background, told to me by a witness who was closely concerned, can also be described as a 'mistake'. A lady had been spending the evening out of doors with her husband, in the company of two other men. One of them was in fact a very intimate friend of hers, but the others did not know that, nor must they. The married couple's friends accompanied them to their door, and said goodbye as they waited for it to be opened. The lady bowed to one of the other men, gave him her hand, and said a few cordial words. Then she took her unacknowledged lover's arm, turned to her husband, and was about to say goodbye to him in the same way. The husband understood, took off his hat, and said with the utmost courtesy: 'Well, goodbye to you too then, ma'am!' The wife, in alarm, let go of her lover's arm, and before the caretaker appeared had just time to sigh: 'Good gracious, what a silly thing to do!' Her husband was one of those married men who like to think it absolutely impossible for their wives to be unfaithful, and he had often said that if he had reason to suspect such a thing, more than one life would be in danger. He therefore had the strongest unconscious motives not to notice the challenge inherent in his wife's mistake.

13) A mistake by one of my patients was repeated with the opposite significance, and is thus particularly instructive: an over-apprehensive young man, after a long internal struggle with himself, had brought himself to promise marriage to a girl who had long loved him, as indeed he loved her. He took his fiancée home, said goodbye, boarded a tram in a state of high delight, and asked the conductor for *two* tickets. Six months later he was married, but he had not yet really adjusted to the benefits of married life. He wondered whether he had done right, he missed his old friends, and he had all kinds of objections to his parents-in-law. One evening he fetched his young wife from her parents' home, got into the tram with her, and on this occasion asked the conductor for a single ticket only.

14) Maeder gives a good example of the way in which a 'mistake'

can grant a reluctantly suppressed wish. A colleague wanted to enjoy a day off work undisturbed; however, he had to pay a call in Lucerne, and he was not looking forward to it. After much thought, he decided that he would pay the call after all. To occupy his mind he read the daily papers on his journey from Zurich to Arth and Goldau, he changed trains at the last-named station, and he continued reading. As the journey went on, the ticket inspector told him that he was in the wrong train: he had bought a ticket to Lucerne, but he was now on his way back from Goldau to Zurich ('Nouvelles contributions', etc., *Archives de Psychoanalyse* VI, 1908).

15) An analogous if not entirely successful attempt to help a suppressed wish to express itself through the same mechanism is described by Dr V. Tausk under the heading 'Going the Wrong Way'.

'I had come on leave to Vienna from the front. A former patient had heard that I was there and sent a message asking if I would visit him, since he was sick in bed. I agreed to his request, and spent two hours with him. When I left him, my patient asked what he owed me. "I'm here on leave, not as a consultant," I replied. "Please think of this visit as an act of friendship." The sick man demurred, probably feeling that he had no right to claim professional services purely out of friendship. However, he finally agreed, saying, in a respectful tone dictated by his pleasure at saving the money, that as a psychoanalyst I must surely know the right thing to do. A little later I myself began doubting whether my high-minded approach had been right, and full of these doubts – which scarcely admitted any ambiguity – I got into the electric tramline X. After a short ride I had to change to tram Y. As I was waiting at the stop, I forgot about the fee and thought of my patient's symptoms. Meanwhile, the tram I was waiting for came along and I got in. But I had to get out again at the next stop. Without noticing, I had boarded an X instead of a Y tram by mistake, and I was going back the way I had just come, as if to visit the patient from whom I had refused to take a fee. *But my unconscious mind did want to take that fee*' (*Internationale Zeitschrift für Psychoanalyse* IV, 1916/17).

16) I once played a trick on myself very similar to the one described

in example 14. I had agreed with my eldest brother, a man of rather strict ideas, to pay him a long-overdue visit at an English seaside resort that summer, and as I was short of time I had decided to go by the shortest route without stopping on the way. I did ask him for an extra day's delay which I could spend in Holland, but he said I could leave that until I was travelling home. So I was going by way of Munich and Cologne to Rotterdam and the Hook of Holland, where I was to catch the boat for the crossing to Harwich at midnight. I had to change in Cologne, and left the train from Munich in order to board the Rotterdam express, but it was nowhere to be seen. I asked various railway officials, was sent from platform to platform, found myself getting very agitated, and soon worked out that during this unsuccessful search I must have missed my connection. On getting confirmation that I had indeed missed it, I wondered whether to spend the night in Cologne. Family feeling among other factors suggested that idea, since according to an old family tradition my forebears had fled Cologne during a pogrom. However, I decided against it and caught a later train to Rotterdam, where I arrived quite late at night, so that now I was in fact obliged to spend a day in Holland. I used the time to fulfil my long-cherished wish of seeing the wonderful Rembrandts in The Hague and the Rijksmuseum. Only next morning, when I was able to gather my impressions together during the railway journey through England, did a perfectly clear memory emerge in my mind of seeing a large notice-board at Cologne station saying 'Rotterdam–Hook of Holland', only a few paces from where I had got out of the Munich train, in fact on the very same platform. The train in which I should have continued my journey was waiting there all the time. I would have had to account for my overlooking this obvious notice and hurrying off to look for my train elsewhere as an incomprehensible instance of 'blindness', had I not assumed that my real intention was to defy my brother's wishes and see the Rembrandts on my outward journey. Everything else, the good show of agitation I put on, the emergence of a pious inclination to spend the night in Cologne, was merely a way of concealing my intention from myself until I had carried it out.

17) J. Stärcke (op. cit.) describes a similar incident from his own

experience, on the face of it caused by 'forgetfulness', but really intended to grant a wish that he had apparently abandoned:

'I was once to give a lecture illustrated by slides in a certain village, but then it was put forward a week. I had answered the letter notifying me of the postponement, and had written down the change of date. I would have liked to visit the same village one afternoon to see a writer of my acquaintance who lived there. To my regret, however, I could find no afternoon free around then, and with reluctance I gave up the idea of visiting my friend.

'When the evening of the lecture arrived, I set off in great haste to the station with a bag full of lantern slides. I had to take a taxi to catch the train (I quite often do leave my departure so late that I have to take a taxi to get to my train on time!). Once I reached my destination I was rather surprised to find no one at the station to meet me (as is usual when one is giving a lecture in a small town or village). Suddenly I remembered that the lecture had been postponed for a week, and I had now made a fruitless journey on the original date. When I had heartily cursed my forgetfulness, I contemplated catching the next train home again. On further deliberation, however, it struck me that I now had an excellent opportunity of making the call I had been wanting to pay, and so I did. Only on the way there did it occur to me that my unfulfilled wish to have time for this visit had hatched an ingenious plot against me. Lugging my heavy bag of slides and hurrying to catch the train were very good ways of concealing my unconscious intention all the better.'

One may not be inclined to think that the kinds of mistakes I have elucidated here are very numerous or particularly significant. However, I think we may wonder whether we should extend the same ideas to assessing those much more important *errors of judgement* made by people in their daily lives and in scientific studies. Only the most unusual and well-balanced minds seem able to preserve the perceived image of outward reality from the distortion it usually suffers by being filtered through the psychic individuality of the subject perceiving it.

Notes

1. 8th edition (*Gesammelte Werke*, vols. II/III).
2. But I was not entirely mistaken! According to the Orphic version of the myth, the act of emasculation was repeated when Kronos was castrated by his son Zeus. (Roscher, *Lexikon der Mythologie*.)

XI

Combined Slips

Two of the examples mentioned above – my error in connecting the Medici with Venice, and the young man's slip in speaking to his lover on the telephone despite my advising him against it – were not described with perfect accuracy, for on careful examination they represent a combination of slips: of forgetfulness with a mistake. The same combination of slips can be demonstrated even more clearly from some other examples.

1) A friend told me about the following incident: 'A few years ago I accepted election to the committee of a certain literary society because I thought it might help me to get the play I had written staged some day, and I attended the meetings, which took place every Friday, regularly if without much interest. A few months ago I was assured that my drama would be produced at the theatre in F., and after that I regularly *forgot* to attend the meetings of the society. When I read what you had written about such subjects I felt ashamed of my forgetfulness, blaming myself for my mean-minded conduct in staying away once I no longer needed these people. I decided that I would be sure not to forget to go on the next Friday. I kept reminding myself of this resolution, until the time came to put it into practice and I was at the committee room door. To my surprise it was closed, and the meeting was already over. I had mistaken the day – it was now Saturday!'

2) The next example combines a symptomatic action with a case in which something was mislaid: it came to me from a good if more remote source.

A lady was travelling to Rome with her brother-in-law, a famous artist. The German expatriates living in Rome welcomed him with great respect, and among other presents given to him was a gold medal of antique classical origin. The lady felt some vexation, believing that her brother-in-law did not value this fine piece properly. When her sister had come to take her place, and she herself was home again, she found on unpacking that she had brought the medal with her. Just how it had happened she could not imagine. She wrote at once to her brother-in-law to tell him about the misappropriated item, and said she would send it back to Rome next day. Next day, however, it had been so skilfully mislaid that it was impossible to find it and send it on, and then the true meaning of her 'absence of mind' dawned on the lady: she really wanted to keep the medal for herself.

3) In some cases a slip is persistently repeated, changing its method of operation in the process:

Jones (op. cit., p. 483) tell us that, for reasons unknown to him, he once left a letter lying on his desk for several days before sending it off. He finally brought himself to do so, but it was returned by the 'dead letter office' because he had forgotten to write the address on it. When he had addressed it he took it back to the post office, but this time he had forgotten to stamp it. He could no longer ignore the fact that he did not want to send the letter at all.

4) A short account by Dr Karl Weiss of Vienna cogently describes unsuccessful attempts to carry out an action to which there is internal opposition:

'The consistency with which the unconscious can make itself felt when it has a reason not to let a project be carried out, and the difficulty of guarding against this tendency, are obvious from the following incident. An acquaintance asked me to lend him a book and bring it round to him next day. I immediately agreed, but with a distinct sense of reluctance which I could not at first explain to myself. Later, I realized why: the man concerned had owed me a sum of money for years, and seemed to have no intention of paying it back. I thought no more of the matter, but I did remember it next morning, with the same sense of reluctance, and told myself at once: "Your unconscious will try to make you forget the book. But you don't want to be churlish, so you will do your best to remember it."

I went home, wrapped the book up in a piece of paper and put it beside me on my desk while I wrote some letters. After a while I went out; having gone a few steps, I remembered that I had left the letters I was going to take to the post on my desk. (In one of those letters, incidentally, I had been forced to express displeasure to someone who was supposed to be supporting me in a certain matter.) I turned back, fetched the letters, and went out again. In the electric tram I remembered that I had promised my wife I would buy her something, and I was pleased to think that it would be only a small packet. Here I suddenly made the association between packet and book, and now I realized that I still did not have the book with me. Not only had I forgotten it the first time I went out, I had also continued to overlook it when I went back to pick up the letters from where it was lying.'

5) A similar illustration is provided by an observation that Otto Rank has analysed in detail:

'A man of meticulously tidy and painfully precise habits told me about the following experience, an extremely unusual one for him. One afternoon, when he was out in the street and wanted to know the time, he realized that he had left his watch at home, which as far as he could remember he had never done before. Since he had an appointment to be kept punctually that evening, and he did not have time to go back for his watch now, he took the opportunity of visiting a lady who was a friend of his to borrow her watch for the evening; this was particularly convenient because he had to visit her again next morning to keep an appointment they had already made, and he promised to return the watch then. However, when he was about to give the borrowed watch back to its owner next day, he realized to his surprise that he had left it at home, putting his own watch in his pocket instead. He made a firm resolution to return the lady's watch in the afternoon, and so he did. But when he was going to look at the time as he left, he found to his great annoyance and amazement that yet again he had forgotten his own watch. The repetition of the slip seemed to this normally well-organized man so pathological that he thought he would like to discover its psychological motivation, which promptly emerged from the psychoanalytical question of whether he had suffered any distressing experience on the crucial day when he first forgot the watch, and if so in what context. He immediately said that after lunch, just before he went out and forgot his watch, he had been talking to his mother, and she told him that a family member with an irresponsible disposition, who had already caused him a great deal of annoyance and expense, had pawned his own watch but needed it at home, so he had left a message asking our well-organized friend to let him have the money to redeem it. This way of borrowing money, almost amounting to blackmail, had affected our subject very unpleasantly, reminding him of all the vexation this family member had caused him over many years. His own symptomatic action thus proved to have been determined in several ways. First, it expressed a train of thought to the effect that he was not going to let anyone extort money from him like this, and if a watch was necessary he would simply leave his own at home; however, as he needed it in order to keep his evening appointment he could carry out that intention only unconsciously and in the form of a symptomatic action. Second, his forgetfulness meant something like: squandering money on that useless creature all the time will ruin me, and I shall have to give up everything. Although he said himself that he felt only momentary annoyance on hearing about the message, the duplication of his symptomatic action showed that it was still at work in his unconscious, rather as if his conscious mind were saying: I can't get this business out of my head.[1] The fact that the same fate then befell the lady's watch that he had borrowed is not surprising, given this attitude adopted by the unconscious mind. But perhaps there were other and more particular motives favouring this transference to the "innocent" lady's watch. The most obvious is that he would probably have liked to keep it to replace his own watch, which he had sacrificed, and so forgot to give it back next day. In addition, perhaps he would have liked to keep the watch as a memento of the lady herself. Furthermore, forgetting the watch belonging to this lady – whom he admired – gave him an opportunity for a second visit to her; after all, he already had an appointment to visit her in the morning on other business, and he seems to have been indicating, by forgetting the watch, that it was a waste to hand her back her own watch casually during a visit that had been planned well in advance. Forgetting his own watch twice, which enabled him to pay another visit in order to return hers, suggests that our man was trying unconsciously to avoid carrying both watches at the same time. He clearly did not want to give such an impression of excess, which stood in stark contrast to his relation's indigence; on the other hand, he also wanted to keep a cautious check on his apparent intention of marrying the lady by reminding himself that he had irremovable obligations to his own family (in the person of his mother). Finally, another reason for failing to return the watch may have been that on the previous evening he had been embarrassed, as a bachelor, to let his friends see him consulting the lady's watch and had done so only on the sly, and to avoid any repetition of this awkward eventuality he did not want to have it in his pocket again. On the other hand, as he had to return it, the result was the unconscious performance of a symptomatic action which took the form of a compromise between his conflicting feelings and the hard-won victory of his unconscious' (*Zentralblatt für Psychoanalyse* II, 5).

The three following observations were made by J. Stärcke (op. cit.):

6) *Mislaying, breaking and forgetting things – as the expression of the suppressed ability of the negative counter-will*: 'One day I was going to lend my brother several items from a collection of illustrations I had made for a scientific work, which he wanted to use as slides in a lecture. Although it did briefly cross my mind that as I had gone to a good deal of trouble to collect these reproductions, I would prefer them not to be publicly shown or published in any way before I could do it myself, I promised him to look out the negatives of the pictures he wanted and make slides of them. However, I could not find the negatives. I looked through the whole stack of boxes of negatives on the subject, I picked up a good two hundred negatives one by one, but those I was looking for were not there. I suspected that I was in fact reluctant to let my brother have the pictures. When I had become aware of these grudging ideas and

had done my best to overcome them, I realized that I had set aside the box on top of the pile without looking through it, and it was the box containing the negatives I was looking for. It had a brief note of its contents on the lid, at which I had probably cast a fleeting glance before setting that particular box aside. In fact I did not quite seem to have got over my reluctance, because all kinds of other mishaps occurred before the slides were ready to be sent off. I broke one of them while I was holding it and cleaning the glass over the picture (and I never usually break slides). When I had made another slide from the plate I dropped it, and saved it from being broken only by putting out my foot to catch it. While I was mounting the slides the whole stack fell to the floor once again, but luckily none of them broke. Finally, however, it was several more days before I actually packed them up and dispatched them. Every day I had planned to do so, and every time I forgot.'

7) *Repeated forgetfulness – actions that miss their mark when they are finally carried out*: 'I once had to send an acquaintance a postcard, but I kept putting it off for days on end, and I had a strong suspicion why: he had written to tell me that someone whom I did not particularly want to see was planning to visit me that week. When the week was over, and the prospect of the visit to which I was not looking forward had become very slight, I finally wrote the postcard and told my acquaintance when I would be available. When I wrote the card I originally meant to say that I had been prevented from writing before because of *druk werk* (the pressure of work), but in the end I left that out: no reasonable person believes in that hackneyed excuse any more. Whether this small untruth still insisted on being expressed in some way I do not know, but when I took the postcard to the letterbox I posted it, by mistake, in the lower slot for *Drukwerk* (printed matter).'

8) *Forgetfulness and mistakes*: 'A girl went out one fine morning to draw the plaster casts in the Rijksmuseum. Although she would rather have gone for a walk on such a nice day, she decided to work hard at her drawing. But first she had to buy some drawing paper. She went to the shop (which was about ten minutes' walk away from the museum), bought pencils and other drawing instruments, but

forgot the paper. Then she went to the museum, and was sitting on her little stool ready to start work when she realized that she still had no paper, so she had to go back to the shop again. Once she had her paper she really did begin drawing, and was getting on well with her work when, some time later, she heard several chimes from the clocktower of the museum. It must be twelve noon, she thought, but she went on working until the bell struck the quarter hour. Oh, she thought, that must be twelve-fifteen, and at this point she put away her drawing instruments and decided to walk through the Vondelpark and go to her sister's house for coffee (as the Dutch call lunch). But on reaching the Suasso Museum she saw, to her surprise, that instead of being twelve-thirty it was only twelve noon! The enticingly fine weather had outwitted her industrious intentions, and when the bell struck at eleven-thirty she had forgotten that a bell in a clocktower strikes the half hours too.'

9) As several of the observations above show, an unconsciously disruptive tendency can also achieve its purpose by persistently repeating the same kind of slip. I take an amusing example of this from a little book called *Frank Wedekind und das Theater* [*Frank Wedekind and the Theatre*], published by the firm of Drei-Masken-Verlag in Munich, but I must leave responsibility for the little story itself, which is told in Mark Twain's style, to the author of the book.

'In Wedekind's one-act play *Die Zensur* [*Censorship*], one of the characters says, at the climax of the play: "Die Furcht vor dem Tode ist ein Denkfehler ['The fear of death is a fallacy']." In rehearsal the author, feeling pleased with this phrase, asked the actor to pause briefly before the word *Denkfehler*. That evening the actor entered fully into the spirit of the thing, inserted the pause precisely where it was required, but then solemnly announced: "Die Furcht vor dem Tode is ein *Druckfehler* [misprint]." The author assured the artist, on being asked about it after the performance, that he had not the slightest objection to the effect of the pause, except that at that particular point his play did not say that fear of death was a *misprint*, and the word was *fallacy*. At the following evening's performance the actor said, at the crucial point, and yet again in the most solemn of tones: "The fear of death is a – *Denkzettel* [memorandum]." Once again Wedekind heaped praise on the actor, merely commenting in passing that he had not said the fear of death was a *memorandum* but a *fallacy*. On the following evening *Die Zensur* was performed again, and when the crucial moment came the actor, with whom the author was on very friendly terms and exchanging views on art by this time, said with the most solemn feeling imaginable: "The fear of death is a – *Druckzettel* [printed pamphlet]." The actor received the author's unstinting approbation, and the one-act play had many more performances, but by now the author had given up his "fallacy" as a lost cause.'

Rank has also studied the very interesting connections between 'slips and dreaming' (*Zentralblatt für Psychoanalyse* II, p. 266, and *Internationale Zeitschrift für Psychoanalyse* III, p. 158), but they cannot be traced without close analysis of the dreams to which the slips related. I once had a rather complicated dream in which I had lost my wallet. In the morning, sure enough, I could not find it when I was getting dressed; I had forgotten to take it out of my trouser pocket and put it in its usual place the night before my dream. I was not unaware, therefore, of this act of forgetfulness, which was probably intended to express an unconscious idea ready to surface in the context of a dream.[2]

I do not claim that such cases of combined slips can tell us anything we could not learn from cases of slips in isolation, but this change of the form of the slip, while the result is the same, does give the distinct impression that the will is trying to achieve some definite purpose, and strongly contradicts the idea that slips simply happen by chance and need no interpretation. It is also striking that in these examples a conscious intention entirely fails to prevent the slip from occurring. My friend did not manage to attend his committee meeting; the lady was unable to part with the Roman medal. The unconscious motive opposing their intentions found another way to express itself when foiled on the first occasion. Something more than a conscious intention is necessary to overcome an unconscious motive; it takes psychic investigation to bring something unknown to the attention of the conscious mind.

Notes

1. This continued working in the unconscious mind can also be expressed in the form of a dream following the slip, or sometimes in the repetition of the slip, or in omitting to correct it.

2. It is not unusual for a slip such as losing or mislaying something to be corrected by a dream in which the dreamer discovers where to find the missing item, but there is nothing occult about it so long as the dreamer is the same as the person who suffered the loss. A young lady wrote: 'About four months ago, in the bank, I found that I had lost a very pretty ring. I searched every corner of my room, but could not find it. A week ago I dreamed it was near the cupboard beside the radiator. Of course the dream would not let me rest, and sure enough, I found it there next morning.' She was surprised by the incident, but said it often happened that her ideas and wishes were fulfilled in this way, although she did not ask herself what change had occurred in her life between her loss of the ring and its recovery.

XII

Determinism – Belief in Chance and Superstition – Some Points of View

The following statement may be made as the general conclusion to be drawn from the various discussions above: *certain inadequacies in our psychic performance* – the character they all share will be more closely defined below – *and certain actions performed apparently unintentionally prove, when methods of psychoanalytical investigation are applied to them, to be well motivated and determined by factors of which the conscious mind is unaware.*

To be classified with phenomena capable of explanation in this way, a psychic slip must fulfil the following conditions.

a) It must not go beyond a certain point, a point that is established by our judgement and complies with our ideas of what is 'within the range of normality'.

b) It must have the character of a brief and temporary disturbance. We must have carried out the same action correctly before, or believe ourselves capable of carrying it out more correctly at any time. If someone else corrects our slip, we must immediately acknowledge the justice of the correction and the malfunctioning of our own psychic process.

c) If we notice the slip at all, we must not recognize any motivation for it in ourselves; instead, we must be tempted to put it down to 'carelessness' or 'chance'.

The category of psychic slip, therefore, comprises cases of forgetfulness, mistakes that we make although we know better, slips of the tongue, slips in reading, slips of the pen, inadvertent actions and so-called fortuitous actions.

The same word formation, with the prefix *ver-* [in German, all the nouns Freud uses but one derive from verbs beginning *ver-*:

vergessen, versprechen, verlesen, verschreiben and *vergreifen*; the odd one out is *Zufallshandlungen*, fortuitous actions] gives a linguistic indication of the internal similarity of most of these phenomena. However, a series of comments which may be of further interest can be connected with the explanation of the psychic processes thus defined.

A) By saying that some of our psychic actions cannot be explained as the work of intention, we fail to recognize the extent of determination present in our mental life. It goes further, both here and in other areas, than we suspect. In 1900 I explained in an essay on the literary historian R. M. Meyer in *Die Zeit*, illustrated by examples, that it is impossible to compose something entirely nonsensical intentionally and voluntarily. For quite a long time I have known that one cannot contrive to think of either a number or a name completely at random. If we study a number apparently plucked from thin air jokingly or in high spirits, a number which may perhaps run to several digits, it will become evident that it is really strictly determined, unlikely as that might have seemed. I will begin with a brief account of a first name arbitrarily chosen, and then analyse a similar example of a number 'unthinkingly thrown out'.

1) When I was writing up the case history of a woman patient of mine for publication, I wondered what first name to give her. I seemed to have a very wide choice; of course certain names excluded themselves from the start, first and foremost her real name, then the names of my own family, something to which I would object, and in addition any really unusual women's names; but that surely left a wide range available. One would expect, and I myself did expect, that a whole host of women's names would suggest themselves to me. Instead, only a single name came into my mind: the name *Dora*. I wondered what had determined it. Who else was called Dora? I felt like rejecting the next idea to occur to me as incredible, for it told me that the nanny who looked after my sister's children was called Dora, but I had enough self-discipline, or enough experience of analysis, to follow that idea and take it further. I immediately thought of a small incident the previous evening, which

brought me the association determining the name I was seeking. I saw a letter addressed to 'Fräulein Rosa W.' lying on the table in my sister's dining room. In surprise, I asked who that was, and learned that the nanny Dora was really called Rosa, but had been obliged to change her name on entering the household because my sister is a Rosa too and could have taken the name to mean herself. I said, sympathetically: Poor servants, they can't even keep their own names! And now that I came to think of it, I said no more for a moment, but began meditating on various serious subjects. My thoughts trailed vaguely away, but I could now easily recall them to my conscious mind. So when next day I was looking for a name for someone *who could not be allowed to keep her own*, only *Dora* sprang to mind. In this instance the fact that it was the sole name to occur to me was based on a strong similarity of content, for in my patient's case history the crucial influence on her course of treatment had also been exerted by someone working in the capacity of a servant in a strange house, this time as a governess.

This little incident had an unexpected sequel years later. One day, when I brought up the case history of the girl I had called Dora in a lecture – the case history itself had been published long before – I realized that one of the two women in my audience was also called Dora, a name I would have to mention very often and in very many different contexts during the lecture. I turned to my young colleague, who was also a personal acquaintance of mine, and apologized, saying that I really hadn't stopped to think that her own name was Dora, and I would be happy to replace the name I had given my patient by another in today's lecture. Then I had to think of a name in a hurry, and was just telling myself that I must not set a bad example to my psychoanalytically trained colleagues by hitting upon the first name of the other woman present. So I was pleased when the name Erna occurred to me as a replacement for Dora, and I made use of it in the lecture. Afterwards, I wondered just where the name Erna had come from, and could not help smiling when I realized that the possibility I had feared in choosing a replacement name had in fact happened, at least in part. For the other lady's surname was Lucerna, ending in '-erna'.

2) I wrote to a friend telling him that I had finished reading the proofs of the *Interpretation of Dreams*, and was not going to change anything else in the work 'even if there turned out to be 2467 mistakes in it'. I immediately tried to account to myself for this number, and added my little analysis as a postscript to my letter. I think I had better quote exactly what I wrote when I had caught myself in the act:

'So here, briefly, is another contribution to the psychopathology of everyday life. You will find in this letter the number 2467, given as a high-spirited, arbitrary assessment of the number of errors that might be found in the dream book. I meant it to suggest just any very large number, and so indeed it does. But there is nothing arbitrary or undetermined in the workings of the mind. You will also, and correctly, expect that my unconscious set to work in a hurry to decide on the number that my conscious mind was to produce. Well, I had just been reading a piece in the newspaper about the retirement of one General E. M. as master of ordnance. I take an interest in the man: when I was doing my military service as a medical student he was a colonel. At the time he fell ill, and told the doctors: "You'd better cure me within the week. I have work to do, and the emperor is waiting for it." I determined then and there to follow the man's career, and now (this was in 1899) he had come to the end of it, having retired with the rank of master of ordnance. I tried working out how long it had taken him, and supposed I must have met him in the hospital in 1882. That would make it 17 years. I told my wife, and she commented: "Then I suppose you'll soon be retiring too." To which I protested: "Heaven forbid!" After this exchange I sat down at my desk to write to you, but my previous train of thought continued, and for a very good reason. My calculation had been wrong, and I had a clear point of reference for that fact in my memory. I had reached my majority, I mean my 24th birthday, while I was under military arrest for going absent without leave. That was in 1880, and thus 19 years ago. So there's the reason for the "24" in 2467! Now, take my age at present, 43, add 24 years, and the result is 67! Which means that when my wife suggested I might feel like retiring, my wishful thinking added another 24 years of work to my age now. I was clearly feeling vexed that during the whole period over which I had followed Colonel M.'s career I had not got very far myself, yet I felt a kind of triumph at the thought that he was now retired while I still had everything ahead of me. So I may legitimately say that not even the number 2467, which I brought out without any conscious intention, was not determined by my unconscious mind.'

3) Since studying this first example of the explanation of a number apparently chosen at random, I have tried the same experiment many times, and with equal success, but most of these cases are so intimate in their content that they cannot be passed on.

For that reason, however, I will add here a very interesting analysis of a 'chance number' that Dr Alfred Adler of Vienna heard from an acquaintance whom he describes as a 'very sound source'.[1] 'Yesterday evening,' said this man, 'I was reading the *Psychopathology of Everyday Life* [an earlier edition], and I would have finished the book there and then had not a curious incident prevented me. For when I read the passage claiming that every number we call into our conscious minds, apparently quite arbitrarily, has a meaning of its own, I decided to try an experiment. The number 1734 occurred to me. *And now the following ideas came at a headlong pace:* 1734 ÷ 17 = 102; 102 ÷ 17 = 6. Then I divided the digits of the number into 17 and 34. I am 34 years old. As I think I once told you, I regard one's 34th year as the last year of youth, so I felt extremely gloomy on my last birthday. I had entered upon a very enjoyable and interesting period of development at the end of my 17th year. I divide my life up into 17-year sections. So what is the meaning of my division sums? I thought of the number 102, which is the number given to Kotzebue's play *Menschenhass und Reue* [*Misanthropy and Remorse*] in the Reclam Universal Library series.

'My present psychic condition, as it happens, is one of misanthropy and remorse. No. 6 in the Universal Library (and I know a good many of the numbers in that series off by heart) is Müllner's *Die Schuld* [*Guilt*]. I am constantly tormented by the idea that I am to blame for my own inability to become what I could have been. It also occurred to me that No. 34 in the Universal Library series is a story also by Müllner, entitled *Der Kaliber* [*The Calibre*]. I divided the word into "Ka-liber", and it then struck me that it contains the words "Ali" and "Kali" [potassium]. This reminded me that I was once playing at making up rhymes with my 6-year-old son Ali. I asked him if he could find a rhyme for Ali. He couldn't, and when he asked me for one I said: "Ali reinigt den Mund mit hypermangansaurem Kali' [Ali cleans his mouth with potassium permanganate]," and we had a good laugh. Ali was a very *lieb* [sweet] child at this time, but recently I have been sorry to notice that he is *ka (kein) lieber Ali* [no longer a sweet Ali].'

'So then I asked myself, what book is No. 17 in the Universal Library? I couldn't remember. However, I must certainly have known once, so I supposed that I had forgotten the number on purpose. I racked my brains to no avail. I meant to read on, but I was reading only automatically, without understanding a word, because that teasing No. 17 was on my mind. I put out the light and went on thinking. Finally it struck me that No. 17 must be a play by Shakespeare. But which play? I thought of *Hero and Leander*. Obviously a silly attempt of my will to distract me. Finally I got up and looked for the Reclam Universal Library catalogue. No. 17 is *Macbeth*. To my surprise, I realized that my mind could dredge up almost nothing about the play, although I have paid it as much attention as other dramas by Shakespeare. All I could think of was: murderers, Lady Macbeth, witches, "Fair is foul", and the fact that I had once thought Schiller's version of *Macbeth* very good. No doubt I had wanted to forget the play. Then it occurred to me that 17 and 34 divided by 17 give 1 and 2. Nos. 1 and 2 in the Universal Library contain the text of Goethe's *Faust*, and I once thought I saw many of Faust's characteristics in myself.' It is a pity that medical discretion did not allow us more of an insight into the meaning of this train of thought. Adler comments that the man did not succeed in synthesizing his ideas, which would hardly seem worthy of note if the rest of them had not produced something providing a key for the understanding of the number 1734 and the whole series of ideas.

'This morning,' Adler's source continued, 'I had an experience that provides strong support for Freud's theory. My wife, whom I had woken when I got up in the night, asked me what I was doing with the Universal Library catalogue. I told her the story. She thought it was all just hair-splitting, except – and this is very interesting – that she fancied there must be something in the idea of *Macbeth*, which I had so firmly rejected. But she added that if she thought of a random number she herself could associate no ideas with it. I said: "Let's try." She gave me the number 117. I replied at once: "17 refers to what I've just told you, and, what's more, I was telling you only yesterday that there's too much of an age difference between a woman of 82 and a man of 35." For I had been teasing my wife over the last few days by pretending she was a little old lady of 82 – and 82 + 35 = 117.'

So the man who could not work out the determination of his own number immediately found the answer when his wife gave him a number apparently chosen at random. In fact the wife had a very good idea of the complex that had given rise to the figure thought up by her husband, and took her own from the same complex, which they must both have shared because it concerned their respective ages and, as Adler indicates, the husband's suppressed wish which, followed out to its conclusion, would have run: 'The only right sort of wife for a man of 34, like me, would be a girl of 17.'

Lest we should be over-inclined to dismiss such 'parlour games' as beneath consideration, I will add something I recently heard from Dr Adler: a year after the publication of this analysis, the man concerned was divorced from his wife.[2]

4) Adler gives similar explanations for the occurrence of obsessive numbers, and the choice of what are described as 'favourite numbers' is not without some connection to the life of the person who chooses them, and has a certain psychological interest. A man who admitted to a particular preference for the numbers 17 and 19 added, after a little thought, that when he went to university at the age of 17 he had at last attained the academic freedom for which he longed, while at the age of 19 he had gone on his first major journey and soon afterwards made his first scientific discovery. However, his preference did not become fixed until a decade later, when the same numbers acquired significance in his love life. In fact even those numbers that are used with particular frequency in certain circum-

stances, although apparently at random, can be traced back to an unexpected significance through analysis. For instance, it occurred to a patient of mine one day that when he was annoyed he was particularly apt to say: 'I've told you that 17 to 36 times before,' and he wondered whether there was some motivation for it. It struck him at once that he had been born on the 27th of a month, while his younger brother was born on the 26th of a month, and he felt justified in complaining that fate had deprived him of many of the good things of life in order to give them to his younger brother. He depicted this favouritism of destiny in his mind by subtracting ten from his own date of birth and adding that number to his brother's birthday. 'Even though I'm the elder brother I've been short-changed.'

5) I will dwell a little longer on the analysis of ideas connected with numbers, for I know of no other isolated observations that so strikingly prove the existence of extremely complex thought processes inaccessible to the conscious mind, nor of any better example of analysis in which influence by the doctor (through suggestion), something often suspected, can so definitely be ruled out. With his consent, I will therefore give an account of the analysis of a numerical idea produced by one of my patients. I need say of him only that he is the youngest of a large family and lost his father, whom he greatly admired, while he was a small child. In a particularly cheerful frame of mind, he thought of the number 426718 and asked himself: 'Now, what do I associate with that? Well, first of all there's a joke I heard: "If a doctor treats your cold it will last 42 days, and if you leave it untreated it will go on for 6 weeks."' This matches the first digits in the number: $42 = 6 \times 7$. When he hesitated after producing this first idea, I pointed out that the 6 figure number he had chosen contained all the digits up to 8 except for 3 and 5. At once he went on with his interpretation. 'Well, there are 7 siblings in our family and I am the youngest. No. 3 in order of age is my sister A. and No. 5 is my brother L. – they were both my enemies. As a child I used to ask God in my prayers every evening to remove my tormentors from this life. I think I was fulfilling that wish myself: I passed over 3 and 5, my nasty brother and the sister I hated.' 'So if the number refers

to your brothers and sisters, what about the 18 at the end? There were only 7 of you.' 'I often thought that if my father had lived longer then I wouldn't have been the youngest child. If there had been another "1", then there would have been 8 of us, and being the elder I'd have had a younger brother or sister to boss about.'

So the number was accounted for, but we still had to find out the connection between the first part of the interpretation and the rest of it. That was explained very easily from the circumstances that had put the last two digits into the subject's head, as he thought that 'if his father had lived longer' he would not have been the youngest. $42 = 6 \times 7$ expressed his low opinion of the doctors who had been unable to help his father, and thus a wish that he had not died. The whole number really reflected the granting of his two childish wishes about his family circle: he wanted the brother and sister he disliked to die, and he wanted another little sibling after him in the family: or to reduce the idea to its essence: if only those two had died instead of my dear father![3]

6) Here is a little example from my correspondence. A telegraph director in L. wrote to tell me that his son, aged 18½, who wanted to study medicine, was at present interested in the psychopathology of everyday life and was trying to convince his parents that my views were correct. I reproduce one of the attempts the young man had made, without any comment on the discussion to which it gave rise.

'My son was talking to my wife about what is usually called chance, and told her she could not really claim that any song or even any number came into her mind purely "by chance". The conversation went on like this. Son: Give me a number – any number. Mother: Very well, 79. Son: What do you associate with it? Mother: It makes me think of the pretty hat I saw yesterday. Son: What did it cost? Mother: 158 marks. Son: There you are, then: $158 \div 2 = 79$. The hat was too expensive, and I expect you were really thinking: "If it cost only half that, then I'd buy it."'

'At first I objected to my son's ideas, pointing out that ladies in general are not particularly good at arithmetic, and his mother had probably not worked out that 79 was half of 158, so his theory rested on the unlikely notion that the unconscious was better at arithmetic than the normal conscious mind. "Not at all," he told me. "I'll admit that Mother didn't do the sum ($158 \div 2 = 79$), but she could well have seen the equation by chance; or indeed, she could have been thinking of the hat in her dreams and working out what it would cost at only half the price." '

7) I take the analysis of another number from Jones (op. cit., p. 478). A gentleman he knew thought of the number 986 and then challenged him to connect it with anything he could think of. 'Using the free-association method he first recalled a memory, which had not previously been present in his mind, to the following effect: Six years ago, on the hottest day he could remember, he had seen a joke in an evening newspaper, which stated that the thermometer had stood at 986° F., evidently an exaggeration of 98.6° F. We were at the time seated in front of a very hot fire from which he had just drawn back, and he remarked, probably quite correctly, that the heat had aroused this dormant memory. However, I was curious to know why this memory had persisted with such vividness as to be so readily brought out, for with most people it surely would have been forgotten beyond recall, unless it had become associated with some other mental experience of more significance. He told me that in reading the joke he had laughed uproariously, and that on many subsequent occasions he had recalled it with great relish. As the joke was obviously a very tenuous one, this strengthened my expectation that more lay behind. His next thought was the general reflection that the conception of heat had always greatly impressed him; that heat was the most important thing in the universe, the source of all life, and so on. This remarkable attitude in quite a prosaic young man certainly needed some explanation, so I asked him to continue his free associations. The next thought was of a factory-stack that he could see from his bedroom window. He often stood of an evening watching the flame and smoke issuing out of it, and reflecting on the deplorable waste of energy. Heat, fire, the source of life, the waste of vital energy issuing from an upright, hollow tube – it was not hard to divine from such associations that the ideas of heat and fire were unconsciously linked in his mind with the idea of love, as is so

frequent in symbolic thinking, and that there was a strong masturbation complex present, a conclusion which he presently confirmed.'

I would suggest that anyone wanting to get a good impression of
the way in which unconscious thought works on numbers should
read C. G. Jung's article 'Ein Beitrag zur Kenntniss des Zahlen-
traumes' ['A Contribution to the Understanding of the Numerical
Dream'] (*Zentralblatt für Psychoanalyse* I, 1911), and another by
E. Jones ('Unconscious Manipulations of Numbers', ibid. II, 5,
1912).

In my own self-analyses of this kind two things in particular have
struck me: first, the almost somnambulistic certainty with which I
make for my unknown aim, immersing myself in a train of thought
that involves calculations and then suddenly arrives at the number
I was seeking, not to mention the speed with which my mind
performs the rest of the work; and second, the fact that the numbers
are so readily available to my unconscious, although I am not good
at arithmetic and have the greatest difficulty in consciously remembering dates, house numbers, and so forth. I actually find that this
unconscious mental manipulation of numbers shows an inclination
to superstition in me, although I had long found its origin a mystery.[4]

We shall not be surprised to find that not only numbers but also
verbal ideas of a different kind regularly prove to be well determined
when they are subjected to analytical investigation.

8) A good example of the derivation of an obsessive word, one that
haunts the mind, is given by Jung (*Diagnostische Assoziationsstudien*
IV, p. 215). 'A lady told me that for some days she had had the word
"Taganrog" [a Russian place-name] always on the tip of her tongue,
and she had no idea where it had come from. I asked the lady about
any events of an emotional nature and any suppressed wishes of hers
in the recent past. After some hesitation, she told me that she would
have liked to have a *Morgenrock* [morning coat], but her husband
did not show the interest she would have liked in it. "Morgenrock –
Tag-an-rock [literally, 'day-on-coat']"; the partial relationship of
the words in sense and sound is obvious. The determination of the
Russian form of the word derives from the fact that at about the
same time the lady had met someone who came from Taganrog.'

9) I owe Dr E. Hitschmann the explanation of another case where a couple of lines of verse kept obtruding themselves in a particular location, although their origin and the connections were not obvious.

'Told to me by Dr E., a doctor of law: Six years ago I was travelling from Biarritz to San Sebastian. The railway line crosses the river Bidassoa, which is the boundary between France and Spain at this point. There is a splendid view from the bridge, with a broad valley and the Pyrenees on one side and the sea stretching away on the other. It was a fine, bright summer's day, everything was flooded with bright sunlight, I was on holiday and looking forward to arriving in Spain – when these lines of verse came into my mind:

> *Aber frei ist schon die Seele,*
> *Schwebet in dem Meer von Licht.*

[Free as air the soul is flying, hovering in the sea of light.]

'I remember that at the time I wondered where these lines came from, and could not remember; judging by their metrical form, they must be part of a poem, but it eluded my memory completely. I think I recollect that later, as the lines kept returning to my mind, I asked several people about them, but no one could place them.

'On my way back from a trip to Spain last year, I was travelling on the same stretch of railway line. It was night, pitch dark, and raining. I looked out of the window to see if we were coming to the frontier station yet, and noticed that we were on the Bidassoa bridge. The lines quoted above immediately came back into my mind, and yet again I could not remember where they came from.

'Several months later, I happened to pick up the poems of Uhland at home. I opened the volume, and my glance fell on the lines: "Free as air the soul is flying, hovering in the sea of light", which form the conclusion of a poem entitled 'Der Waller' ['The Pilgrim']. I read the poem, and now remembered, very vaguely, that I did once know it, many years ago. It tells a story which is set in Spain, and this struck me as the only connection the quotation had with the part of the railway line that I have described. But I was not entirely satisfied with my discovery, and went on leafing automatically through the book. The lines "Free as air the soul is flying," etc., were the last printed on a certain page. Turning it, I found a poem entitled 'The Bidassoa Bridge' on the next page.

'I should add that the content of this second poem seemed to me even stranger than the subject of the first, and that its opening lines run:

> *Auf der Bidassoabrücke steht ein Heiliger altersgrau,*
> *Segnet rechts die span'schen Berge, segnet links den fränk'schen*
> *Gau.'*

[On the Bidassoa bridge stands a saint both old and grey, blessing Spain to his right hand, blessing France the other way.]

B) The light thus cast on the determination of names and numbers apparently chosen at random may perhaps help to clear up another problem. Many people, as we know, cite a special conviction of the existence of free will in order to reject the assumption of consistent psychic determinism. Their sense of conviction is real, and does not give way to a belief in determinism. It must, like all normal feelings, have something to justify it. However, so far as I can see, it does not express itself in major and important decisions, occasions on which we are more inclined to feel a sense of psychic compulsion, to which we readily appeal for support ('Here stand I; I can do no other'). On the other hand, people like to think that in making trivial decisions of little importance they could just as well have decided differently, and that they acted from free will and not pre-motivation. Our analyses show that there is no need to dispute a person's right to feel convinced of his free will. If we distinguish between conscious and unconscious motivations, this sense of conviction tells us that conscious motivation does not extend to all our motor decisions. *Minima non curat praetor* [The praetor does not concern himself with minor matters]. But what is left free by one side receives motivation from the other, from the unconscious, and so determination in the psychic area is duly carried out after all.[5]

✻

C) Although in the nature of things an understanding of the motivation of the slips described above must elude the conscious mind, it would be good to find psychological evidence of its existence, and in fact it is probable, for reasons that emerge from closer study of the unconscious, that such evidence is indeed to be found somewhere. Phenomena which seem to correspond to an unconscious and therefore displaced understanding of that motivation can actually be shown to exist in two areas:

a) It is a conspicuous and generally observed feature of the conduct of paranoiacs that they attribute the utmost importance to certain small details of other people's behaviour which the rest of us disregard; they interpret them in certain ways and draw wide-ranging conclusions from them. For instance, the last paranoiac I saw believed that all around him were in collusion because they waved one hand in a certain way when he was leaving the railway station. Another man carefully noted the way people walked down the street swinging their walking sticks, and so on.[6]

The category of fortuitous behaviour which does not need motivation, and which a normal person considers to form part of his own psychic operations and mental slips, is thus dismissed by the paranoiac where other people's psychic expressions are concerned. Everything he notices about them is significant, everything can be interpreted. How does he come to see it in this way? Here, as in so many similar cases, he is probably projecting into the mental life of others factors that are unconsciously present in his own. In paranoia, moreover, all kinds of ideas which in normal people and neurotics cannot be traced as present in the unconscious except through psychoanalysis make their way, instead, into the conscious mind.[7] Here the paranoiac is partially correct; he recognizes something that eludes normal perception, and sees more keenly than someone with a normal mind, but his perceptions are invalidated by the displacement of what he recognizes in this way on to other people. I trust I shall not be expected to justify individual paranoiac interpretations. However, the modified amount of justification that we may allow to paranoia in this view of fortuitous actions will facilitate psychological understanding of the conviction which all these interpretations carry in the paranoiac's mind. *There is some truth in it*; our own errors of judgement, errors that need not be described as pathological, acquire their characteristic sense of conviction in just the same way. Such feelings are justified in relation to a certain part of a mistaken train of thought, or the source from which it comes, and we extend them to the rest of the context.

b) Another sign of our unconscious and displaced understanding of motivation in fortuitous actions and slips is conveyed by the phenomenon of superstition. Let me explain what I mean by discussing the little incident that was my point of departure for these reflections.

On returning from holiday I immediately thought about the patients with whom I was to be occupied in the new working year. My first call was paid to a very old lady for whom I had been carrying out the same medical tasks twice a day for years (see p. 169 above). Because of the monotony of my visits, unconscious ideas very frequently expressed themselves on my way to see her and while I was treating her. She was over ninety years old, so it was natural to wonder at the beginning of every year how much longer she had to live. On the day in question I was in a hurry, so I took a cab to her home. Every cab-driver on the rank outside the building where I live knows the old lady's address, for they have all driven me there quite often. Today it so happened that the driver did not stop at her home, but outside the building of the same number in a nearby street running parallel, which in fact looked much the same. I pointed the driver's mistake out to him, and he apologized. Was there any significance in the fact that I had been driven to a building where I would not find the old lady? Not to me, certainly, but had I been *superstitious* I would have seen an omen in this incident, a prophecy on the part of destiny that this year would be the last of the old lady's life. A great many omens mentioned in historical records were based on symbolism just as flimsy as this, although I myself would explain this incident as chance, without any further significance.

It would have been quite different if I had made my journey on foot, and then, 'lost in thought' and 'absent-mindedly' had gone to the building in the parallel street instead of the one where I was expected. I would explain that not as chance, but as an action performed with unconscious intent and calling for interpretation. I would probably have interpreted my mistake as suggesting that I did not expect to be visiting the old lady much longer.

I would distinguish myself from a superstitious man, therefore, as follows: I do not believe that an event not caused in any way by my own mental life can tell me any hidden facts about the future structure of reality, but I do believe that an unintentional expression of my own mental processes can reveal some hidden factor which itself belongs to my mental life alone. I may believe in outer (real) chance, but not in fortuitous inner (psychic) actions. A superstitious man will see it the other way around: he knows nothing of the motivation of his fortuitous actions and slips, he believes fortuitous psychic factors exist, and he is inclined to ascribe a significance to outside fortuitous events that will make itself felt in reality, and to see chance as a means of expression for something hidden that is outside him. There are two differences between me and the superstitious man: first, he projects a motivation on to something outside him, while I look for it within myself; and second, he interprets chance as some incident that has happened, while I derive it from an idea. However, what seems to him concealed corresponds to the unconscious in me, and we share an urge not to see chance as solely accidental but to place some kind of interpretation on it.[8]

I assume that this conscious ignorance and unconscious understanding of the motivation of psychic fortuitous events is one of the roots of superstition. *Because* a superstitious person is ignorant of the motivation of his own fortuitous actions, and because that motivation is clamouring to be recognized, he has to accommodate it in the world outside himself by displacement. If there is a connection of this kind it will scarcely be confined to this one case. In fact I believe that a large part of any mythological view of the world, extending a long way even into the most modern forms of religion, is nothing but *psychology projected into the outside world*. The vague recognition (it might be called endopsychic perception) of psychic factors and circumstances[9] in the unconscious is reflected – it is difficult to put it any other way, so here I must call on the analogy with paranoia – is reflected in the construction of a *supernatural reality*, which science will transform back into the *psychology of the unconscious*. The myths of Paradise and the Fall, of God, good and evil, immortality, and so on could be understood in this way, turning *metaphysics* into *metapsychology*. There is less of a gulf between paranoiac and superstitious displacement than may at first glance appear. When human beings first began thinking, as we know, they felt compelled to resolve the outer world, anthropomorphically, into a diversity of personalities in their own image; the chance events that they interpreted in superstitious terms were therefore the actions and expressions of persons. They were just like those paranoiacs who draw conclusions from the trivial signs they observe in other people, and like all those healthy people who, correctly, judge character by the fortuitous and unintentional actions of their fellow men. Superstition seems misplaced only in our modern, scientific but by no means complete view of the world; as the world appeared to pre-scientific ages and peoples, superstition was legitimate and logical.

Relatively speaking, therefore, the Roman who abandoned some important enterprise if he saw birds flying in the wrong formation was right; he was acting logically in line with his assumptions. But if he abstained from the enterprise because he had stumbled on the threshold of his door (*un Romain retournerait* [a Roman would turn back], as they say), he was definitely superior to us unbelievers, and a better psychologist than we are, despite our current efforts. His stumbling showed him that some doubt existed, something in him was working against his enterprise, and its power could impair his own ability to carry out his intention just as he was on the point of performing it. One can be sure of success only if all mental forces are united in making for the desired aim. As Schiller's Wilhelm Tell, having hesitated for a long time before shooting the apple from his son's head, says when asked by the governor why he had taken a second arrow too:

Mit diesem zweiten Pfeil durchschoss ich – Euch,
Wenn ich mein liebes Kind getroffen hätte,
Und Euer – wahrlich, hätt' ich nicht gefehlt.

[If I had killed my dear beloved child, the second arrow would have been for you. And that shot – truly – would have found its mark.]

D) Anyone who has had an opportunity of studying the hidden emotions of the human mind by psychoanalytic methods can also contribute some new ideas about the quality of the unconscious motives expressed in superstition. It is particularly easy to see how superstition arises from suppressed hostile and cruel feelings in neurotics, who are often very intelligent but afflicted with compulsive ideas and obsessions. Superstition is to a high degree an expectation of bad luck, and anyone who frequently ill-wishes other people, but has repressed such ideas because he has been brought up to wish them well instead, will be particularly likely to expect bad luck to descend upon him from outside as a punishment for his unconscious ill-will.

Admittedly I have by no means exhausted the psychology of superstition with these remarks, but I must at least touch on the other side of the question: can we dismiss the existence of any real roots for superstition entirely, and are we sure that presentiments, prophetic dreams, telepathic experiences, expressions of supernatural powers, and so forth have no basis in fact? I am far from wishing to dismiss out of hand phenomena that have been observed in circumstantial detail even by the intellectually outstanding; it would be better to take them as a subject for further investigation. One might even hope that some of those observations will be elucidated by our dawning knowledge of unconscious mental processes without obliging us to make drastic alterations to our present views.[10] Should other phenomena, such as those to which spiritualists lay claim, be capable of proof, then we would have to make the modifications demanded by this new discovery to our 'laws', without letting our belief in the consistency of terrestrial manifestations be shaken.

In the context of these remarks, I can answer the questions that arise only subjectively, that is to say, from my own experience. Unfortunately I must confess that I am one of those unworthy individuals before whom ghosts desist from their haunting, and the supernatural eludes me, so I have never been in a position to experience anything that might persuade me to believe in signs and wonders. Like everyone else, I have had presentiments and I have known misfortune, but the two kept their distance from each other: nothing happened to justify the presentiments, and misfortune struck out of the blue. When I was a young man living alone in a foreign city, I often enough heard my name suddenly called by a beloved and unmistakable voice, and made a note of the exact moment in time when this aural hallucination occurred, thereafter asking my family anxiously what had been happening at home just then? The answer was nothing. Conversely, on a later occasion I was working with my patients, my mind at ease and without any presentiment of misfortune, at the very time when my child was in danger of bleeding to death. And I have never been able to acknowledge any of the presentiments reported to me by my patients as real phenomena. But I must admit that in recent years I have had several remarkable experiences that could have been explained easily enough if we assumed that telepathic thought-transference exists.

Many people believe in prophetic dreams, a belief resting on the fact that many future events really do turn out as our wishes have pre-constructed them in dreaming.[11] That is not surprising in itself, and as a rule extensive divergences that the credulous dreamer prefers to ignore exist between the dream and its fulfilment. A good example of a dream that can accurately be called prophetic was once offered to me for precise analysis by an intelligent and truthful patient. She told me she had once dreamed of meeting her former friend and family doctor outside a certain shop in a certain street, and when she went into the inner city next morning she really did meet him at the place specified in the dream. I may add that this remarkable coincidence did not prove significant in relation to any subsequent experience, so that there was nothing in the future to account for it.

But careful questioning established the absence of any actual proof that the lady had remembered her dream as soon as she woke up in the morning, and before she went for a walk and met her friend. She could not object to a version of the facts that deprived the event of any element of the marvellous, leaving only an interesting psychological problem. She had gone down the street in question one morning, had met her former doctor outside a shop, and was convinced at the sight of him that she had dreamed of their meeting in that very place the night before. My analysis could then suggest, with a high degree of probability, just how she had come to feel so sure, for as a general rule conviction can claim a certain right to credibility. Meeting at a predetermined place when you have been expecting such a meeting is very much in the nature of a rendezvous. Her former doctor reminded her of old days in which meetings with a *third* person, also a friend of the doctor's, had been significant to her. She was still involved with this other gentleman, and had been expecting to see him the day before her alleged dream, but he never turned up. If I felt it permissible to give a fuller account of the circumstances in this case, I could easily show that her illusion of having had a prophetic dream when she saw her friend from the past was equivalent to her saying something like: 'Oh, doctor, you remind me so much of the past! I never had to wait in vain for N. when we had a rendezvous in those days.'

I myself have had a simple and easily interpreted experience of the famous 'strange coincidence' of meeting someone of whom one has just been thinking, and it may well be a good model for similar cases. A few days after I was granted the title of professor, which confers much prestige in monarchical states, I was walking through the inner city when my thoughts were suddenly diverted into a childlike fantasy of revenge against a certain couple who had called me in to examine their little daughter a few months earlier. She had shown signs of an interesting symptom of obsession in connection with a dream. I was intrigued by her case, and thought I saw how her obsession had developed, but her parents declined to let me treat her, informing me that they were thinking of going to a foreign doctor who used hypnosis as a cure. I was now fantasizing that his efforts had failed completely, whereupon the parents begged me to begin treatment, saying they now had total confidence in me, and so forth. However, I replied: Oh, so now that I'm a professor myself you trust me, do you? My title makes no difference to my abilities; if you didn't want me when I was a mere lecturer you can do without my services as a professor. At this point my fantasy was interrupted by a loud greeting of: 'Good day, Professor!' and I looked up to see, coming down the street, the same couple on whom I had just been revenging myself by refusing their request. My next idea did away with any notion of the marvellous. I had been walking along a straight, wide and almost empty thoroughfare, in the opposite direction from the girl's parents, I had caught sight of their imposing figures as I briefly looked up when I was some twenty paces away from them, but rejected my sighting of them – as if it were a negative hallucination – for those emotional reasons that then expressed themselves in what had appeared to be the spontaneous emergence of a fantasy.

I take the following account of another 'explanation of an apparent presentiment' from Otto Rank:

'Some time ago I myself experienced a curious version of the "strange coincidence" of meeting a person when one has just been thinking about him. Just before Christmas I was on my way to the Austro-Hungarian Bank to exchange a note for ten new crowns in silver, which I planned to give as presents. Deep in grandiose fantasies connected with the contrast between my own small means and the money piled high in the bank, I turned into the narrow street where its building stands. I saw an automobile at the main entrance, and a great many people coming in and out. Well, I said to myself, I suppose the bank clerks will have time to deal with my few crowns, and anyway I shan't keep them long; I shall just hand in the note I want changed and say: I'd like this changed into gold, please! I immediately noticed my mistake – it was *silver* I was going to ask for – and came down to earth from my daydreams. I was now only a few paces from the entrance, and saw a young man coming towards me who looked familiar, although as I am short-sighted I could not recognize him for certain. When he came closer I recognized him as a school friend of my *brother's*, a man called *Gold*, and I had hoped for a good deal of support from this man's own brother, a well-known writer, when I embarked on a literary career. However, it was not forthcoming, and nor as a consequence was the material success I had hoped for, a subject that had been occupying my imagination on my way to the bank. Deep in my fantasies, I must therefore have unconsciously seen Herr Gold coming towards me, and my conscious mind, dreaming of financial success, had transformed this incident into a form which made me think of asking the cashier for gold instead of the less valuable silver. On the other hand, the paradox of the fact that my unconscious could perceive something which my eye recognized only later seems partly explicable from what is called (by Bleuler) a "complexive readiness", concentrating on financial matters and guiding me all along, contrary to what I really knew, to a place where in fact they deal only with transactions in gold and paper money' (*Zentralblatt für Psychoanalyse* II, 5).

Also in the category of the amazing and uncanny is that curious sensation felt so often, and in so many situations, of having had an experience already, or having been in the same place before, although one can never succeed in remembering what seems to have been that earlier occasion. I know that I am simply adopting an imprecise verbal convention in calling what we feel at such moments a sensation: it is a process of judgement involving identification, but these cases have their own unique character, and one must not forget that it is never possible to locate the memory being sought. I do not know if this phenomenon of *déjà vu* has ever been cited in proof of an individual's earlier psychic existence, but psychologists have turned their attention to it, trying to solve the riddle in all kinds of speculative ways. None of the attempts that have been made to explain it strikes me as satisfactory, because none of them takes anything into account but the concomitant features and conditions encouraging the phenomenon. Those psychic processes which, so my observations suggest, are solely responsible for elucidating the sense of *déjà vu*, that is to say, unconscious fantasies, are still generally ignored by psychologists today.

I think it is a mistake to describe the sensation of having had an experience already as an illusion. More probably, at such moments it touches on something one has indeed already experienced, but the experience was never conscious and so cannot be consciously recalled. The sensation of *déjà vu*, in short, is the memory of an unconscious fantasy – for unconscious fantasies (or daydreams) do exist, just like the conscious fantasies with which we are all familiar from personal experience.

This subject, as I am aware, deserves extremely close study, but here I will cite only the analysis of a single case of *déjà vu* where the sensation was notable for its particular intensity and duration. A lady who is now 37 very clearly remembered her first visit to school friends in the country when she was 12½. When she went into the garden of their house she immediately felt that she had been there before; she had the same sensation when she went into the living rooms, and even seemed to know in advance which room adjoined which, what the view from it would be, and so on. However, as her parents confirmed, it was quite out of the question for her sense of familiarity to have arisen from some previous visit to the house and the garden, perhaps in very early childhood. The lady who told me this was not looking for any psychological explanation, but thought that her sensation foreshadowed the importance these friends of hers would assume in her emotional life later. Investigation of the circumstances in which the phenomenon occurred, however, pointed the way to a different concept. When she made her visit she knew that the daughters of the family, her friends, had an only brother who was seriously ill. She saw him during her visit, and thought that he looked very sick indeed and on the point of death. As it happened, her own only brother had been dangerously ill with diphtheria a few months before, and during his illness she had spent several weeks away from her parents' house with a female relative. She thought that her brother had in fact been with her on this visit to her friends in the country, and even that it was his first expedition of any length after his illness, but her memory was curiously vague on these points, although she remembered all the other details very clearly, in particular the dress she had been wearing that day. It will not be difficult for anyone versed in such matters to conclude, from these indications, that expectation of her brother's death loomed large in the girl's mind at the time, but either it had never been consciously present or she had vigorously repressed it when, fortunately, he recovered. If he had not, she would have been in mourning and wearing a different dress. She found the same kind of situation at the home of her friends in the country, where their only brother was in danger of dying, and he did indeed die soon afterwards. She should have remembered consciously that she had been in the same situation herself a few months earlier, but instead she was prevented from recollecting it by repression, instead transferring her sense of something remembered to the house and garden of her friends' home, and she fell victim to the *fausse reconnaissance* of having seen all those things before. We may conclude from what she repressed that her expectation of her brother's death at the time was not so very far in nature from a wish-fulfilment fantasy: if he died she would be the only child in the family. She suffered from neurosis in later life, and was terrified by the fear of losing her parents. Analysis, as usual, revealed an unconscious wish to that effect behind her fear.

I have been able to trace back my own fleeting experiences of *déjà vu* in a similar way to the emotional circumstances of the moment. 'Here is another occasion to revive the fantasy (unconscious and unrecognized) that I formed at such and such a time in order to express my wish for the situation to improve.' This explanation of *déjà vu* has so far been accepted by only one observer. Dr Ferenczi, to whom the third edition of this book owes so many valuable contributions, has written to me on the subject: 'Both in myself and in others, I have become convinced that the inexplicable sense of familiarity can be derived from unconscious fantasies of which one is unconsciously reminded in an actual situation. The case of one of my patients appeared different, but in fact was quite similar. He had a sense of *déjà vu* very often, but it regularly proved to be the result of a *forgotten (or suppressed) dream* of the night before. It seems, then, that *déjà vu* can arise not only from daydreams but also from nocturnal dreaming.'

I later learned that in 1904 Grasset explained the phenomenon in a manner very close to my own.

In 1913 I wrote a short paper[12] describing another phenomenon which is very similar to *déjà vu*. It is *déjà raconté*, the illusion of having already said something, and it is particularly interesting when it emerges during psychoanalytical treatment. The patient then claims, with every sign of subjective certainty, to have told the doctor about a certain memory long ago. However, the doctor is sure his patient never mentioned it, and can usually convince the patient that he is mistaken. The explanation of this interesting slip is probably that the patient did intend to describe the memory but omitted to do so, and is now substituting the memory of the previous intention for the later failure to put it into practice.

Similar, and probably operating in the same way, are the 'supposed slips' mentioned by Ferenczi.[13] We think we have forgotten, mislaid or lost some object, but we can convince ourselves that nothing of the kind happened and everything is in order. For instance, a patient comes back to the doctor's room for the umbrella she says she has left there, but the doctor sees that she actually has the umbrella in her hand. She therefore had an urge to make such a slip, and it was enough to act as the substitute for actually making it. Apart from this difference a supposed slip is just the same as a real one, but might be described as costing one less.

E) Not long ago, when I was telling a colleague with a training in philosophy some instances of the forgetting of names, and their analysis, he immediately replied: 'Yes, that's all very well, but I don't forget names in the same way at all.' Obviously this is not an easy question; I don't think that my colleague had ever before thought of analysing the forgetting of a name, so he could not say in just what way he did it differently. But his comment does touch on a problem which many people will be inclined to point out: is the account I have given here of slips and fortuitous actions generally or only occasionally valid, and, if it applies only in certain cases, then in what circumstances may it be cited to explain phenomena that could be caused in other ways? My experience fails me when it comes to answering this question. I can only warn against considering that connections of the kind I have explained here are unusual, for whenever I have put my theory to the test with myself and my patients it has proved accurate, as in the examples given above, or at least there have been good reasons for assuming it to be accurate. It is not surprising if one sometimes fails to find the hidden meaning of a symptomatic action, since the amount of inner resistance to that solution must be regarded as a crucial factor. Nor can one always interpret every single dream of one's own or one's patients, but to make a little further progress into its hidden meaning is enough to confirm the general validity of the theory. The dream that resists interpretation the next day can often be made to reveal its secret a week or a month later, when some real change in the conflicting strength of psychic factors has occurred. The same applies to the explanation of slips and symptomatic actions; the example of my misreading 'in a tub through Europe' (see pp. 104ff.) gave me a chance to show how a symptom that could not at first be understood may become susceptible of analysis when *real* interest in the suppressed idea has died down.[14] As long as there was a chance that my brother would get the coveted title of professor before me, the misreading I mentioned withstood repeated efforts at analysis; after it had turned out that he was unlikely to do so, I was suddenly able to see my way to solving it. It would therefore be wrong to say that all cases which resist analysis arise through some psychic mechanism other than the one set out here; negative evidence is not enough for such a supposition. And the readiness probably generally present in healthy people to believe in some other explanation of slips and symptomatic actions is devoid of any value as evidence; it naturally expresses the same mental forces as those that caused the mystery and are therefore working to maintain it and resist its explanation.

On the other hand, we must not overlook the fact that repressed ideas and emotions do not of their own accord cause their expression in symptomatic actions and slips. The technical ability of innervations to make slips like this must operate independently; that ability is then gratefully exploited by the intention of something repressed to make itself consciously felt. In the case of verbal slips, extensive studies by philosophers and philologists have tried to establish the structural and functional relationships that make themselves available to carry out such an intention. If we distinguish the unconscious motive from the opposing physiological and psycho-physical factors conditioning the slip or symptomatic action, it is still an open question whether, within the range of normal behaviour, there are other factors which may produce slips and symptomatic actions in line with those relationships, resembling but acting as substitutes for the unconscious motive. It is not within the scope of this book to answer that question.

Nor is it my intention to exaggerate the differences between the psychoanalytic and the popular concept of slips, which are wide enough anyway. I would point, instead, to cases where those differences are a good deal less clear-cut. Highly complicated interpretations are not needed for the simplest and least striking examples of slips of the tongue and pen, for instance where words are compressed or words and letters omitted. From the psychoanalytic viewpoint, it must be said that in these cases some kind of disruption has indicated an intention, but there is no saying what caused the disruption or what its intention was. All it has done is to announce its presence. In cases like this conditions encouraging a slip, as I myself have never disputed, are encouraged by relationships of sound and obvious psychological associations. However, it is scientifically appropriate to ask for such rudimentary slips of the tongue or pen to be judged in relation to more conspicuous slips, those from which, when investigated, unambiguous conclusions can be drawn for the reasons behind slips as a whole.

F) Since my comments on slips of the tongue, I have contented myself with showing that there is a concealed motivation for slips of various kinds, and have been working towards an understanding of this motivation with the aid of psychoanalysis. So far I have left the general nature and peculiarities of the psychic factors expressed in such slips almost out of consideration, or at least I have not yet made any attempt to define them more closely and test them for regularity. Nor am I going to embark on a thorough study of the subject here, since the initial stages of any such study soon show that it is better approached from another direction.[15] But several questions may be asked at this point, and I will at least mention them and give a brief outline of their extent: 1) What is the content and origin of those ideas and emotions that indicate their presence through slips and fortuitous actions? 2) What are the conditions that induce an idea or emotion to use these incidents as a means of expression and enable them to do so? 3) Can constant and unambiguous connections be traced between the nature of a slip and the character of what it expresses?

I will begin by assembling some material to help us answer the last question. In discussing examples of slips of the tongue, it was found necessary to go beyond the content of what the speaker intended to say, and search outside that intention for the cause of the speech disturbance. In a number of cases that cause was then evident, and was known to the speaker's conscious mind. In the apparently simplest and most obvious examples it was another version of the idea concerned, which sounded equal in status but disrupted its expression, although one could not say why one idea was suppressed and the other made itself felt (Meringer and Mayer's 'contaminations'). In a second group of cases, the suppression of one concept was motivated by something which did not, however, prove strong enough to obliterate it entirely (*zum Vorschwein gekommen* instead of *zum Vorschein gekommen*). The suppressed concept was still obvious. The only thing that can be said without reservation of the third group is that in those cases the disruptive idea was different from the intended idea, and here we can make what looks like an essential distinction. The disruptive idea is either connected with the idea it disturbed by means of associated ideas (disturbance through inner resistance), or it is different in nature, and the word that has been disturbed is linked with the often unconscious idea disturbing it through a disconcerting *outward* association. In the examples I have cited from my psychoanalyses, the whole speech is influenced by ideas which have been simultaneously activated but are entirely unconscious, and which reveal themselves either through the disturbance itself (*Klapperschlange*

– *Kleopatra*) or exert indirect influence, enabling various parts of the consciously intended speech to disturb each other (*Ase natmen*, against the background of *Hasenauerstrasse* and reminiscences of French people who were known to the speaker). The withheld or unconscious ideas disrupting speech are of many different origins. My survey, then, does not reveal a general rule tending in any direction.

Comparative study of examples of misreadings and slips of the pen leads to the same results. Individual cases, as in slips of the tongue, seem to owe their occurrence to compression without any other motivation (for instance, *der Apfe*). However, it would be interesting to know whether special conditions must after all be met for such compressions to occur – compressions that regularly occur in dream work but appear wrong in our waking minds – and the examples themselves do not lead us anywhere. However, I would not draw the conclusion that no special conditions exist other than, for instance, failing to pay conscious attention, since I know from other sources that activities automatically performed are particularly notable for their correct and reliable nature. Instead I would emphasize that here, as so often in biology, normal or approximately normal subjects are less useful objects of research than their pathological counterparts. I expect to have light cast on what is still obscure in the explanation of these very mild disruptions by the elucidation of more severe disturbances.

Nor is there any shortage of examples of misreadings and slips of the pen allowing us to recognize a more distant and complicated motivation. The misreading of 'In a tub through Europe' (*Im Fass* for *Am Fuss*, on foot) can be explained by the influence of an idea remote and different from the real phrase, arising from repressed emotions of envy and ambition, and using the 'bridge' of the two meanings of the word *Beförderung* as a link with a neutral, innocuous theme. In the case of 'Burckhard' the name itself acted as a 'bridge'.

It is obvious that disturbances of the functions of speech arise more easily and make fewer demands on the disruptive forces than those of other psychic phenomena. We are on different ground when we come to study forgetfulness in the real sense, that is, forgetting past experiences (forgetting proper names and foreign words, as described in sections I and II, could be distinguished from this forgetfulness in the strict sense as "omission"). The basic conditions affecting the normal process of forgetting are not known.[16] We must also bear in mind that not everything thought to be forgotten actually is. My explanation here relates only to those cases in which we are surprised to find that we have forgotten something because our slip contravenes the rule that the memory forgets unimportant matters but retains what is really important. Analysis of examples of forgetfulness which seem to me to require special explanation always shows that the motive for forgetting was an aversion to remembering something which would arouse distressing sensations. One comes to suppose that this motive strives to express itself generally in psychic life, but is somehow prevented from making itself felt regularly by other forces working against it. The most careful psychological study of the extent and significance of an aversion to remembering painful impressions seems called for, and outside this wider context one cannot say what particular circumstances make this generally desirable form of forgetting possible in individual cases.

Another factor comes to the fore when we study the forgetting of intentions; here, the conflict that we only suspect to be involved in the repression of painful memories becomes tangible, and analysis of examples regularly reveals a negative force opposing but not eliminating the intention. As in slips discussed earlier, two types of psychic process can again be recognized; the negative counter-will either aims directly at the intention (when it is one of some importance), or in itself it is alien to the intention and creates a link with it through some *outward* association (in relatively unimportant intentions).

The same conflict dominates the phenomenon of inadvertent actions. The impulse expressed in the disruption of the action is often a counter-impulse, but more frequently still is a completely alien one, expressing itself by disturbing the execution of the action. The cases in which disturbance occurs through some internal contradiction are more significant and affect more important actions.

Internal conflict is less and less important in fortuitous and symptomatic actions. The conscious mind thinks little of these motor expressions, or ignores them entirely. They serve to express many kinds of unconscious or suppressed emotions, and generally tend to be symbolic of fantasies or wishes.

As for the first of my three questions, about the origin of those ideas and emotions which express themselves in slips, it may be said that in a good many cases the disruptive ideas can be shown to originate in suppressed emotions in mental life. In normal people selfish, jealous and hostile feelings and impulses, upon which the pressure of moral teaching weighs very heavily, quite often make use of slips in order to find some way of expressing their forces, forces that are undeniably present but are not recognized by the higher authorities in our minds. Permitting these slips and fortuitous actions to occur reflects, to a considerable extent, a useful toleration of amorality. Sexual currents of many kinds figure prominently among these suppressed emotions, and it is because of the chance nature of the material here that few of them are found among the ideas revealed by analysis in my examples. As the cases I have analysed are taken mainly from my own mental life, my choice of material was obviously partisan from the first and likely to exclude sexual matters. On other occasions, perfectly innocuous objections and considerations seem to be at the root of the disruptive ideas.

We now face the second question, of the psychological conditions that account for an idea's seeking expression not in full but in what might be called parasitical form, as the modification and disturbance of another idea. The most striking examples of slips suggest that these conditions should be sought in relation to their capacity to enter the conscious mind – in the more or less strongly marked character of their 'repression'. However, following this idea through our series of examples dissolves that character into increasingly vague indications. An inclination to ignore something regarded as a waste of time – an assessment of an idea as not really relevant to a certain subject – would seem to motivate the suppression of an idea which then resorts to expressing itself by disrupting another idea, playing the same part as the moral condemnation of an unseemly emotion or derivation from entirely unconscious trains of thought. We can gain no insight into the general nature of the factors conditioning slips and fortuitous actions in this way. Such studies produce a single significant fact: the more innocuous the motivation of the slip, and therefore the less offensive and thus less inaccessible to the conscious mind is the idea expressed in the slip, the more easily is the phenomenon explained once attention is drawn to it; the simplest cases of slips of the tongue are immediately noticed and spontaneously corrected. Motivation by genuinely repressed ideas calls for solution by careful analysis, which may itself sometimes encounter difficulties or fail.

It is justifiable, then, to see the results of this last investigation as suggesting that a satisfactory explanation of the psychological conditions for the occurrence of slips and fortuitous actions is to be found by approaching the matter from another direction and along another path. The forbearing reader may therefore see in these remarks evidence of certain ragged edges where the subject was rather arbitrarily removed from a wider context.

G) I should end with a few words at least indicating the way to this wider context. In its essentials, the mechanism of slips and fortuitous actions, as we have seen through analysis, agrees with the mechanism of dream formation as I studied it in the section on 'dream work' in my book on the interpretation of dreams. Compressions and compromise formations (contaminations) occur in both phenomena; the situation is the same in that unconscious ideas express themselves in unusual ways, through external associations, as the modification of other ideas. The inconsistencies, absurdities and mistakes of the content of dreams, which have largely prevented them from being recognized as the product of psychic processes, arise in the same way, although admittedly with freer use of the means available, as do the common slips in our everyday life; in both, *the appearance of an incorrect function is set off by the curious interference with each other of two or more operations functioning correctly*. We may draw an important conclusion from this contingency: the curiously functioning operation, the results of which are most strikingly evident in the content of a dream, cannot be derived from the fact that the dreamer's mental life is asleep at the time, if slips provide so much evidence that it works in waking life. The same context also prevents us from seeing the extensive disintegration of mental activity in a morbid state functioning as the condition for these psychic processes, abnormal and strange as they may seem to us.[17]

A correct assessment of the strange psychic activities which allow both slips and dreams to arise can be made only once we have recognized that psycho-neurotic symptoms, particularly psychic forms of hysteria and compulsive neurosis, also show all the major features of this method of functioning in their mechanism. Our investigations may continue from this point. I feel, however, that it is particularly interesting to look at slips, fortuitous and symptomatic actions in the light of this last analogy. If we equate them with the operations of psychoneuroses, that is to say, with neurotic symptoms, there is a good deal of sense in, and support for, the claims often made that the borderline between nervous normality and abnormality is a fluid one, and that we are all slightly neurotic. One does not need medical experience to call to mind various types of neuroticism that are merely indicated – neurotic *formes frustes*: cases where there are only a few symptoms, or they appear rarely or not violently, their diminution being expressed in the number, intensity and frequency of occurrence of the morbid phenomena. Perhaps, however, one would not guess which type seems to convey most frequently the transition between health and sickness. The type in question, expressing its signs of sickness in slips and symptomatic actions, is notable for the transference of its symptoms to the least important psychic procedures, while everything that can claim a higher psychic value remains undisturbed. The reverse accommodation of symptoms, when they appear in the functions most important to both individuals and society and disrupt eating and drinking, sexual intercourse, professional work and social life, is found in severe cases of neurosis, and is more characteristic of them than, for instance, the variety or vehemence of their signs of sickness.

However, the common characteristic of both the mildest and most severe cases, a characteristic also shown by slips and fortuitous actions, lies in the fact that *the phenomena can be traced back to incompletely suppressed psychic material which, although displaced from the conscious mind, is not, however, deprived of all ability to express itself.*

Notes

1. *Psychische-Neurotische Wochenschrift* no. 28, 1905.
2. In explanation of the point about *Macbeth* as No. 17 in the Universal Library, Adler tells me that when the man concerned was in his seventeenth year he joined an anarchist society, which planned to assassinate the king. No doubt that was why he had forgotten the story of *Macbeth*. At that time the same person had received a coded letter in which the characters of the alphabet were replaced by numbers.
3. For the sake of simplicity, I have left out several other and equally cogent ideas on the patient's part.
4. Herr Rudolf Schneider, in Munich, has raised an interesting objection to the evidential force of such analyses of numbers ('Zu Freud's analytischer Untersuchung des Zahleinfalles' ['On Freud's Analytical Study of Numerical Ideas'], *Zeitschrift für Psychoanalyse* I, 1920). He chose certain numbers, for instance one that first met his eye in a historical work when he opened it, or he faced someone else with the number he had chosen and waited to see if the apparently determining ideas that had emerged in connection with that number occurred to that other person too. This was in fact the case; in one example concerning himself which he gives, the ideas produced as rich and evocative a line of determination as we found in our analyses of spontaneously occurring numbers, while the number in Schneider's experiment, coming from outside, did not need determination. In a second experiment with someone else, he obviously made the task too easy for himself by giving his subject the number 2, with which everyone is bound to connect some determining factor or other. R. Schneider draws two conclusions from his work: first, 'the psychic is as easily able to associate with numbers as with words', and second, the emergence of determining ideas connected with spontaneously produced numbers proves nothing about the origin of those numbers from the ideas found in their 'analysis'. The first conclusion is undoubtedly correct. One can just as easily associate some suitable idea with a given number as with a word that is called out, perhaps even more easily, since the few digits available to us can give rise

to a particularly wide range of possible associations. We are then simply in the situation of what has been called the association experiment, which has been studied in its many manifestations by the Bleuler–Jung school. In this situation the idea (or reaction) is determined by the given word (or stimulus). But such reactions may be of various different kinds, and Jung's experiments have shown that even the wider distinction is not left to 'chance' but that unconscious 'complexes' play a part in its determination if they are affected by the stimulus. Schneider's second conclusion goes too far. The fact that suitable ideas emerge in connection with given numbers (or words) says nothing about the derivation of spontaneously emerging numbers (or words) which could not have been taken into consideration before the knowledge of that fact. These ideas (verbal or numerical) could be indeterminate, or determined by the ideas that emerge in analysis, or by other ideas that do not surface in analysis, in which case the analysis has misled us. One must reject any impression that the problems with numbers and verbal ideas are different from each other. A critical study of the problem, and thus a justification of the psychoanalytical technique of ideas, is outside the scope of this book. In analytical practice, one sets out from the presumption that the second proposition is correct, and can be used in the majority of cases. Studies carried out by an experimental psychologist have shown that it is far the most likely (Poppelreuter). (And cf. in this connection Bleuler's valuable comments in his book *Das autistisch-undisziplinerte Denken* . . . [*Autistic and Undisciplined Thinking* . . .], 1919, part 9: 'On the probabilities of psychological perception'.

5. These views on the strict determination of apparently arbitrary psychic actions have already borne much fruit for psychology – and perhaps for the administration of justice. In this sense, Bleuler and Jung have made it possible to understand reaction in what is known as the association experiment, in which the person being studied responds to a word which is uttered with whatever idea occurs to him (in reaction to the stimulus word), and the time he takes to do so is calculated (reaction time). In his *Diagnostische Assoziationsstudien* (1906) Jung has shown what a subtle test of psychic conditions the association experiment can be when it is interpreted in this way. Wertheimer and Klein, who have studied with H. Gross, the Prague lecturer in criminal law, have developed a technique for 'diagnosing of the facts of a case', which is being tested by psychologists and lawyers.

6. Those setting out from other points of departure have classified this judgement of other people's trivial and coincidental means of expression as 'delusions of reference'.

7. The fantasies of sexual and cruel abuse that can be brought to the consciousness of hysterics sometimes coincide in every particular with the complaints of persecution made by paranoiacs. It is remarkable, but not incomprehensible, that we encounter exactly the same content in the activities in which perverts really engage in order to satisfy their desires.

8. I will add a good example employed by N. Ossipow to illustrate the difference between a superstitious, a psychoanalytic and a mystic concept ('Psychoanalyse und Aberglauben' ['Psychoanalysis and Superstition'], *Internationale Zeitschrift für Psychoanalyse* VIII, 1922). Ossipow had married in a small Russian provincial town, and directly afterwards travelled to Moscow with his young wife. At a station two hours from their journey's end, he felt a wish to go out of the station and take a look at the town. He thought the train would be stopping long enough, but when he came back a few minutes later it had already left, with his wife on board. On hearing of this accident, his old nurse at home said, shaking her head: 'Dear me, that marriage will never turn out well.' At the time Ossipow laughed at her prophecy. But since he separated from his wife five months later, he could not help, in retrospect, seeing his leaving the train as an 'unconscious protest' against the marriage. The town where he committed this slip acquired great importance for him years later, since it was the home of someone else with whom he was to be linked closely. The very existence of this person was entirely unknown to him at the time. But the *mystic* explanation of his conduct would be that he had left the train to Moscow, with his wife on it, in that particular town because of a premonition that he was to enter a relationship with that other person in the future.

9. Which of course do not have anything of the character of cognition.

10. E. Hitschmann, 'Zur Kritik des Hellsehens' ['On Clairvoyance'], *Wiener Klinische Rundschau*, 1910, no. 6, and 'Ein Dichter und sein Vater. Beitrag zur Psychologie religiöser Bekehrung und telepathischer Phänomene' ['A Writer and his Father. A contribution to the psychology of religious conversion and telepathic phenomena'], *Imago* IV, 1915/16.

11. Cf. Freud, 'Traum und Telepathie' ['Dreaming and Telepathy'] (*Imago* VIII, 1922. Also in vol. XIII of the *Gesammelte Werke*).

12. 'Über *fausse reconnaissance* ("*déjà raconté*") während der psychoanalytischen Arbeit' ['On *fausse reconnaissance* ("*déjà raconté*") during Psychoanalytic Work'] (*Internationale Zeitschrift für Psychoanalyse* I, 1913). In Vol X of *Gesammelte Werke*.

13. *Internationale Zeitschrift für Psychoanalyse* III, 1915.

14. There are some interesting problems of an *economic* nature connected with this, questions relating to the fact that the psychic processes aim at gaining pleasure and eliminating a sense of aversion. How it becomes possible to win back a name forgotten because of aversion by the use of substitute associations is an economic problem. An excellent work by Tausek ('Entwertung des Verdrängungsmotivs durch Rekompense' ['Cancellation of the Motive for Suppression by Recompenses'], *Internationale Zeitschrift für Psychoanalyse* I, 1913) cites good examples of the way in which a forgotten name can be recovered if it can be associated with something, and that association can then maintain equilibrium between it and the sense of aversion expected in reproducing it.

15. This work has been purposely kept on a popular level, and intends only to ease the necessary acceptance of *unconscious yet effective* mental processes by citing a number of examples, while avoiding all theoretical assumptions about the nature of the unconscious mind.

16. I can give some indication of the mechanism of genuine forgetting, as follows: the material in the memory is in general subject to two influences, compression and distortion. Distortion is the work of the tendencies dominating mental life, and turns chiefly against those traces of memory that still have emotional connotations and are more resistant to compression. Traces that have become indifferent fall victim to the compression process without putting up any opposition, but we may observe that over and above this fact, tendencies to distortion will affect indifferent material if they cannot find satisfaction in material they would like to express themselves. Since these processes of compression and distortion influence the transformation of the material in the memory, it may be thought that the passage of time makes memories uncertain and unclear. However, forgetfulness is very probably not a directly temporal function. When traces of memory are repressed they can be shown to have undergone no change over quite a long period. The unconscious is timeless anyway. The outstanding and most surprising character of psychic fixation is that all impressions are retained just as they were absorbed, and moreover are retained in all the forms they assumed in further developments, a relationship which cannot be explained by any comparison from another sphere. According to this theory, therefore, every earlier stage of any material contained in the memory would be available for recollection, even if its elements have all long since changed their original connotations for later ones.

17. Cf. *The Interpretation of Dreams* [VII.E], p. 362 (8th edition, *Gesammelte Werke*, vols II/III).

FOR THE BEST IN PAPERBACKS, LOOK FOR THE

In every corner of the world, on every subject under the sun, Penguin represents quality and variety—the very best in publishing today.

For complete information about books available from Penguin—including Penguin Classics, Penguin Compass, and Puffins—and how to order them, write to us at the appropriate address below. Please note that for copyright reasons the selection of books varies from country to country.

In the United States: Please write to *Penguin Group (USA), P.O. Box 12289 Dept. B, Newark, New Jersey 07101-5289* or call 1-800-788-6262.

In the United Kingdom: Please write to *Dept. EP, Penguin Books Ltd, Bath Road, Harmondsworth, West Drayton, Middlesex UB7 0DA.*

In Canada: Please write to *Penguin Books Canada Ltd, 10 Alcorn Avenue, Suite 300, Toronto, Ontario M4V 3B2.*

In Australia: Please write to *Penguin Books Australia Ltd, P.O. Box 257, Ringwood, Victoria 3134.*

In New Zealand: Please write to *Penguin Books (NZ) Ltd, Private Bag 102902, North Shore Mail Centre, Auckland 10.*

In India: Please write to *Penguin Books India Pvt Ltd, 11 Panchsheel Shopping Centre, Panchsheel Park, New Delhi 110 017.*

In the Netherlands: Please write to *Penguin Books Netherlands bv, Postbus 3507, NL-1001 AH Amsterdam.*

In Germany: Please write to *Penguin Books Deutschland GmbH, Metzlerstrasse 26, 60594 Frankfurt am Main.*

In Spain: Please write to *Penguin Books S. A., Bravo Murillo 19, 1° B, 28015 Madrid.*

In Italy: Please write to *Penguin Italia s.r.l., Via Benedetto Croce 2, 20094 Corsico, Milano.*

In France: Please write to *Penguin France, Le Carré Wilson, 62 rue Benjamin Baillaud, 31500 Toulouse.*

In Japan: Please write to *Penguin Books Japan Ltd, Kaneko Building, 2-3-25 Koraku, Bunkyo-Ku, Tokyo 112.*

In South Africa: Please write to *Penguin Books South Africa (Pty) Ltd, Private Bag X14, Parkview, 2122 Johannesburg.*

CLICK ON A CLASSIC
www.penguinclassics.com

The world's greatest literature at your fingertips

Constantly updated information on more than a thousand titles, from Icelandic sagas to ancient Indian epics, Russian drama to Italian romance, American greats to African masterpieces

•

The latest news on recent additions to the list, updated editions, and specially commissioned translations

•

Original essays by leading writers

•

A wealth of background material, including biographies of every classic author from Aristotle to Zamyatin, plot synopses, readers' and teachers' guides, useful web links

•

Online desk and examination copy assistance for academics

•

Trivia quizzes, competitions, giveaways, news on forthcoming screen adaptations

"Freud ultimately did more for our understanding
of art than any other writer since Aristotle."
—Lionel Trilling

The Schreber Case
Translated by Andrew Webber
Introduction by Colin MacCabe
In 1903, Judge Daniel Schreber, a highly intelligent and cultured man,
produced a vivid account of his nervous illness dominated by the desire
to become a woman, terrifying delusions about his doctor, and a belief
in his own special relationship with God. Eight years later, Freud's penetrating insight uncovered the impulses and feelings Schreber had
about his father, which underlay his extravagant symptoms.
ISBN 0-14-243742-5

The "Wolfman" and Other Cases
Translated by Louise Adey Huish
Introduction by Gillian Beer
When a disturbed young Russian man came to Freud for treatment, the
analysis of his childhood neuroses—most notably a dream about wolves
outside his bedroom window—eventually revealed a deep-seated trau-
ma. It took more than four years to treat him, and "The Wolfman"
became one of Freud's most famous cases. This volume also contains
other case histories, all of which show us Freud at work, in his own
words. *ISBN 0-14-243745-X*

The Joke and Its Relation to the Unconscious
Translated by Joyce Crick
Introduction by John Carey
In a rich collection of puns, witticisms, one-liners, and anecdotes, Freud
answers the question "why do we laugh?" *The Joke and Its Relation to
the Unconscious* explains how jokes provide immense pleasure by releas-
ing us from our inhibitions and allowing us to express sexual, aggressive,
playful, or cynical instincts that would otherwise remain hidden.
ISBN 0-14-243744-1

The Psychopathology of Everyday Life
Translated by Anthea Bell
Introduction by Paul Keegan
Starting with the story of how he once forgot the name of an Italian painter—and how a young acquaintance mangled a quotation from Virgil through fears that his girlfriend might be pregnant—*The Psychopathology of Everyday Life* brings together a treasure trove of muddled memories, inadvertent action, and verbal tangles. Freud's dazzling interpretations provide the perfect introduction to psycho-analytic thinking in action.   *ISBN 0-14-243743-3*

Coming in September 2003

The Uncanny
Translated by David McClintock
Introduction by Hugh Haughton
Freud was fascinated by the mysteries of creativity and the imagina-tion. His insights into the roots of artistic expression in the triangular "family romances" (of father, mother, and infant) that so dominate our early lives reveal the artistry of Freud's own writing. Freud's first exercise in psychobiography, his celebrated study of Leonardo, bril-liantly uses a single memory to reveal the childhood conflicts behind Leonardo's remarkable achievements and his striking eccentricity.

The Psychology of Love
Translated by Shaun Whiteside
Introduction by Jeri Johnson
This volume brings together Freud's illuminating discussions of the ways in which sexuality is always psychosexuality—that there is no sexuality without fantasy, conscious or unconscious. In these papers Freud develops his now famous theories about childhood and the transgressive nature of human desire.